BRIGHT SATANIC MILLS

Bright Satanic Mills

Universities, Regional Development and the
Knowledge Economy

Edited by

ALAN HARDING
University of Salford, UK

ALAN SCOTT
University of Innsbruck, Austria

STEPHAN LASKE
University of Innsbruck, Austria

CHRISTIAN BURTSCHER
University of Innsbruck, Austria

ASHGATE

Published with the support of the Austrian Federal Ministry for Education, Science and Culture.

Published by
Ashgate Publishing Limited
Gower House
Croft Road
Aldershot
Hampshire GU11 3HR
England

Ashgate Publishing Company
Suite 420
101 Cherry Street
Burlington, VT 05401-4405
USA

Ashgate website: http://www.ashgate.com

British Library Cataloguing in Publication Data
Bright satanic mills : universities, regional development
    and the knowledge economy
    1. Universities and colleges - Economic aspects
    2. Knowledge management - Economic aspects 3. Community
    development 4. Universities and colleges - Public relations
    I. Harding, Alan, 1958-
    378.1

Library of Congress Cataloging-in-Publication Data
Bright satanic mills : universities, regional development, and the knowledge economy /
    edited by Alan Harding ... [et al.].
        p. cm.
    Includes bibliographical references and index.
    ISBN-13: 978-0-7546-4585-6 (alk. paper) 1. Education, Higher. 2. Regional planning.
    I. Harding, Alan, 1958-

LB2326.4.B75 2007
338.4'3378--dc22
                                                          2006031441

ISBN: 978-0-7546-4585-6

Printed and bound in Great Britain by MPG Books Ltd, Bodmin, Cornwall.

Contents

List of Figures and Tables

Figures

Tables

List of Contributors

Todd Bridgman is a lecturer in organizational behaviour at Victoria University of Wellington, New Zealand. He was previously an ESRC postdoctoral fellow at the Judge Business School, University of Cambridge, where he completed his PhD. His doctoral thesis, which was judged best doctoral thesis in Critical Management Studies at the Academy of Management 2005, investigates the commercialization of the academic's public role, in the context of UK research-led business schools. He is currently co-editing a *Handbook of Critical Management Studies*.

Christian Burtscher recently completed an MA in law at the University of Innsbruck, and is currently a doctoral candidate in the Department of Sociology. He is co-editor of and contributor to *Wirtschaft, Demokratie und soziale Verantwortung* (Vanndenhoeck und Ruprecht, 2004), and co-author of 'Universities and the Regulatory Framework: The Austrian University System in Transition' (*Social Epistemology*, 2006). He is also chair of the Grüne Bildungswerkstatt Tirol (an educational organization of the local Austrian Green Party). He was part of the organization team of the Universities and Regional Development conference in Innsbruck in December 2002, from which this volume stems.

Dolores Byrnes is currently an instructor in peace and conflict studies at Colgate University. She received her PhD in anthropology at Cornell University in 2001. Her fieldwork with the state government in Guanajuato, Mexico allowed her to conduct an in-depth ethnographic study of a public policy created by Vicente Fox. The resulting book, *Driving the State*, was published in 2003 (Cornell University Press). She won a 2003–4 Knight Postdoctoral Fellowship, which supported her research into disciplinary boundaries created through language. Her professional background also includes research and writing positions in the private and non-profit sectors.

David R. Charles holds the David Goldman Chair of Business Innovation and is Director of Research in the University of Newcastle upon Tyne Business School. David also co-ordinates the research group on innovation, learning and knowledge in the Centre for Urban and Regional Development Studies. His research interests include innovation management, the role of universities in regional development, regional innovation policy and city-region development. His work on universities includes a major EU project on universities and regional development (UNIREG) and work on HE business interaction for the UK Higher Education Funding Councils and Office of Science and Technology. He is currently leading an EU research network on processes of learning in city regions.

Maximilian Egger has been the director of SoWi-Holding since 1996. The holding is non-profit organization associated with the University of Innsbruck, currently comprising three business units: PINN (Patenschaftsmodell INNsbruck), EUROMOBIL, and the Placement Center. The main objective of SoWi-Holding is to promote cooperation between students, academics and businesses in order to create competitive advantages for all participants. He studied in Innsbruck, London and New York, and has master's degrees in economics and business education, and in language and literacy. He has, in addition, been active in various fields of the business for more than twenty years.

Huib Ernste is Professor of Human Geography and Head of Department at Radboud University, Nijmegen, Netherlands. He studied human and economic geography, and research methods at the University of Groningen (Netherlands) and took his PhD in human geography at the Swiss Federal Institute of Technology, Zurich, where he was also a lecturer and associate professor. He is co-founder of a research and consultancy firm in Switzerland and has been Visiting Professor at the University of Utrecht, the University of Salzburg, UCLA and the University of Münster. Recently he initiated the Alexander von Humboldt Lectures in human geography in Nijmegen. His research interests lie in social theory and human geography, especially spatial action theory, spatial decision models and economic geography. His current research focuses on borders in the framework of the Nijmegen Centre for Border Research. As Head of Department, he is much involved in strategy and organization of scientific knowledge production and academic teaching.

Davydd J. Greenwood is the Goldwin Smith Professor of Anthropology and Director of the Institute for European Studies at Cornell University, where he has served as a faculty member since 1970. He has been elected a corresponding member of the Spanish Royal Academy of Moral and Political Sciences. He served as the John S. Knight Professor and Director of the Mario Einaudi Center for ten years, and was president of the Association of International Education Administrators. He also has served as a programme evaluator for many universities and for the National Foreign Language Center. His work centres on action research, political economy, ethnic conflict, community and regional development, the Spanish Basque Country, Spain's La Mancha region and the Finger Lakes region of upstate New York, where he carried out a three-year action research and community development project with communities along the Erie Canal corridor. His current work focuses on the impact of corporatization on higher education, with a particular emphasis on the social sciences, and he is the principal investigator with an international team of twenty-three scholars on a Ford Foundation-supported project, the Social Science and Higher Education Network. Among his books are *Unrewarding Wealth: The Commercialization and*

Collapse of Agriculture in a Spanish Basque Town (Cambridge University Press, 1976), The *Taming of Evolution: The Persistence of Non-evolutionary Views in the Study of Humans* (Cornell University Press, 1985), *Introduction to Action Research: Social Research for Social Change* (Sage, 2nd Edition, 1998), and he edited *Action Research: From Research to Writing in the Scandinavian Action Research Program* (John Benjamins, 1999).

Alan Harding is co-director of SURF and Professor of Urban and Regional Governance at the University of Salford. He works on the broad themes of urban and regional development, policy and governance and has led and taken part in a large number of applied academic and consultancy studies focusing on the way in which local and regional economic development and regeneration initiatives are conceived, promoted, delivered and evaluated, domestically and internationally. Clients for this work have included the European Commission, national government departments, regional development agencies, local authorities, other public agencies, charitable trusts and foundations, national research councils, private sector umbrella organisations and individual corporations. Alan has advised a range of local, regional, national and international agencies and organizations on issues related to his research. He currently co-edits the *International Journal of Urban and Regional Research.*

Michael Harloe is Vice-Chancellor of the University of Salford and a social scientist who has worked for many years on issues of urban and regional development. He was the founder editor (1977-97) of the *International Journal of Urban and Regional Research*. His most recent (co-authored) book is *Working Capital. Life and Labour in Contemporary London* (Routledge, 2002), which is based on one of the major projects in the recently completed ESRC Cities Programme. He was formerly Dean of Social Sciences and Pro-Vice-Chancellor Research at the University of Essex and became Vice-Chancellor of Salford University in October 1997. He is a member of the Academy of the Learned Societies in the Social Sciences.

Stephan Laske is Professor of Business Management and Business Education, and Dean of the School of Management at the University of Innsbruck. He has taught at the universities of Munich, Wuppertal, Hanover and Linz, and has been a visiting scholar in the Graduate School of Management, Griffith University (Brisbane, Australia) and the School of Economics and Commercial Law, Gothenburg University (Sweden). He has wide experience in higher-education management. As chair of the university's academic senate, he was responsible for a two-year organization development programme, and he has also chaired the Austrian Association of Senate Leaders. Currently, he is member of the board of governors of Innsbruck Medical University, and of the Scientific Commission in Lower Saxony (Germany), an advisory body to the minister of science. He has published widely on university management and personnel policy, and is currently leading a research project on university governing boards supported by the Austrian National Bank (ÖNB).

Morten Levin is a professor in the Department of Industrial Economics and Technology Management of the Faculty of Social Sciences and Technology Management at the Norwegian University of Science and Technology in Trondheim. He holds graduate degrees in engineering and in sociology. Throughout his professional life he has worked as an action researcher with particular focus on processes and structures of social change in the relationships between technology and organization. The action research has taken place in industrial contexts, in local communities, and in university teaching where he has developed, and been in charge of, PhD programmes in action research. He is author of a number of books and articles, including *Introduction to Action Research: Social Research for Social Change* (with Davydd Greenwood, Sage 1998), *Researching Enterprise, Development and Change as Practice* (John Benjamins, 2002). He serves on the editorial boards of *Systems Practice and Action Research, Action Research, The Handbook of Qualitative Inquiry* and *The Handbook of Action Research*.

William Lovegrove is Vice-Chancellor and President of the University of Southern Queensland. He is internationally known for his research in the areas of visual information processing and dyslexia, and has been involved in developing international programmes and in building staff performance and extensive commercial links with industry and government. He was previously Deputy Vice Chancellor (Research, Internationalization and Commercialization) at Griffith University and has had responsibilities at Griffith for teaching and learning (including flexible learning), academic and staff issues, and strategic planning and quality. He has represented the Australian Vice-Chancellors Committee on many occasions and been the chair of the Pro Vice-Chancellors/Deputy Vice-Chancellors (Research) Subcommittee of the AVCC (1998) and of the research working group on the McKinnon Benchmarking Report (1999), as well as a member of the standing committees on research and international issues.

Tim May is a director of the Centre for Sustainable Urban and Regional Futures (SURF), a largely self-financing, multi-disciplinary research centre at the University of Salford, which works on issues associated with regeneration, housing, city and regional policy, and territorial knowledge, science and technology. Its funders include research councils, development agencies, the EU, central and local government, universities, health and private sector organizations (see www.surf.salford.ac.uk for more information). As well as journal articles and book chapters, Tim May has authored and edited books on social theory, research methods and methodology, organizational decision-making, identity and transformation, and is co-author (with Zygmunt Bauman) of *Thinking Sociologically* (Blackwell, 2001). He is the series editor of an international books series (Issues in Society, McGraw-Hill/Open University Press) and is currently writing a book on the analysis of social relations (Sage) and preparing new editions of books on social theory and social research.

Claudia Meister-Scheytt is a lecturer in the department of organization and learning of the school of management at Innsbruck University. Her main research interest lies in processes of organizational change in universities, changing governance structures and management practices. She is co-editor of and contributor to *Management von Universitäten, Personalentwicklung und universitärer Wandel* and *Universität im 21. Jahrhundert* (Rainer Hampp Verlag). She is chair of the Witten-Herdecke University Association, the alumni organization of Germany's first private university. She is also director of the sub-commission on higher education management of the Verband der Hochschullehrer für Betriebswirtschaft (the German association of university teachers of business administration) and acts as a consultant to higher education institutions and policy-making bodies.

Beth Perry joined SURF in October 2000 after completing degrees in European integration and modern languages at the Universities of Manchester (1999) and Bradford (2000). She has worked on a number of SURF consultancy and research projects, including the Liverpool–Manchester Vision Study; a cost-benefit analysis of the Commonwealth Games; an evaluation of regeneration in Hulme; an ODPM New Horizons project on Urban Futures; the 'Rethinking the University' project within Salford and a scoping study on innovation drivers. Her main conceptual interests are in urban and regional policy and governance, particularly in relation to theories of multi-level governance and the role of universities in regional development and the knowledge economy. Beth is currently leading a two-year programme of work funded by the ESRC Science in Society programme looking at comparative regional science policies in Europe and the multi-level governance of science. This builds on a previous one-year project that focused on evaluating the regional dimensions to science policy in the UK through a case study of the North West. Other current research includes examination of inter-relationship between universities and health and social sectors, with a particular focus on issues of knowledge transfer in the NHS.

Alan Scott is Professor of Sociology at the University of Innsbruck, and convener of the School of Political Science and Sociology's 'Contemporary Europe: Governance and Civil Society' research programme (www2.uibk.ac.at/gcs/). His main research interests lie in political sociology, organizational governance and social theory. He is project leader of a NODE (New Orientations for Democracy in Europe) research project on post-democracy (www.node-research.at). As a member of the Social Science and Higher Education Research Network, he co-organized the 'Universities and Regional Development' conference, and a conference on 'Cultural Studies and Trans-disciplinarity' (published as *Politik der Cultural Studies,* Turia + Kant, 2006). Other recent publications include, as co-editor, the *Blackwell Companion to Political Sociology* (Blackwell, 2001/04) and a co-translation of Georg Simmel's *Rembrandt* (Routledge, 2005).

Christine Smith is Professor of Economics at Griffith University in Australia. She is currently Acting Pro-Vice-Chancellor (Business and Law), was dean of the Griffith Business School from 2003–4 and head of the School of Economics from 1998–2003. Her area of expertise is regional and urban economics. She is the author and co-author of a number of books including *Productivity and Regional Economic Growth Performance in Australia, Integration of Multiregional Models for Policy Analysis: An Australian Perspective,* and *Conflict Analysis and Practical Conflict Management Procedures.* She is the editor of the *Australasian Journal of Regional Studies* and a member of the editorial board of *Papers in Regional Science.* In addition, she has acted as an advisor to federal, state and local governments on regional and urban development issues, modelling the economic impacts of various policy initiatives, and alternative dispute resolution procedures.

Hugh Willmott is Professorial Research Fellow in Organizational Behaviour at Cardiff University's business school, prior to which he was Diageo Professor of Management Studies and Director of the PhD Programme at the Judge Institute of Management at the University of Cambridge. He is currently working on a number of projects whose common theme is the changing organization and management of work. His books include *Making Quality Critical* (Routledge, 1995), *The Re-engineering Revolution* (Sage, 2000), *Managing Knowledge* (Macmillan 2000*), Management Lives* (Sage, 1999), *Studying Management Critically* (Sage, 2003), and *Fragmenting Work* (OUP, 2004). He has published widely in social science and management journals, and is currently an editorial board member of the Academy of Management Review, *Organization Studies* and the *Journal of Management Studies.* Further details can be found on his homepage: http://dspace.dial.pipex.com/town/close/hr22/hcwhome.

Acknowledgements

Several of the chapters that appear in this volume started life as presentations to the Universities and Regional Development Conference in Innsbruck in December 2002 jointly organized by the SoWi (Social Science) Faculty, University of Innsbruck and the Centre for Sustainable Urban and Regional Futures (SURF), University of Salford (http://www.surf.salford.ac.uk/). Our thanks to the conference sponsors: Land Tirol (Tyrolean Provincial Government), Tiroler Zukunftsstiftung, RLB Tirol, the British Council and the Bank Austria Stiftung. This conference emerged from the work of the Social Science and Higher Education Network (http://www.einaudi.cornell.edu/sshen/), several members of which are represented in the collection (Byrnes, Greenwood, Levin, May, Scott). Publication of this volume was supported by grants from the Austrian Ministry for Educational, Science and Culture (BM:BWK). Our thanks too to Stephen Curtis for his efficient preparation of the manuscript and to Ashgate's Senior Social Science Editor, Caroline Wintersgill, for her encouragement and support.

ACKNOWLEDGEMENTS

Chapter 1

Introduction: Universities, 'Relevance' and Scale

Alan Scott and Alan Harding

University A 'aims to achieve and sustain excellence in every area of its teaching and research, maintaining and developing its historical position as a *world-class* university, and enriching the *international*, *national* and *regional* communities through the fruits of its research and the skills of its graduates'.

We at University B 'will continue to serve [our host *city*] and [its surrounding *region*] using our skills and knowledge and drawing on our *international* reputation to promote social and cultural well-being and to aid economic growth and regeneration'.

University C 'is a national institution with *international* perspectives, but it gives particular attention to the economic and social well-being of its *local* and *regional* environment'.

University D aims '[t]o advance as a new generation civic university [by, for example] providing … a portfolio of undergraduate and higher level learning skills and opportunities relevant to *local* and *regional* needs and attractive to *local* and *regional* learners'.

A key aim of University E 'is to play a leadership role in the cultural, social, economic and intellectual life of the *local*, *regional* and wider communities we serve and be known for our expertise in supporting economic and social regeneration'.

University F 'promotes access to excellence to enable you to develop your potential. Our aim is to ensure being a student at [University F] is affordable to as many people as possible. We have introduced generous bursaries and scholarships to provide our students with a comprehensive financial support package'.

Farewell, 'Prospectus Age'

Not so long ago, in a dimly remembered world, universities were in the habit of advertising themselves principally through the medium of the prospectus. Prospectuses varied enormously in their length, their design quality and their command of grammar, in the ease with which they fitted through the average letter box and in their propensity to induce premature sleep amongst their readership. In essence, though, they were simple documents whose basic format varied little between institutions. They had a single, well-defined audience – potential students

– and were dominated by factual content which alerted this readership to the courses on offer at any one time. A secondary aspiration of prospectuses, achieved with varying degrees of success, was to give an upbeat view of the environment – be it scholarly, social, cultural or economic – that students would encounter upon taking up their studies.

Today, the armoury of university self-promotion is vastly enlarged, and its weapons are trained on a broader array of targets. The gentle, if loaded, competition for students that characterized the 'prospectus age' has given way to a thinly disguised war for investment waged, in part, through a multitude of branding exercises in which universities – and, increasingly, their component faculties, schools, departments, research centres and even individual academics – parade their ostensible strengths and draw a discrete veil over any weaknesses. Whilst prospectuses have certainly not disappeared, they now jostle for attention, in the labyrinth that is the modern university website, with a battery of annual reports, benchmarking exercises, performance reviews and corporate mission statements. The sample quotes, above, come from the virtual vaults of a selection of UK universities, large and small, celebrated and less so, but they might easily have been taken from equivalents anywhere across the developed world. They show that universities are no longer content to advertise themselves only to prospective students, largely on the basis of their pedagogical achievements, but feel the need to demonstrate, or at least proclaim, that the world would be an infinitely poorer place without them.

The two foundation stones upon which the modern university bases its enlarged sales pitch are *relevance* and *scale*. Thus, for example, our sample universities promise to: 'enrich' the many communities that benefit from their teaching and research; 'serve' the cities and regions in which they sit and 'give particular attention to' their economic, social and cultural well-being; 'aid' local economic growth and regeneration; and, generally, be 'leaders' of cultural, social, economic and intellectual life. In pursuing these ambitions, universities seemingly do not feel themselves constrained by size, history or reputation. Whether they consider themselves 'world class' and in possession of an 'international' reputation (Universities A and B) or as essentially 'national' or 'civic' institutions with fewer international credentials, particularly in research (C, D and E), most claim to produce eminently useful knowledge that can be utilized by a huge range of 'communities' but is especially valuable to those living, metaphorically speaking, on the university's doorstep. Only when there is little else to sell do universities fall back upon the traditional pitch to potential students, using the ultimate consumerist message: 'come here, we're cheap' (University F).

The contributions to this volume, like many of their authors' papers to the international conference on which it is based, take the notions of relevance and scale and subject the common assumption that they increasingly 'drive' what academics actually do to a greater degree of critical scrutiny than has been common heretofore. The task we have set ourselves is to take a step back from the current – often polemical, sometimes highly rhetorical – debates about higher education, and to examine the reality of universities' relationship to their external environment (Part 1) and how it impacts upon and/or is conditioned by the changing inner life of higher-education institutions (Part 2). Our aim is to avoid the kinds of argumentative shortcut that characterize much of the debate about, and often the practice of, university governance, and to take a more theoretically and empirically informed – if inevitably selective – view of the factors that influence the way universities perceive the world beyond the campus and organize themselves in order to engage and interact with it. The volume concentrates, in particular, on the local and regional scale. It asks a number of inter-related questions designed to promote more critical discussion about the degree to which universities have made the transition from the archetypal 'ivory towers' of the prospectus age to the 'bright satanic mills' of the emerging, global knowledge economy. Specifically, our contributors help us understand:

- What has changed to encourage universities to take 'local and regional missions' more seriously?
- Through what mechanisms have these changes been transmitted?
- How have universities, as institutions, and academic communities more generally, responded to the key changes in their operating environments that have encouraged 'regionalization'?
- How have recent changes affected traditional conceptions of the 'role of the academic', based upon dispassionate, detached, discipline-specific, curiosity-driven inquiry?

Our job in this opening chapter is to rehearse the context in which these questions have become more pressing and describe the way in which the rest of the volume approaches the task of addressing them.

The Demand-side Revolution

It is relatively easy to make the case that universities should have become more concerned – and confident – about their 'relevance' in an age in which information has become an increasingly important factor of production. There are also in-principle reasons to expect that universities' 'relevance' to local and regional development and wellbeing, in the broadest sense, should have become more important. Indeed, this case could be summed up in a simple hypothesis: universities are to the 'information age' what coal mines and steel mills were to the industrial economy, that is to say spatially rooted engines of economic, social and environmental change. Underlying this bold, even bald, claim is a chain of logic which suggests that there is such a thing as the 'knowledge economy', that universities play a crucial role in servicing the needs of people, organizations and firms that operate within it, and that – arguably – it is at the sub-national, rather than national, scale that we find the critical sites where this key function is articulated and delivered. Three overarching and inter-related tendencies, in particular, can be argued to have combined to transform demand for what universities provide so as to encourage a sharper focus on 'relevance' and more intense engagement with immediate localities and regions: globalization, the 'information revolution' and the 'massivication' of higher education. We comment upon these below.

Towards Glocal Universities?

The notion of 'globalization' has become so ubiquitous in recent years that there is, as Albrow (1996: 85) has rightly pointed out, a danger that the term 'is used as explanation, rather than as something to be analysed, explored, and explained'. In other words, globalization is too often seen as a causal factor in the absence of a clear understanding of what, precisely, are the agents of change. However let us take, as a starting point, Appadurai's (1990) assertion that globalization is not a single 'thing' but rather a multifaceted set of processes involving unprecedented acceleration in the international circulation of people, goods, services, money, images and ideas. On the face of it, Appadurai's checklist suggests a number of routes through which universities – along with other sorts of organization – might have become more 'globalized', for example through attracting non-domestic staff and students, competing internationally for research funding, prioritizing international audiences for academic work, and so on. Indeed it is possible to see the last twenty years as a period in which the notion of the 'global university' has become established in principle, for example through a variety of international ranking exercises based on comparable sets of performance metrics, and to a certain extent in practice. The formation of cross-national networks of 'elite' institutions, the international franchising of degree courses, the expansion of the 'transfer market' for iconic academics and research groups and the growth of distance-learning packages are obvious examples of universities' attempts to grow the global market for, and profile of, their services, sometimes in collaboration and sometimes in competition with one another.

In this volume, Huib Ernste describes how certain Dutch universities have developed 'globalization' strategies, at least implicitly, in the attempt to maintain or enhance their positions within a European higher education 'system' that is witnessing gradual cross-national convergence designed – at least in the minds of European Commission bureaucrats – to enable the free flow of EU students. In anticipating a future 'hub and spoke' scenario for European universities, whereby a number of 'global' hubs are linked to or co-exist with an array of (local and regional) spokes, however, Ernste effectively suggests three things which question the assumption that future institutional survival depends upon 'going global'. First, the 'shake-out' that will produce the 'hubs' is likely to benefit relatively few institutions; in other words the key 'global players' will be a small minority. Second, elite universities' 'global' functions will be delivered alongside – and indeed be virtually indistinguishable from – their more traditional roles which, at least in the Dutch case, have long focused upon catering for the (perceived) needs of essentially regional markets. And third, the 'regional embeddedness' of even the most internationally orientated institutions is likely to be strengthened rather than weakened by impending changes.

In short, location will continue to matter. The University of Amsterdam, on this analysis, cannot be compared with a footloose American sports franchise that can move around, geographically, in search of a broader base of support and richer sponsors. Rather, it is attempting to find ways in which the Amsterdam brand can be expanded in ways that are less constrained by, but still substantially dependent upon, 'domestic' demand, be it at the Greater Amsterdam, Randstad or Netherlands level, whilst also providing material and symbolic benefits at these spatial scales.

The merit of Ernste's analysis is that, in taking a long-run historical perspective on the degree of 'regionalness' or 'globalness' of Dutch universities, he makes it clear that change is invariably gradual rather than explosive. In particular he points to the longstanding importance, following the great age of nation-state formation, of national government investment in the HE sector in conditioning university behaviour. This provides a useful warning that the university of the future – even when it is self-consciously pursuing a global mission – will continue to be shaped substantially by public policies and resource transfers within a particular national context. Thus, for example, whilst it would be hard to deny that HE institutions in the UK's so-called 'Golden Triangle' linking London, Oxford and Cambridge have pursued, and continue to pursue, variants of a 'globalization strategy', it is clear that the context in which they do so is heavily influenced by national regulations and policy aims. Hence the huge rise in international students is driven not so much by a world-wide search for the 'best' candidates, but by the fact that differential fee structures make the attraction of non-EU nationals highly lucrative. Similarly, the concentration of an ever-higher proportion of public research funding into a dwindling number of institutions is more the result of a national policy aspiration for UK universities to compete with 'world class' institutions elsewhere – especially in the US – than the product of individual institutional strategies.

This observation leads us neatly into an alternative, and apparently paradoxical, 'take' on globalizing processes: that they are associated as much with 'regionalization' or 'localization' as they are with global forms of action or organization. It has become commonplace across the social sciences during the last two decades to stress the importance of 'the sub-national' – whether 'regional', 'urban' or 'urban-regional' – in an age in which the dominance of the nation state, 'national' economies and cultures and national regimes of economic, social and environmental regulation have been challenged, in theory and in practice, by processes of globalization. Beck and Sznaider (2006: 3) find, in this gradual conceptual re-orientation, evidence of the beginning of the end of 'methodological nationalism', which:

> equates societies with nation state societies and sees states and their governments as the primary focus for social scientific analysis. It assumes that humanity is divided into a limited number of nations, which organize themselves internally as nation states and externally set boundaries to distinguish themselves from other nation states.

Recent work on the importance of 'the sub-national' that, at least implicitly, challenges methodological nationalism can be found across the social science spectrum. This literature is too voluminous to summarize here but includes, for example, analyses of: the rise of innovative local and regional production complexes (Storper, 1997); the importance of spatial 'clusters' of advanced economic activity to national competitiveness (Porter, 1990); the increasingly critical roles of major cities and city-regions as 'switching points' in global circuits of production, distribution and exchange (Sassen, 1991; Scott, A.J., 2001); processes of decentralization and devolution of erstwhile national government powers and responsibilities (Jones and Keating, 1995; Le Galès, 2002); the emergence of (sub-national) territorial competition (Jensen-Butler *et al.*, 1997; Cheshire and Gordon, 1998); and the key – and differentially effective – role played by sub-national governments (Putnam, 1993) within an emerging 'system' of multi-level governance (Bernard, 2002). In summarizing key elements of this literature, Buck *et al.* (2005) identify the emergence of a 'new conventional wisdom' which has it that an effective trade-off between economic competitiveness, social cohesion and responsive governance increasingly needs to be struck at the sub-national, rather than national, scale.

In a compelling schematic overview of this highly fragmented literature, Brenner (2004) has recently suggested that it is possible to discern a common, cross-national, direction of travel in what he argues to be interlinked processes of spatial policy reform and sub-national institutional restructuring, at least in Europe. The result, he suggests, has been the progressive abandonment of the 'spatial Keynesianism' that dominated the mid-to-late 20th century and in which considerable attention was paid by national governments to spatial equity, a redistributive approach to public investment and common standards in the delivery of life-sustaining sub-national services. In its place have emerged much more regressive regimes in which welfare is more closely tied to labour market participation and 'spatial policy' has been thoroughly recast. Instead of pursuing redistributive goals through various policies designed to decentralize economic activity and/or promote development in economically vulnerable or marginal areas, Brenner suggests, national governments have increasingly found ways of (a) supporting further growth in those sub-national – and invariably metropolitan – areas that are already 'successful', and (b) distancing themselves from responsibility for the consequences of uneven spatial development through various forms of decentralization and devolution. Crudely summarized, he sees contemporary spatial policy as being about rewarding 'winners' and leaving 'losers' to their own devices.

Brenner is too subtle an analyst to suggest that processes of spatial policy change and sub-national institutional restructuring necessarily take identical forms in different national contexts. Nor does he reflect very directly on the role of higher-education policies. The broad narrative he develops, however, provides a number of interesting avenues for empirical work on HE policy and the extent to which it has been refocused around the perceived needs of economic competitiveness and become more explicitly 'spatialized'. David Charles's contribution to this volume provides precisely this sort of detail through a comparative analysis of the overt relationship between university activity and the development of public policies on spatial economic 'clusters'. In tracing the development of this relationship in very different national and regional economic and political-administrative contexts

– the 'lagging' North East region of England within the traditionally centralized UK and the more prosperous South East Queensland area within federal Australia – he demonstrates the way in which a variety of actors, within universities, across levels of government and administration and in non-statutory sectors, have coalesced around regionally specific sets of 'entrepreneurial' activities more or less exclusively focused, at least in principle, upon improving regional competitiveness.

Charles's chapter uncovers specific instances of the way that academics' concerns with relevance and scale have been brought together around regional economic development activities. He does not argue that these activities are necessarily representative of a new approach to university governance, but the inference that can be drawn from his contribution is that such activities are increasingly privileged within the complex relationship between university managers and academics, on one hand, and their statutory and non-statutory paymasters, clients and 'users', on the other. In this sense, they can be seen as symbolic of the rethinking of relevance and scale brought about by the two other overarching processes we referred to earlier – the 'massivication' of the HE sector and the role of universities in an emerging 'knowledge economy'. These processes, and the extent to which they represent a fundamental break with the past, are addressed in the other two chapters in Part 1.

Universities as Spatial Knowledge Factories

Perry and Harloe examine key aspects of the literatures on the knowledge economy, the 'informational mode of development' and 'knowledge capitalism' and there is little to be gained from rehearsing their analysis here. Suffice it to say that they remain resolutely sceptical about the extent to which the phenomena described within this literature are genuinely new, as opposed to the result of an acceleration of long-established processes (de-industrialization, growth of tertiary sector employment, etc.) whose long-term implications have been recognized for some time – at least since Bell's (1973) seminal work on post-industrialism. What they make clear, however, is the readiness with which the knowledge economy 'narrative' has been seized upon by policy-makers and opinion-formers. Their analysis of policy changes and declarations at the European scale, in particular, demonstrates just how totemic the pursuit of a 'Europe of knowledge' has become and the importance that is attached to HE sector activities in delivering it. At this scale, worries are expressed that Europe's competitive advantage is steadily being eroded not just by established competitors in North America and the Pacific Rim but also by rapidly developing countries elsewhere in Asia – most notably China and India – and in Latin America. This is argued to be the case not just within manufacturing, where the international decentralization of production to countries with lower labour costs and looser regulatory regimes is longstanding, but also, increasingly, within service sectors, where the global 'offshoring' of back office functions has grown apace in recent years (Schleicher, 2006).

Universities, it is argued, are critical to European efforts to counter this 'threat' as a result of their roles in imparting high-level skills to the workforce of the future, providing opportunities for 'lifelong learning', delivering breakthroughs in fundamental research, enabling the commercialization of innovative products, services and processes, and disseminating 'useful' knowledge that can directly benefit wealth-creators and cadres of professional leaders. The 'relevance' of universities, here, is largely taken on trust, the assumption being that some version of the South Korean or Singaporean 'miracles', whereby high rates of economic growth have gone hand in hand with rapid expansion of the HE sector, can also be engineered at the European scale. Given that those nations that have the most 'successful' economies usually have the highest percentages of people educated to degree level or above, this faith appears to be justified. (There have been historical exceptions, however. It could be argued, for example, that the level of faith placed in higher education in the Republic of Ireland for many years generated as many benefits to the US and UK economies as to the domestic one.) The key points to note, however, are that (a) 'relevance' is more assumed than required or organized, given that the impact of European institutions is inevitably indirect and dependent upon choices made at national, sub-national and individual institutional levels, and (b) comparatively little attention is paid to geography and scale in this analysis, the implicit presumption being that a formula that 'works' for, say, Cambridge University in the western European 'core' can be replicated, and have similarly positive effects, at the University of Maribor in Slovenia, in the eastern periphery.

Perry and Harloe do not attempt a comparative review of similar developments in high-level policy at the national scale. Had they done so, however, the conclusion would surely have supported their contention that 'internal restructuring, where it is occurring, does not reflect "intentional design" towards a [local or] regional mission' but rather an attempt to reposition particular universities within various markets for their services, including local and regional ones. The sorts of debate that have recently been grappled with at the European scale have a longer history at the national level. In the case of the UK, for example, they date back at least as far as the green paper on *The Development of Higher Education into the 1990s* (1985), published at a time when Keith Joseph, a keen political champion of neo-liberalism, was Secretary of State for Education. That document, like many that followed it across the globe, called for universities to be more responsive to their external environment – and particularly towards labour market requirements – as well as more entrepreneurial. Since that time, a variety of initiatives, orchestrated by a host of government departments and public agencies, have attempted to bring about closer engagement between universities and external (and often local and regional) 'stakeholders'. However, it would be difficult to sustain the argument that these initiatives have been more than marginal within HE policy in the round.

In the UK, for example, in addition to the 'cluster' initiatives mentioned by Charles and associated with the Department of Trade and Industry, the Department for

Education and Science and its organizational offshoots have devoted comparatively modest resources to university 'reach-out' programmes, targeted mainly on the business community, and made 'policy relevance' and 'user engagement' part of the criteria against which peer-reviewed research bids are assessed. For the most part, however, debate about the importance of universities to sub-national (and therefore also national) competitiveness continues to be largely symbolic. Thus, on one hand, national reviews of sub-national development policy (ODPM, 2006) posit a relationship between the presence of a major research university and relatively high rates of spatial economic growth, but do not identify any sort of causal link between them or set out detailed policy implications. Similarly, individual universities continue to invest significant resources in estimating their local and regional economic impact, but more as a way of demonstrating positive returns on investment in HE than as a guide to what they themselves could or should do differently in order to maximize that impact. Instead, and as Perry and Harloe also discuss in their chapter, relatively abstract debates about the development of 'Mode 2' universities (or parts thereof) provide much of the available ammunition to demonstrate the need for the structures and modes of operation of university governance to change, from the traditional 'Mode 1', in order to better reflect changing circumstances.[1]

What has proven far more important, both in terms of national HE policy and the 'will to engage' amongst universities, is the massivication of the sector. Whilst the extent of the increase in student numbers, along with the way in which it has been financed, varies significantly across OECD countries, there has been a general tendency, over the last 20-30 years, for a greatly increased percentage of the cohort of school leavers to attend university, for older groups within the workforce to 'top up' their knowledge and skills through HE provision, and for the proportion of national populations that are degree-educated to rise accordingly. As a result, universities no longer cater only for the small percentage of the future workforce that is expected to take up leadership positions, but also provide skills and advanced learning capacity to a much larger group that, in many cases, represents the majority of new entrants to, and aspirational movers within, the labour market. This trend could not, by any stretch of the imagination, be said to have been driven by local and regional needs and demands. It is more the product of increasing personal and familial aspirations, the 'ratcheting up' of entry-level qualifications by employers and the tendency of many national governments to set much more ambitious targets for university recruitment. One of its effects, however, has been to provide greater incentives for interaction between universities and the local and regional consumers of their services.

---

1   The notion of Mode 1 and Mode 2 forms of knowledge production was introduced by Gibbons *et al.* (1994). Mode 1 refers to traditional disciplinary scholarship conducted in 'freedom and isolation'; Mode 2 to more problem-oriented and team-based research. Gibbons *et al.* claim a gradual transition from Mode 1 to Mode 2. This claim is controversial, with critics arguing that these two modes of knowledge production were 'virtually joined at the hip at birth' (Fuller, 2000: 80).

This has happened in two main ways. First, the transition from 'elite' to 'mass' HE provision has been built substantially upon universities' ability to open up access to a broader base of entrants who, typically, tend to be less mobile than the traditional school leaver, particularly when the tendency for levels of financial support to students to fall is factored into the equation. Whilst those institutions where demand for places is highest have managed to expand provision through increased applications at the national and international scale, most have relied upon expanding the number of students recruited locally and regionally. Indirectly, this has provided greater incentive for universities to take the current and potential future state of sub-national labour markets more carefully into consideration. Second, the massivication process, far from being cost-neutral, has tended to be accompanied by a fall in the unit cost per student provided out of general taxation. In part, the financial gap this has imposed upon individual universities has been offset by productivity improvements (larger class sizes, use of less labour-intensive teaching methods, etc.). But some of the shortfall has necessarily been made up from expansion of other income sources. Here, once again, whilst the lucky few institutions have been able to tap new income streams at the national and global scale, for example through alumni benefactions, the overall effect has been to encourage greater engagement with the most promising fee-earning clients closer to home.

In summary, then, the combined effects of globalization, greater demand for inputs of knowledge into the productive process and the massivication of the HE sector have been to sharpen the questions asked about the relevance of the services universities provide and to deepen the reliance of the bulk of institutions upon local and regional consumers and clients.

Quite how university managers and the academic community more generally have, or should have, responded to these pressures and with what consequences form the main themes of the chapters in Part 2 of the volume. Before considering these, however, we need to mention the final scene-setting chapter in Part 1 since it provides a crucial link between the demand-side changes discussed thus far and the factors influencing the supply-side responses in Part 2. In his chapter, Morten Levin makes the ostensibly simple point that universities that engage effectively with their localities and regions must, effectively, produce valuable 'regional knowledge'. He then goes on to show just how difficult and yet essential it is to define and distil the notion of regional knowledge and contrasts the possibilities that are available in principle with the poverty of approaches which assume that specific, generalizable knowledge is produced by academics and the only trick that needs to be performed is its transfer into regional contexts of application. In arguing that 'knowing how' rather than 'knowing what' provides the basis of meaningful knowledge transfer, and in setting out the challenges that would need to be faced by academics and non-academics alike in making it a reality, he provides some pointers as to what 'Mode 2' university activities might comprise and what changes would be needed in the expectations and behaviour of external groups to maximize their regional value.

Herding the Supply-side Cats?

Simply because a number of 'demand-side' pressures have ostensibly encouraged universities, as institutions, to be more 'relevant' and 'engaged', and more attentive to the geographical-economic contexts in which they work, it does not follow that academic communities have adjusted, automatically, in ways that can be shown to contribute to local and regional development needs and priorities. The factors that influence the extent to which there has been and should be such a response are assessed in Part 2 of the volume, which focuses upon the internal governance of universities and the interaction between internal organization and external environments.

Within the often historically foreshortened vision of policy and academic debates on relevance and scale, it is easy to forget that such issues, and the dilemmas with which they are associated, have a long history. In his influential *The Decline of the German Mandarins*, Fritz Ringer traces the ultimately doomed resistance of late nineteenth- and early twentieth-century German academics to the effects of modernization on the universities. 'Most German academics,' he observes, 'were no longer willing to consider any compromise with the modern age' (1969: 80). Ringer is far from unsympathetic with their struggle to maintain the integrity of universities and standards in the face of external pressure brought about by industrialization and the expansion of the state, but is critical of the conflation of these legitimate concerns with a wider set of value-conservative and ultimately elitist cultural prejudices. Thus, of the activities of the Corporation of German Universities in the Weimar Republic he writes:

> as a group they did not offer positive proposals. Refusing to admit that there was anything wrong with the old school system, they took an uncompromising and often purposely disdainful stance. Above all, they failed to disentangle the problem of academic standards from the *whole complex of social prejudices* that had grown up around the idea of classical 'cultivation' [*Bildung*]. (Ringer 1969: 78, emphasis added)

The longer-term consequence of such a fundamental resistance to the implications of changes in the external environment was not the safeguarding, but the destruction of those academic values that were potentially worthy of preservation. Inability to reform from within ultimately provoked a political response that changed universities from without, but with little regard to what was and what was not of value in traditional academic practices. In this way the academics themselves may be said to have contributed to a process in which their own core values were displaced. In a comment that has contemporary resonance, Ringer notes that 'a nostalgic and rigid attachment to the values of the past prevented even the kinds of conservative reforms that might have rescued some of those values for the present' (1969: 57).

Although Ringer is analysing a particular historical case, the responses of the Wilhelmian and Weimar Republic universities are by no means unfamiliar. They seem to represent a kind of pattern or dynamic that reproduces itself – with thematic variations – historically and geographically. The account he gives is familiar to many present-day higher-education managers and policy-makers, and, indeed, to many academics themselves. The self-destructive nature of the cultural conservatism and elitism that characterizes the academic profession is, for example, strongly criticized in this volume by Tim May (chapter 7) for whom a defence of the university in terms of traditional notions of 'academic freedom' is no longer enough, or simply looks like a rationalization that will be stifled under the weight of accountability demands and audit requirements. What is it about universities as institutions that sets this dynamic in train? And what conclusions are to be drawn?

Complaints about the inflexibility and irresponsiveness of universities are familiar, and indeed well captured in such witty (or morbid) similes as 'herding cats' and 'moving graveyards'. Ringer's characterization of the traditional (largely self-governed) 'Humboldtian' university as an unhappy place once more provides a telling historical example:

> one cannot avoid the impression that interpersonal relations within the scholarly community were never particularly satisfactory, whether between students and teachers, between younger and older faculty members, or even between colleagues. There was an unhealthy atmosphere of rank-consciousness, favouritism, and mutual resentment. [...] Situations arose in which even the strongest advocates of academic self-governance were inclined to welcome the intervention of the ministry against the prejudices of this or that faculty. (Ringer 1969: 55–6)

Nor are such problems confined to the *Ordinarienuniversitäten* (universities run by – and largely for – professors) that Ringer is characterizing here. For example, in the 1970s experiments in democratizing internal university decision-making (co-determination) in parts of continental Europe were successful in empowering previously exploited junior faculty (and even students), but this did not have the hoped for effect of creating strong, dynamic and progressive universities (see Burtscher, Pasqualoni and Scott, A., 2006). On the contrary, left to themselves, individual departments, or whole institutions, can drift towards what the anthropologist Mary Douglas has labelled 'backwater isolation' – i.e. highly ritualized and rule-bound communities (high grid) but with low levels of mutual trust and solidarity (low group) (e.g. Douglas, 1996). Under these conditions, 'self-made rules' (e.g. concerning disciplinary boundaries) lower levels of interaction by inhibiting 'free transaction' (Douglas and Isherwood, 1979: 22). The philosopher Martin Hollis offered a wonderful imaginary account of what such an academic community might look like:

> St Jude's is an obscure college at an old university. Its cellars have always been excellent, its dons mediocre and waspish. Predictably, it has a long history of opposition. In the last four centuries, the Fellows of St Jude's have opposed popery, Oliver Cromwell, the Industrial Revolution, the holding of services in English, electricity, women, the General Strike and colour television. But principally, of course, they have opposed one another. (Hollis 1970: 32)

Hollis ironically concludes that such a life is not as vapid as it may appear to an outsider since: 'the Fellows are engaged at full stretch on the delicate task of embodying a tradition.' But we no longer live in a world in which embodying a tradition is thought to be an activity on which taxpayers' money should be spent. As Davydd Greenwood puts it in his contribution to this volume, 'many professors and administrators appear to have forgotten this debt to the public and consider the flow of tax money in their direction as a fundamental, pre-political right' (p. 98).

Douglas's grid-group model has been most fruitfully developed in the analysis of public management by Christopher Hood (1998). The phenomenon that Ringer captures historically and Hollis in the form of a paradox (Are they doing nothing? No, they are embodying tradition!), Hood calls 'elitist' or 'sequestrated' egalitarianism: a form of socialism among peers, or within a status group, in which there is an 'emphasis upon participation in communal activity and control of individuals through processes of mutuality' (1998: 134). In egalitarian communities, he notes, 'it is hard to resolve disputes' because there is no effective mechanism for expelling 'deviants and heretics' (*ibid.*: 142), who exercise a de facto veto over their expulsion. Such communities are thus prone to long-running feuds since they fail to reach the decisions that would end feuding. Thus, paradoxically given its emphasis on the community over the individual, egalitarian management, on Hood's account, is likely to encourage free riding (e.g. unwillingness to take on unpleasant tasks), and can easily degenerate into a form of mutual tolerance ('coexistence'): a 'tendency for each of the colleagues in the group to avoid asking awkward questions about the behaviour of other colleagues' (*ibid.*: 41). Institutions run on egalitarian principles also necessarily cut themselves off from their surroundings because strict boundary maintenance is a condition of mutuality. The traditional university – whether in its professor-dominated or democratized form – can come to approximate Hood's sequestrated egalitarian ideal type.

So, we can easily identify a set of more-or-less familiar problems concerning the inner life of universities:

- Problems of ossification and stasis;
- The tendency towards backwater isolation that can easily develop behind the real and imaginary walls of academia;
- The failure to distinguish genuine questions of quality in research and teaching from the 'whole complex of social prejudices' that Ringer identifies;
- The problem of making those who are inclined to 'embody a tradition' responsive to changes in the external environment;
- Making universities answerable to those whom they serve, and who finance them.

But if these problems are familiar, so too by now are the solutions that have been adopted, and these solutions are everywhere the same: organizational re-engineering with an emphasis upon target-setting and auditing, already familiar within the English-speaking university systems – and to a degree pioneered in Australia (see Marginson and Considine, 2000) – is now spreading throughout continental Europe (see, for example, Schimank, 2000) and beyond. However, while university governance practices inspired by new public management ideas may be successful in disrupting deeply embedded and self-reproducing 'patterns' (DiMaggio and Powell, 1991) of the type discussed above, there is now growing evidence that: (a) they create new risks and inefficiencies; (b) because they are grounded in a general theory of organizations qua organizations, they tend to be insensitive to qualities that may be necessary for a specific type of organization to perform its particular functions; and (c) they are much less effective than their modernizing rhetoric asserts.

With respect to the first of these types of criticism, there is now an extensive analysis of outcomes of auditing and 'just do it' cultures, which have displaced – or have been said to displace – traditional organizations, including the traditional university (Power, 1997, du Gay, 2000, and Strathern, 2000 are among the major references). The key arguments can be listed briefly as follows:

- Control by total quality management (TQM) and audit are low-trust modes of management destructive of organizational culture in general, and thus perpetuate the problems they claim to address (O'Neill, 2002);
- They are destructive in particular of the culture of public service upon which publicly-funded institutions especially are dependent (du Gay, 2000);
- Creating auditable subjects is a costly 'ritual of verification' in which the control mechanisms rather than performance itself are assessed. The effort is frequently disproportional to the pay-off, and behaviour adjusts to targets. Thus, we can be assured that 'the system works well even when substantive performance is poor' (Power, 1997: 60);
- Low trust and audit regimes are self-confirming and self-reproducing. In a downward spiral, they lower the level of public trust in institutions, thus increasing the demand for further control and surveillance (Power 1997; Marquand 2004);
- New forms of management encourage authoritarian and monological leadership styles (Willmott, 1993), and undermine social (and organizational) pluralism (Palumbo and Scott, A., 2005);
- Imitation of the market model (internal markets, teaching and research audit (e.g. the Research Assessment Exercise (RAE) and Total Quality Assessment (TQA) in the UK), and emphasis on national and global competition – often via the surrogate of league tables, etc.) leads to a breakdown of institutional 'pillarization' and thus opens universities to corporate interests and pressures (see Monbiot, 2001 for a journalistic account, Crouch, 2004 for a sociological one, and Slaughter and Leslie, 1997 for a discussion with specific reference to higher education, particularly the USA).

Such considerations have been fed into the debate about higher education, notably by Simon Marginson and Mark Considine (2000) who offer a detailed empirical analysis of the effects of organizational change and new management styles on the Australian university system. Similarly, Chris Shore and Susan Wright (2000) have applied this type of critique of modern public management to university governance via the notion of 'coercive accountability', and have argued that 'the time has come to hold audit itself to account so that we may realize the true extent of the disastrous social costs of the coercive new form of governance' (2000: 85). One sub-theme of Part 2 of this volume is how one might support such a conclusion other than on the basis of an uncritical attitude towards what went before, or blindness to its weaknesses. This concern is particularly marked in the contributions of Davydd Greenwood and Tim May, neither of whom would wish to fall for either the pathos of the defence of the status quo ante, nor the modernizing rhetoric of new public management. Their concern – and a central concern of the collection – is to think beyond these polar options. As Greenwood puts it 'unlike private corporations, driven by market tests of profitability of particular goods and services, universities are composed of a mixed, confusing, and even contradictory set of activities' (p. 98). It is this plurality of functions that requires us, in his view, to extend the list of those with a legitimate 'stake' in the university beyond the narrow economic interests so often invoked in policy debate (cf. Slaughter and Leslie, 1997).

With this argument we already touch on the second of the above types of criticism of new public management, namely its failure to adequately address, or arguably even pose, the question: what kind of management is fit for what kind of task? The limits of the one size fits all/one best way logic become particularly apparent if it can be shown that some of the 'dysfunctions' of universities are unavoidable outcomes of the tasks that they are bound to undertake. This argument has been powerfully made by Susanne Lohmann (2004), who argues that ossification lies in the nature of the scientific or scholarly enterprise itself. This enterprise is one of deep specialization, and this is both the source of its extraordinary historical achievements and its inability – left to its own devices – to counter its ossifying tendencies:

> The tendency of the university to ossify is an integral aspect of its positive function to enable deep specialization. [...] But the constituent elements of the university – deeply specialized scholars and discipline-based departments – cannot easily change their stripes simply because their stripes are the way they are for a reason. (Lohmann, 2004: 78)

What is a necessary *defence* can all too easily become a *defect*. The walls between the university and the outside world and the (disciplinary) walls within the university are necessary conditions for deep specialization, but they can also keep redundant practices running in perpetuity: 'one important function of the disciplines is to protect the established lines of inquiry, and when those lines become obsolete, they keep right on protecting' (*ibid*.: 82). If correct, Lohmann's analysis has a number of implications of which two are particularly important: first, the self-government of university affairs by academics cannot address the problem of ossification because it is governed by the same logic that led to that ossification in the first place. Secondly, what has, over the last quarter of a century, generally come to be seen as '*the* solution' to this problem – namely the highly managed model with centralized authority and weak devolution of power (Clark 1998) – is hardly less problematic since it seeks to offer generalized solutions to problems that are unavoidable by-products of features necessary for this particular organization to perform its function.

Similar concerns are raised in this volume by Dolores Byrnes (chapter 8), and by Todd Bridgman and Hugh Willmott (chapter 9). Both Byrnes and Bridgman and Willmott see shifts in institutional arrangements as posing identity problems for collective and individual agents. Byrnes's study is based upon ethnography of three US universities, and a number of academic disciplines. She identifies the implications of an increasingly hegemonic discourse based upon the natural sciences and economic instrumentalism for disciplines (such as philosophy), which do not and cannot convincingly embody those virtues. She shows that they have (or believe themselves to have) little option but to adopt the hegemonic discourse, but are thereby forced into defensive strategies that fail to resolve, or may even exacerbate, problems of legitimation and self-presentation. This also makes clearer why it is increasingly problematic to appeal to principles that would have once had purchase, such as academic freedom or the spirit of criticism (May's point); in the current context these look increasingly like empty gestures. Bridgman and Willmott pose a similar dilemma for the 'public intellectual'. Like Byrnes, they argue that one can be damned if one does (conform to the hegemonic discourse) and damned if one doesn't. However, the conclusion they draw is that under these conditions it is better to adopt what may appear to be the higher-risk and defiant strategy and (contra Scott, A., 1997) ignore Weber's advice about self-restraint in matters of value judgement, which, Weber believed, places a defensive shield around academic freedom. This view raises the intriguing counter-factual possibility that Ringer's German professors might have been no better off had they open-mindedly embraced modernity. For Byrnes, and for Bridgman and Willmott, the prospect for universities is one of the decline of pluralism as all activities come to be measured by a limited numbers of criteria of success (or failure). Bridgman and Willmott see the role of the public intellectual as an alternative to the client-orientation that is held up as the model for the academic's relationship to the wider world, and as one way of resisting processes of homogenization.

But how hegemonic is this discourse really? Is new public management as effective as both its proponents and critics tend to assume? This is the third strand of criticism identified above. While among contemporary university managers large-scale organizational reform is frequently viewed as the measure of first resort, and sometimes as a cure-all, such thinking is prone to what Albert Hirschman has dubbed 'fracasomania' (failure complex): 'by invoking the desperate predicament in which a people is caught, as well as the failure of prior attempts at reform, it is implicitly or explicitly argued that the old order must be smashed and a new one rebuilt from scratch *regardless* of any counterproductive consequences that might ensue' (Hirschman, 1991: 162). Hirschman argues that such a logic leads to a vacillation between polar alternatives (a view that coincides with Hood's – see below), and produces results that are only marginally, if at all, more rational than those of dyed-in-the-wool conservatism. A similar line of thought, with a similar emphasis upon irrational outcomes, is developed by James Scott for whom 'cadastral rule' (rule by the plan and by the organizational chart) tends to vastly overestimate the power of the plan to alter behaviour on the ground:

> Redesigning the lines and boxes in an organizational chart is simpler than changing how that organization in fact operates. Changing the rules and regulations is simpler than eliciting behavior that conforms to them (Scott, J.C., 1998: 255).

Once organizational reforms have been carried through, the work has (formally) been completed, and those affected (including managers) are left to make the best of the new circumstances. However, this is precisely where there is scope for subverting the intention of the planner, and this leads us straight back to Hood's analysis. Hood identifies the problem here not merely as one of side-effects (in the traditional sense of unforeseen and unintended consequences) but also of 'reverse effects': achieving the 'very opposite of the desired effect' (1998: 210). Organizational re-engineering encourages such 'reverse effects' in all the manifestations that Hood identifies. As he notes, 'the more reliance is placed on any given polar approach to public management, the more serious its "blind spots" are likely to become, producing unexpected reverse effects through "functional disruption" and "placation"' (*ibid.*: 217). For example, 'redesigning the lines and boxes' induces – passive and active – resistance, and the inevitable concessions made ('placation') subvert the original intent (*ibid.*: 213). Cadastral rule and 'modernization rhetoric' (Hood, Pt III) share an illusion of which Machiavelli (often invoked by reformers) warned: in order to govern effectively one needs to understand the nature of the *materia* over which one rules. Fracasomania (Hirschman), and utopian planning (J.C. Scott) share an implicit faith that one can reshape that *materia* more-or-less at will. This faith turns out, more frequently than managerialism likes to acknowledge, to be unfounded. Thus, in contrast to some of the critical accountancy takes on new public management, Hirschman, J.C. Scott and Hood all point to the *weaknesses* of organizational redesign rather than its transformative *powers*.

These considerations should give us reason to pause about the conclusion to be drawn from the behaviour of Ringer's German professors and Hollis's fictitious Fellows of St Jude's. The error that Ringer identifies among late nineteenth- and early twentieth-century German academics – the conflation of legitimate concerns about standards with 'a whole complex of social prejudices' – can just as easily be made by the modernizers, but with the opposite conclusion drawn: not the preservation of everything, but its destruction is required. Here all arguments for autonomy, or for traditional modes of academic work (anything that smacks of 'Mode-1ism') can be interpreted as social prejudice and/or as a rationalization of privilege and an instinctive defence of outmoded practices. But the sense of 'public service', the loss of which du Gay (2000) fears in the case of civil servants faced with political pressures in the guise of reform, has its equivalent in academic practice: methodical care; long-term commitment to a discipline and/or a field of research (see Baert and Shipman, 2005); the careful checking of data, results, and textual references; the refusal to rush into publication or tailor results to anticipated end user or sponsor requirements; defence of the autonomy of academic practices from political or commercial interest; rigour. Such an 'ethic of responsibility' and 'conduct of life' *is* inflexible, and precisely therefore protects the integrity of academic practices and the autonomy of academic institutions. Walls protect as well as imprison (cf. Lohmann). It is perhaps no coincidence that it has so frequently been philosophy that has been the lightening conductor for the modernizers' rage, because it, above all, symbolizes these qualities. Furthermore, auditing culture turns what Weber identified as an internalized ethic and life-long commitment to the daemon who, once found, holds the treads of ones life (1919a: 33) into external and measurable (but also fakeable) 'performance'. So we need not assume that Hollis was being entirely ironic about 'embodying tradition'. An institution unable to preserve its autonomy – unable to embody tradition – and that completely subordinates its rituals to demands for efficiency or external pressures will lose its distinctiveness, and this too induces problems of legitimation (Meyer and Rowan, 1991): what exactly is there to preserve? Since not merely the embodiment but also the preservation and handing down of (intellectual and cultural) tradition are among the legitimate functions of the university, acknowledging the plurality of its responsibilities requires recognition of the types and limits of openness that are appropriate to particular levels and tasks. Thus, the call for openness and for a closer relationship between the university and its environment, has to be tempered by a recognition of the specificities of 'science as a vocation' if we are ourselves to avoid slipping into modernizing rhetoric, polar approaches, or simply opening up one more state-sponsored common to commercialization (Palumbo and Scott, A., 2005).

For this variety of (partly contrasting) reasons, we need to start thinking of alternatives to what has become the global alternative to the traditional university: a mix of 'bossism' (the 'hierarchist way') and competition plus rivalry (the 'individualist way'), to use Hood's categories (1998: 56). In this spirit, several contributions in this volume call for a more context-sensitive model; one that does not make overblown claims, nor is based upon the monolithic 'one best way' thinking. The dilemmas they seek to address should be apparent from the foregoing discussion: left to its own devices, the university will be beset by problems of ossification and can drift towards backwater isolation (to this extent there is agreement with the views of higher-educations critics and reformers), but the solutions that have been proposed and put into practice are themselves beset with problems and bear quite different risks and absurdities. Neither a backward-looking nor a Panglossian response is therefore appropriate. As Stefan Collini has noted in a challenging essay on higher education in the UK:

> On the one hand, there is the mournful idiom of cultural declinism: 'standards' are falling, 'philistinism' is rampant, 'autonomy' has been lost, and even the barbarians are going to the dogs. And on the other, there is the upbeat idiom of brave new worldism: 'challenges' and 'opportunities' abound, 'partnerships with industry'

beckon, 'accountability' rules, and we're all 'investing in the future' like billy-oh. As with larger questions of social and cultural change, it can be difficult to escape the magnetic pull of these extremes, difficult to get the measure of the changes that have been taking place without either falling into the absurdity of suggesting that everything would be all right if we could just go back to universities as they were *c.*1953, or the equal absurdity of proposing that more ruthless cost-cutting and more aggressive marketing could soon have HiEdbizUK plc showing healthy profits for shareholders. (Collini, 2003)

Seeking to avoid this polarization, the contributions here tend to argue not against (the necessity of) management, but rather against managerial*ism* in its gung-ho mode. But what are such arguments in favour of? Here is a first summary of some of the points that will be made in more detail in the chapters that follow:

- *Treating organizational change as a process not as an end in itself;* not a guarantee of 'happiness, efficiency and usefulness' but, at best, a way of removing 'mechanical constraints' (Weber 1918: 134), for example by facilitating the negotiation of (provisional) solutions.[2] This recognition of the limits of organizational reengineering has practical implications: removing constraints requires not primarily holistic measures but pragmatic ones. Examples might include: building parallel and cross-cutting structures that will eventually displace those that are unredeemably ossified; moving frustrated faculty out of positions in which they can block any change (cf. Lohmann, 2004: 83); creating structures (outside traditional departments) in which those who are willing to cooperate and exchange can do so (rather than trying to force cooperation on these accustomed to solitary scholarly activity). Such strategies are not quick fixes but they do, in contrast to a fundamental opposition to management of the kind sometimes found among academics, entail a degree of central decision making and direction; and are thus also an acknowledgement of the limits of self-governance and co-determination;

- *Sensitivity to context and function; not treating organization as* sui generis. As Tim May observes in his contribution: 'sensitivity to context is precisely the element that is missing' (p. 131). A century of criticism of positivism has done little to shift the simplistic view that there are general laws of social life from which not merely predictions, but also controls can be deduced. In contrast, universities are here viewed as having specific characteristics given by their functions, and we may even have to recognize that ossification and inefficiencies are inherent in scientific and scholarly practice. We cannot know for sure what will and will not be important and dynamic in the mid to long range, so *a degree of* slack is

---

2   Weber's observation here is on the role of constitutional reform, but it also provides a useful corrective to modernizing rhetoric by insisting that rational reform is, at best, a means to an end, and that that end is itself relatively modest: the removal of mechanical constraints (*mechanische Hemmnisse*).

necessary to insure the longer-term viability of the system. Slack is an investment in an unknowable future. Paradoxically, the outcome of the failure to recognize this can be the conservative and timid policy of imitating that which appears to have worked elsewhere.[3] In these respects, a black and white problem-solution mindset is inappropriate. Unavoidable but undesirable side-effects of necessary practices cannot be 'solved' (i.e. eradicated); they can only be moderated and managed in such a way as to minimizing their undesired effects;

- *Acknowledgement of the specificities of universities as organizations.* Public management practices treat all organizations as though they were – or ought to be – firms (Marquand, 2004) and seek to create quasi-markets, but, as Greenwood notes in his contribution, 'market behaviour with a significant workforce that cannot be fired is impossible' (p. 100). Most of the contributions to Part 2 of this volume which address the question of the *internal* university governance are in general agreement with David Marquand's view that, as institutions within the 'public domain',[4] universities require a form of steering that is not state (the pre-Humboldtian university), not familial (the Humboldtian university), and not quasi-market (the modern centrally managed, corporate university), and seek to identify at least the outline of what such a 'fourth way' might be;

- *Linking internal reform to the external environment.* This is a key theme of this volume, and one particularly manifest in the discussion of ways of extending the range 'stakeholders' with a legitimate claim to have a say in internal university affairs (especially the chapter by Greenwood, but also Levin in Part 1). The stakeholder issue is in fact closely related to the above considerations. If, on the basis of its own resources, neither the self-governed nor the centrally managed corporate university is able to address its problems adequately, the drawing in of a broader set of external interests (and not just powerful vested interests) has to be locked into internal reform processes. This also is necessary for the university's external legitimation and broadens the notion of 'accountability' away from auditing discourse and practice: 'instead of a defensive and/or arrogant university reaction to these pressures and instead of handing the university over to a group of accountants, a more intelligent response would be to evaluate the depth of the crisis universities find themselves in and to engage in a public process of the redesign of university work life with the legitimate problem owners' (Greenwood).

These are wide-ranging and, as put above, rather abstractly expressed responses. In the latter half of Part 2 of the volume, we seek to make some of this more concrete by offering specific case studies where such strategies were – in part at least – attempted.

---

3   For an influential discussion, see DiMaggio and Powell, 1991 on 'institutional isomorphism', particularly in its 'mimetic' form.

4   For his definition of the 'public domain', see Marquand, 2004: 26–9.

Here the concerns of the volume's two parts – internal governance and external relations – come together. The chapters by Stephan Laske, Maximilian Egger and Claudia Meister-Scheytt (chapter 10), by Christine Smith and William Lovegrove (chapter 11) and the final chapter, which takes the form of an interview undertaken by two of the co-editors (Laske and Scott) with Lothar Zechlin, Founding Rector of the University of Duisburg-Essen, examine three cases in which universities have sought to reposition themselves, strategically, within their respective regions through processes of engagement with local actors, in the former two cases, and through the merger of two formerly independent institutions in the latter case. The three regions in questions – the Austrian Tyrol, the Brisbane (Australia) area and the Ruhrgebiet in Germany – are areas of contrasting economic fortunes and trajectories. There is contrast, too, in the nature of regional engagement activities examined. Smith and Lovegrove focus upon the impact of a university campus on an urban area in (relative) decline. Laske, Egger and Meister-Scheytt demonstrate the sensitivity and complexity of the negotiations needed to secure a working relationship between university and regional actors. Zechlin, by contrast, describes how the merger process was negotiated and implemented in the face of very different sets of internal and external aspirations, expectations and pressures.

All three, however, illustrate just how far the mundane reality of building solid coalitions for change – whatever the scale – is from the rhetoric of the knowledge society, cluster building, knowledge transfer, and the rest. They also make the case (and here is a direct link with issues of internal governance) that suitable internal structures are required to facilitate the region-university relationship and to establish the legitimacy of any new departure. In an interesting twist, they argue that while traditional university structures made regional partnerships difficult, the modernized university – with its emphasis upon international reputation and competition – risks making it even more so by creating disincentives; for example by rewarding academic endeavour (in research and publication) that is decontextualized and oriented away from the locality. Except at a rhetorical level, relevance and international competition are not easily squared. The case study chapters nevertheless make the case that the effort can be worth it and can impact upon the quality of teaching as well as tying university and regions more closely together. Smith and Lovegrove, for example, note that high-level decisions within the university are necessary to initiate partnership relations, but more sustained and grassroots commitment is needed to realize their full potential. Zechlin, in his interview, is more candid still in asserting the importance of resolving internal organizational-cultural issues as a precondition for creating a settled institution that can survive the competing pressures generated within a fragmented and politicized regional environment. The implicit lesson all three chapters draw is that 'learning regions' require learning universities. These examples offer general support to May's call for greater management and policy sensitivity to context, and to Greenwood's proposal for extending the range of stakeholders to a wider (also local or regional) community.

Ultimately, the challenge set by Part 1 of this volume – for faculty as well as university managers – is to understand and make sense of the pressures that will continue to demand at least a partial 'regionalization' of HE business in such a way that universities have credible responses to those who would question their 'relevance'. The challenge issued by the contributions in Part 2 is to take seriously the proposition that this re-orientation cannot be achieved effectively through managerialist fiat or external audit but must entail the active renegotiation of both internal and external relations. The price for not doing so, according to the consensus of the many and varied contributions that make up this collection, is likely to be a continuing vacillation between management styles, and a continuing loss of external legitimacy.

PART 1
Local and Regional Engagement Strategies: Dilemmas and Options

Chapter 2

External Engagements and Internal Transformations: Universities, Localities and Regional Development[1]

Beth Perry and Michael Harloe[2]

Introduction

The development of the knowledge economy is placing universities at the heart of economic and social development processes in relation to their teaching, research and outreach functions. While this is by no means an exclusively contemporary phenomenon, and certainly not an uncontroversial one, emphasis is increasingly being placed on the contribution of universities to their localities and regions in political, economic, social and civic terms. For those keen to exploit the opportunities this presents, a consideration of the need for internal transformations within the university is required in order to make it 'fit for purpose' to meet new 'entrepreneurial' roles. A core concern here is how best to reorientate or remould the university in such a way as to meet new challenges while guarding the 'essence' of the academic enterprise. What is needed is further empirical work which considers the relationship between external engagements and internal transformations in different national and sub-national contexts.

It is widely accepted that the university is assuming growing importance in policy terms as an engine of economic growth and social transformation. Consequently, universities across both the developed and developing worlds are being encouraged, and in some cases coerced, into greater engagement with their localities and regions. In this chapter we consider first, in general terms, the drivers that are bringing about such increased engagement with wider economic, societal and political actors and the increasing centrality of the university within economic

1 This chapter is a significantly revised version of the keynote lecture given by Michael Harloe and Beth Perry at the conference on Universities, Localities and Regional Development held at the University of Innsbruck in December 2002. The original lecture, in modified and lengthened form, was printed in the *International Journal of Urban and Regional Research* (Harloe and Perry, 2004).

2 We gratefully acknowledge support of the ESRC Science in Society programme through Award Numbers L144250004 and RES-151-25-0037 for funding research on which the observations in this paper are based.

and social development processes. This process is highlighted through a discussion of emerging European frameworks for higher education and research. For many, the emphasis on new roles for the university implies the need for internal reform of university governance structures and organizational arrangements. Second, then, the chapter moves on to review the current literatures on university reform in face of the 'entrepreneurial' challenge and the different kinds of reorientations that are seemingly underway. More than external engagements, such internal transformations pose core challenges in terms of the extent to which making the university 'fit for purpose' and transforming it into a twenty-first-century institution undermine the essence of what has traditionally been seen as the core of the academic enterprise. A pivotal question here is how to preserve what is distinctive about the university as a site of knowledge production, at the same time as ensuring that external expectations can be met and roles fulfilled. In the final section of the chapter, we consider the range of factors that enable or constrain the particular responses of universities to the dual-edged demands of the internal–external dichotomy. In doing so, this chapter offers an overview of recent literatures to contextualize the range of contributions in this collection, as well as highlighting the need for change from within as a precursor to meaningful external engagements.

Knowledge Economies, Capitalisms and Scales

The Knowledge Economy

It is widely recognized that we now live in a knowledge-based economy, where knowledge has superseded physical and tangible assets as the key foundation for wealth creation and economic growth. Accounts of this change and its many implications can be found across a wide range of disciplines from management studies to sociology, from political studies to geography, from economics to science and technology studies and so on (Gibbons *et al.*, 1994; Neef, 1998; Burton-Jones, 1999; Allen, 2000; Bryson *et al.*, 2000. Dunning *et al.*, 2000. Fuller, 2000. Delanty, 2001. May, 2001. Hellstrom and Ramen, 2001; Bowring, 2002). Such is the trans-disciplinary relevance of changes related to the role, value and economics of knowledge, that most accounts of change are incomplete if read in isolation.

Most writers on the subject date the concept of the knowledge economy in the academic literature back to the influential work of Bell in 1973 who is acknowledged as one of the first to recognize the key role of knowledge as a factor in the production and reproduction of economies and societies (Allen, 2000; Bryson *et al.*, 2000; Scarborough, 2001; Drennan, 2002). Bell's seminal work, *The Coming of Post-Industrial Society* (1973) charts the perceived shift from manufacturing to a less tangible world of services and information. For Bell, this shift represents a key step along the path towards a post-industrial economy in which the singular driving feature is knowledge, and, in particular, codified abstract knowledge (Allen, 2000). Putting it simply, the 'new' economy is based on creating, doing things to or with knowledge: '...the action of knowledge upon knowledge is the main source of productivity' (Castells, 1996). In the knowledge-driven economy what counts are knowledge, skills, innovation and creativity. It is not that land and labour are no longer important, rather that they are seen as increasingly secondary to knowledge in wealth creation. This change is often characterized as an economic shift from action-centred to intellectual skills (Bryson *et al.*, 2000), from brawn to brains, or from natural, tangible to intangible, created assets.

A number of key characteristics have been highlighted as evidence of the knowledge economy. For some, the most obvious of these are the proliferation of high-tech industries and the expansion of the scientific base, the move away from manufacturing to a service-based economy and the development of new information technologies and accelerated technological change (Neef, 1998). Others stress the growth of symbolic goods, demassification and the boundary-less firm (Burton-Jones, 1999: 13). Information technologies, while important, are only one catalyst to the increasing role and importance of knowledge in the economy, as growing recognition is being given to the economic value of tacit knowledges and extra-economic resources in creating competitiveness. More significant evidence of the fundamental shifts that have taken place in the economy can be seen, rather, in the increasing complexity and sophistication of processes of production and products, the necessity for and increasing reliance on specialist and idiosyncratic skills, the rising importance of the use and transfer of knowledge for economic activities and the application of knowledge to knowledge (Bryson *et al.*, 2000: 2).

While policy discourses have become permeated with knowledge economy rhetoric and have accepted the existence of the knowledge economy as a seemingly unchallengeable fact, academic writings have remained more sceptical. One core debate concerns whether the knowledge economy is spin or substance and whether it is fundamentally 'new' (Weingart, 1997). Some authors do see the knowledge economy in a historical context as a new phase of economic development on a par with the agricultural or industrial revolutions. Thus, 'informationalism' is but the latest stage of development after industrialism and agriculture (Jessop, 2000: 64) as the 'limits of the productivity revolution' (Drucker, 1998) have been reached. Castells recognizes that knowledge has always played an important economic role, but that it is the application of knowledge to the production of knowledge that is new. In this respect, the move from industrialism to informationalism apparently heralds a new mode of production in which 'knowledge capitalism' characterizes the contemporary economic, social and institutional world (see Gibbons *et al.*, 1994; Jessop, 2000). Similarly, Drucker (1998) argues that the primary importance of knowledge as *the* resource, rather than *a* resource, has led to a post-capitalist society that fundamentally changes the structure of society, the economy and the political world.

Such accounts are linked by the common assumption that there is inherently something different about the dynamics of knowledge itself in the knowledge economy, representing a fundamental departure from previous paradigms. Others argue, however, that capitalism has not been rivalled by the knowledge economy, insofar as the fundamental tenets of capitalism remain valid. Burton-Jones (1999) asserts that capitalism and knowledge capitalism both thrive on capital accumulation, open market competition, free trade, the power of the individual and the survival of the fittest. In this sense, he argues that it is the 'equipment' used by the players that changes, rather than the 'rules of the capitalist game'. Knowledge capitalism is seen as a generic form of capitalism based on the accumulation of knowledge, not monetary and physical forms of wealth, and as such may replace previous national models of capitalism (Burton-Jones, 1999: 22). His assertion that the trend towards a global knowledge-based economy will eliminate regional differences ignores the context-specific determinants of knowledge production and important differences between heterogeneous systems. Yet such accounts remain useful in emphasizing elements of continuity as well as change. The same is true of others who argue that our societies have always been 'knowledge societies' (Stehr, 1994) and that it is the speed and permeation of knowledge into society that is particularly distinctive in modern times (de Weert, 2001).

Changing Notions of Space and Scale

A second key driver of current socio-economic transformations is the restructuring of notions of space and scale, made apparent by numerous urban and regional scholars over the last thirty years (see Perry and Harding 2002). Here we refer to changing notions of scale and their resultant implications for national states as appropriate units of analysis as well as for the actors within them. Much has been written about globalization and the so-called 'death of distance' thesis which sees the rise of information technologies and dissolution of national boundaries in trade, investment, finance, goods, people and services leading to a disembeddedness in which space, place, distance and even time are collapsed (Ohmae, 1995; Morgan, 2001). On the other hand, a range of authors focus more upon the ways in which territory and scale are becoming more, not less important as economic synergies, clusters and tacit knowledge spillovers require proximity and a continued emphasis on face-to-face contact (Cooke *et al.*, 1997. Savitch, 2002). Here, reference to 'industrial complexes', 'innovative mileux' or 'creative places' draws attention to the relationship between place, assets and competitive success (Gordon and McCann, 2000; Florida, 2002). Such processes have been referred to as 'glocalization' (Swyndegouw, 1992) to reflect the harnessing of specific local assets as a mechanism for achieving global competitiveness. What is clear in all such debates is that space is being rescaled and reorganized in a number of complex and interdependent ways – with global, European, national, regional, city-regional and local processes of restructuring (Brenner, 1998; Salet *et al.*, 2003). In this respect, it is increasingly more appropriate to speak of 'nested scales of activities' rather than to subscribe glibly to simplistic dichotomies between the global and local, the embedded or disembedded (Taylor, 1996). As activities are rescaled and/or responsibilities redistributed vertically between territorial levels of government, we see also a shift in the horizontal distribution of capacities and capabilities between actors. Processes of liberalization, regulation, deregulation and privatization have combined over recent years to strengthen the movement from 'government' to 'governance', bringing new actors and institutions into policy arenas (Stoker and Mossberger, 1994; Storper, 1995; Soja, 2000). Power is more dispersed between and within institutional actors and contexts, with the result that partnerships are increasingly seen as necessary to reach policy goals.

The Knowledge Economy and the University

What does this mean for the university? Such drivers, it is said, combine to place universities at the heart of economic and social development processes (Castells and Hall, 1994; Goddard and Chatterton, 2001). Taking the supranational level of the European Union as an example, we see increasing concern with the roles and diverse functions of the university through policies designed to realize the knowledge economy at nested scales of activity. In recognition of the movement towards a knowledge society, the European Commission has set a number of initiatives in place to ensure that innovation, research, education and training are core to the EU's internal policies. From an initial focus on education, training and employment set out in 'Towards a Europe of Knowledge', which aims to 'promote the highest level of knowledge for its people through broad access to education and its permanent updating' (European Commission, 1997), developments since have concentrated more specifically on higher education. Building on the Sorbonne Declaration of 1998, the Bologna Process committed signatory member states to a process of coordination towards the creation of a European Higher Education Area (EHEA) by 2010. The EHEA focuses on coordinating the policies of member states to achieve six related goals on comparable degree structures, system cycles, credit systems, mobility, quality assurance and European dimensions in higher education (Joint Declaration of European Ministers of Education, 1999). European higher education ministers met again in September 2003 in Berlin to reaffirm commitment to the EHEA and to review progress on meeting the original objectives, as well as to undertake some additional actions – for instance, including the doctoral cycle in the aims for common degree systems (Communiqué of the Conference of Ministers Responsible for Higher Education, 2003). At the Lisbon European Council meeting in 2000, the target for Europe to become 'the most competitive and dynamic knowledge-based economy in the world, capable of sustainable economic growth with more and better jobs and greater social cohesion' (European Commission, 2003) was set. Core to this was the agreement to create a European Research Area (ERA) to lay the foundation for a common science policy across the EU through coordinating national research policies in order to combat fragmentation and duplication. The agreement also has considerable financial implications: to increase EU total expenditure on research to three per cent of GDP by 2010 to compete with the United States and Japan (European Commission, 2000).

A separate Commission Communication deals with the regional dimensions of the ERA and sees that the ERA concept implies that efforts should be deployed effectively at different administrative and organizational layers (European

Commission, 2001). The Communication states that the role of each of the actors, public and private, needs to be re-examined to establish synergies and take advantage of complementarities among European national and regional instruments to achieve a 'reinforced partnership' (European Commission, 2001: 9). Here, then, the emphasis is upon new sets of actors working in partnership across sectors and territorial levels to achieve the goals of the European knowledge economy. Among all the challenges posed by the knowledge economy, the local and regional roles of universities and cooperation with industry and enterprise are seen as particularly important. Indeed, the restructuring of space and scale has meant that 'for many universities regional engagement is ...becoming the crucible within which an appropriate response to overall trends in higher education is being forged' (Goddard and Chatterton, 2001).

Both the EHEA and the ERA initiatives aim rather at coordination and harmonization than at the creation of a federal European system of higher education and research. However, the debate over the appropriate levels of coordination in the context of diverse national traditions and cultures remains an open one, particularly in the context of discussions over the potential purpose, scope and role of a European Research Council (Cannell, 2001). What we can say at this stage is that global pressures are leading to varying levels of commitment to coordination and convergence between national systems of higher education and research, with concomitant implications for the university as a site of knowledge production. This too has been the subject of recent Commission Communications. Universities are seen as unique in their contributions to the core functions of the knowledge society in producing new knowledge, in knowledge transfer and transmission and in new industrial processes or services (European Commission, 2003). Yet core issues remain, relating to the global lack of competitiveness of the European university system, the sustainability of university research funding, questions of autonomy and professionalism, the achievement and maintenance of research excellence and the contribution more generally of universities towards the sets of initiatives that comprise the 'Europe of Knowledge'.

Inherent in the above European frameworks is a recognition that realizing the knowledge economy and the external engagements of higher education institutions requires an understanding and re-evaluation of the systems and internal mechanisms of universities themselves. On the one hand, we see the development of a multiscalar knowledge world placing emphasis on universities' external engagements and their roles within society. Although space precludes a more detailed discussion here, this is by no means an exclusively European or Western phenomena (Garlick, 2000; Charles, 2001; Puukka, 2001; Jimenez and Zubieta, 2001). In developing countries the emphasis is as much on the political, social and civic roles of the university as on the need for economic knowledge-driven competitiveness. Indeed, the notion of 'engagement' offers itself to flexible interpretation, meaning different things in different contexts (Bjarnason and Coldstream, 2003). This is all too apparent, for instance, in the potential tensions between commercial and industrial-based engagements, aimed at profit and wealth creation, and socially driven engagements in which the university is better conceived as an instrument of inclusion and participation. Gibbons (2003: 48) notes that our understanding of engagement depends on the nature of the social contract between universities and society. Here we turn from convergence and commonality, in terms of the increasing emphasis on universities, localities and regional development, towards difference and diversity. The social contract between universities and society is historically and contextually defined and subject to constant and variable interpretation across countries. The distinctively different forms of engagement between universities and their localities, involving rather different institutions, thus poses a particularly fruitful area of research. Factors which potentially influence notions of engagement include national political systems, cultural differences, territorial relations, degrees of integration into the global economy, degrees of regionalization, the natures and histories of higher education and funding systems and specific local circumstances and institutional peculiarities, to name but a few.

On the other hand, in the emerging discussions on the university as a site of knowledge production, we see external engagements linked to internal transformations. At the supranational level of policy-making, this is reflected, for instance, in the EHEA initiative itself. But it is at the micro level that institutional change must be put into practice. For Coldstream, 'engagement' is more than links to the outside world and must characterize the 'whole orientation of the university's policy and practice' (2003: 6). Thus a further set of factors influences the nature and form of engagement, namely internal organizational transformations necessary to meet external demands.

Towards the Entrepreneurial or 'Mode 2' University?

Despite political, economic and social upheaval and change, the university remained a relatively stable, though evolving, institution from its medieval roots until the second half of the twentieth century (Barnett, 1990). Its primary functions – the pursuit of knowledge in a range of academic disciplines and the provision of a liberal education to an elite as part of a more general aim to create a more knowledgeable and enlightened population – have shaped and influenced the nature and form of its organization. Neither fully autonomous nor constrained, universities in their historical form have persisted as relatively independent institutions able to determine their own internal structures, values, management and governance. Universities have generally been granted a partial degree of autonomy from the state and society, leading to particular and distinctive forms of self-organization and self-governance. This is epitomized in the traditional image of the curiosity-driven scholar, determining his or her own research agendas, pursuing largely individualized interests, which may or may not meet those of wider society, and with far greater degrees of autonomy than most employees.

The emphasis on the external engagements of the university, particularly its local and regional roles, requires a fundamental re-evaluation of its internal workings in order to make it an institution 'fit for purpose' and to re-educate academics as to their civic and social responsibilities. The potential realization of the knowledge economy rests essentially on the extent to which universities can adapt to the challenges placed upon them. These include (Harloe and Perry, 2004):

- the adoption of quasi-market systems and processes
- a shift from a public service to a performance- and audit-based ethos
- the commercialization of activities in teaching and research
- responding to the needs of government, industry and 'customers'
- linking research to demands for societal and economic relevance
- pressures on traditional methods of management and governance
- revised systems of remuneration and reward linked to revisions in evaluations of worth and status
- individualization and the undermining of the culture of collegiality
- new sites of knowledge production (e.g. corporate and e-learning universities)
- contestability of knowledge claims and delegitimation of the university.

Within this we see issues relating not just to universities as organizations, but also to the staff within them. Indeed, while university managers must forge appropriate responses to external challenges at the strategic level, it is ultimately individual academics who must convert the institutional rhetorics of engagement into reality. We shall return to this important issue later.

Many have seen the knowledge economy and the restructuring of space and scale as presenting opportunities not threats, stressing the wider benefits of a reflexive, innovative and more streamlined university (Clark, 1998; Van der Sijde and Schutte, 2000; Jongbloed and Goedegebuure, 2001). This is embodied in the concepts of the 'entrepreneurial' or 'enterprise' university, actively engaging with stakeholders and societal actors. The term was perhaps most famously used by Clark in his 1998 study of five universities in Northern Europe, recorded in *Creating Entrepreneurial Universities: Organizational Pathways of Transformation.* Through examination of the Universities of Warwick, Strathclyde (both UK), Twente (Netherlands), Joensuu (Finland) and Chalmers University of Technology (Sweden), Clark identified five core elements to the entrepreneurial university: a strengthened steering core, an expanded developmental periphery, a diversified funding base, a stimulated academic heartland and an integrated entrepreneurial culture. There has been much debate on the extent to which this can be seen in practice, indeed, case studies from universities across the globe on institutional responses to these challenges formed the basis of an International Management in Higher Education (IMHE) conference in 2000. The contributions there revealed varying degrees of convergence and divergence in response to external engagements, as well as a 'general supposition that the development of the entrepreneurial/innovative university is likely to be inevitable in most settings, largely because of external circumstances' (Davies, 2000).

Through these and other case studies, we see a number of different institutional responses to the entrepreneurial challenge. These range from focusing on university governance in terms of councils and senates (Bargh, Scott and Smith, 1996), patterns of formal and informal authority (Weber, 2000), entrepreneurial and institutional cultural changes (Davies, 2000; Rosenberg, 2000), management audits (Risbourg and Daumin, 2000) or processes of 'rethinking the university' from below as in the University of Salford. Again, as with the notion of 'engagement', interpretations of 'entrepreneurial' remain variable, ranging from a neo-liberal market-driven conception of entrepreneurialism based on wealth creation and economic growth to a more socially responsive and stakeholder-based approach. The former would seem to be ascendant, if the preponderance of enterprise and entrepreneurship courses springing up, particularly in the UK and US, is anything to go by, with their emphasis on spinning-out, spinning-in, spinning-off and starting-up.

Internal Transformation

A less often touched upon dimension of meeting the entrepreneurial challenge relates to the degree of penetration of internal transformations into the heart of the university. In other words, how far is external engagement dependent upon change in the day-to-day practices of academics? Indeed, for some, the idea of the university as a fundamentally different and evolving institution is predicated not on changes in steering or management, but upon shifts in the practice of science. Here we refer to changes in knowledge production (Gibbons *et al.*, 1994) and the emergence of 'entrepreneurial science' (Etzkowitz, 2002). Taking the first of these, Gibbons, Nowotny and Scott (1994) argue that there is sufficient evidence to suggest that traditional ways of thinking about science and doing science, and the nature of science itself are being challenged by a new mode of knowledge production.

Traditional science, or 'Mode 1' science, has hitherto usually been produced in a context in which problems are set and solved within self-governing and self-regulating academic communities; knowledge production takes place within disciplinary boundaries; research results are communicated through institutional channels; universities are the dominant knowledge-producing institutions and research groups are relatively homogenous and institutionalized. 'Knowledge for knowledge's' sake is the dominant rationale, with less concern for the ultimate use to which science will be put or for producing socially acceptable results, and peer review is seen as the appropriate mode of quality control. This contrasts with the new 'Mode 2' of knowledge production.

Mode 2 is carried out in the context of application, shaped by a diverse set of intellectual, economic and social interests. Problems are set and solved in a transdisciplinary fashion, bringing a number of perspectives to bear on particular issues. As a result, research findings are communicated interactively and continuously throughout the research process itself, by virtue of different organizations participating at different points in time. Research groups, then, are more heterogeneous and transient. Mode 2 is characterized by organizational diversity – not just universities, but other knowledge production sites, linked together through functioning networks of communication. Knowledge production then moves out of disciplinary silos in universities and into new societal contexts. This is accompanied by increased reflexivity on the impacts of research and social accountability. Finally, quality is determined not by peer review, but by a wider set of criteria that reflect the broadening social composition of the review system. It should be noted that the hypothesis put forward by Gibbons *et al.* is not that Mode 2 is replacing Mode 1, but rather that the socioeconomic transformations underway within the auspices of the knowledge economy require a consideration of how, and to what extent, modes of knowledge production are becoming blurred and overlapping.

A fundamental element of the Mode 2 thesis relates to shifting conceptions of academic roles. Whereas Mode 1 is about 'science and scientists', Mode 2 is about 'knowledge and practitioners'. This is perhaps one of the more controversial and sensitive challenges of engagement: through questioning the fundamental premise of academic identity and distinctiveness, the identity of the university itself is also undermined, particularly if one takes the view, less relevant in the current era of university corporate branding and marketing strategies, that the identity of the university is constituted by those that work within it. The implications of this in terms of academic practices and identities lie beyond the scope of this chapter. What is clear is that realizing the 'entrepreneurial university' would seem to be far less controversial than realizing the 'Mode 2 university' in respect of the degrees of superficial or deep-seated change envisaged. If external engagement is to be truly meaningful, then this dimension of change requires greater consideration, yet arguably poses the greatest challenge.

Making Engagement Work in Practice?

So far we have argued that the knowledge economy and the restructuring of space and scale place universities at the heart of economic and social development processes and create increasing demands on universities to engage with a range of political, social, economic and civic actors. This necessitates internal reorientations in addition to external relations and links. A core challenge here is how to preserve the integrity of the academic enterprise, at the individual and collective level, as well as reform the university to meet external challenges. Of course, reform is by no means a universally accepted necessity and debates on the desirability and implications of change are widespread (Readings, 1996; Smith and Webster, 1997; Maskell and Robinson, 2001). In any case, it should be noted that thus far evidence suggests that change may be more perception than reality. For instance, arguing for the 'intelligent regionalization' of universities, Greenwood's analysis (in this volume) relating to the internal and external political economies of universities supports the idea that significant institutional changes will be necessary for public universities to contribute to their regions and localities. Yet Greenwood remains deeply sceptical that this has occurred, seeing universities neither as driving local and regional economies, nor as 'managed with this in mind'. In his account, while there are pressures on universities to adapt internal structures, mechanisms and institutions, current systems orient them everywhere but towards their local surroundings. While this does not accord with our own experiences in the northwest of England, where certain universities are increasingly reorienting themselves towards local and regional economies in the context of the ongoing regionalization and devolution agendas (May and Perry, 2003), as well as in relation to debates on regional innovation systems (Cooke *et al*., 1997; Evangelista *et al*., 2002. Simmie *et al*., 2002), it does remain the case that internal restructuring, where it is occurring, does not reflect 'intentional design' towards a regional mission. Rather, this is better understood as a response to national and global political factors, which, in the UK, are leading to increasing diversification and stratification among universities, one response to which, for some institutions, may be the development of regional engagement. The issue, then, is how pressures impact differentially on varied institutions in diverse contexts and how individual institutions are facilitated or constrained towards meeting the challenges of external engagements, with or without internal change.

Doubts on the extent to which external engagement is accompanied by internal reform are echoed by Davies (2000), who notes that a large proportion of European universities could not be called 'entrepreneurial' in any sense of the word. Instead he refers to several key elements of existing institutional cultures that militate against meaningful external engagements: problem avoidance; internal orientations; individualistic, defensive and isolated patterns of working; fragmented information; low corporate identity and presence; lack of strategic oversight and absence of accountability. Turning rhetorics into reality in terms of regional and local engagements is by no means an easy task. Is it then the case that there are only a handful of institutions that can join the entrepreneurial club, while the majority of institutions do not fit this pattern? Given the range and diversity Clark's original five institutions, that seems unlikely. What we can say is that making engagement work in practice is clearly contingent on a range of context-specific factors.

Most obviously, while common frameworks for action may exist at supranational levels and universities are subject to global pressures, such as in relation to ICTs or globalization (Mansell and Wehn, 1998; Scott, 1998), such pressures are filtered through diverse national sociopolitical, economic and institutional systems, structures and cultures. It is of particular relevance that differences in territorial systems, in terms of degrees of regionalization and devolution, and in higher education and research, from funding to research cultures, influence distinctive institutional responses. Within Europe, while there is undoubtedly limited convergence proposed through the EHEA and ERA initiatives, heterogeneity dominates: 'the aim is to preserve Europe's cultural richness and linguistic diversity, based on its heritage of diversified traditions and to foster its potential of innovation and social and economic development, though enhanced cooperation between European Higher Education Institutions' (Communiqué of the Conference of Ministers Responsible for Higher Education, 2003: 2). This is also obvious from recent comparisons in public sector research systems (Senker *et al*., 1999) and differences in regional and local governance arrangements across member states (Salet *et al*., 2003).

National responses to global pressures, then, tend to take the form of frameworks for action, which again have to be interpreted and filtered through subnational agencies and governments. Here, depending on regional governance arrangements, another set of variables enters into play relating to regional histories, cultures, strengths and weaknesses – both industrially and in terms of research, socioeconomic profile and politics. Relations between regional and local actors, the presence or absence of regional science and innovation policies, intermediary actors in knowledge transfer, and the existence of regional innovation systems all potentially influence universities' external orientations.

The potential for difference in response only increases further at the organizational level. Institutional responses must therefore be forged within and in relation to nested scales of activities. Universities not only have international roles, but also national expectations and regional and local obligations. Whether universities respond proactively, reactively or seek to shape changing environments, and whether change is envisaged at the periphery of the institution or deep within, depends on both external and internal conditions. Strategic leadership and governance, financial robustness, internal systems and histories all combine to shape the potential for internal reform. Of particular importance, it seems, are issues of institutional power and the ability of universities to mobilize different resources and networks to meet organizational aims. Here, positions in international, national and regional hierarchies, as well as networks of influence, are important in determining the relative extent to which institutions are able, if they so desire, to insulate themselves from the harsher aspects of external change. Linked to this are differing perceptions of the value of different types of knowledge, produced within different institutional contexts and according to different sets of criteria. A good example here is provided by the recent emergence of regional science policies in the English regions, which aim explicitly at regional economic and social development, thus implying a focus on relevance and application, yet which seemingly focus resource and support on academic departments rated according to traditional notions of international excellence and basic and curiosity-driven research.[3] The irony here, it seems, is that embeddedness in local and regional economies may not be sufficient to guarantee a dominant position in subnational knowledge hierarchies.

Finally we turn to the micro level, already referred to, in terms of changes to the practice of science and the roles of academics. If knowledge economy rhetorics are to be translated into reality, then case studies of changing modes of knowledge production must surely be core. Issues of implementation and relevance come into conflict with those of academic freedom and autonomy, and little headway has thus far been made in scoping out the middle ground for overcoming this dichotomy. Academics cannot be reduced to 'knowledge workers' within 'knowledge factories'; to do so would be to collapse too far into relativism and undermine the distinctiveness of academic work. Yet meeting albeit worthy external demands in relation to local

---

3   ESRC Award L144250004, 'Making Science History? The Regionalisation of Science Policy'.

and regional development requires some accommodation between the 'rights' of academics and their roles in the implementation of subnational knowledge visions. This is not to divorce institutional context from individual engagement, merely to highlight the disjuncture between rhetorics and a real commitment to change. Incentives are clearly important, at any of the nested scales of activity referred to earlier, to reorientate academic behaviours and reward diverse activities and excellent *relevant* research, in addition to traditional academic functions.

Moving from the macro to the meso and micro levels in this way reveals a dizzying set of factors that interplay to determine universities' institutional responses to the knowledge economy. At each level, the dynamics of socioeconomic knowledge-based transformations are received, translated, acted upon and transferred, in diverse cultural, societal, political, economic and technological contexts. More cross-national and varied case studies of how change is impacting internally on universities and the degrees of penetration of change within the university are clearly needed. Are universities becoming, as Gibbons *et al.* suggest, Mode 2 institutions? How are universities adapting internally to the myriad of pressures placed upon them? Is Mode 1 science being eclipsed, as they also frequently suggest, or is some new accommodation between 'pure' and 'contextualized' research occurring? In either case, what is happening in relation to issues such as academic freedom and the university's ability to pursue research at the frontiers of knowledge and in a critical manner? To what extent can we identify Mode 2 knowledge workers and what are the implications of this shift? How are the diverse sets of factors that influence universities' responses to external engagements manifesting in different contexts? What is needed is further empirical work that considers the relationship between external engagements and internal transformations in different national and subnational contexts. This alone constitutes a large research agenda for urban and regional scholars, but is one that they are well placed to address, given their traditions of interdisciplinary working and their position in relation to policy, practice and research.

Chapter 3

Knowledge and Technology Transfer: Can Universities Promote Regional Development?

Morten Levin

Introduction

In the 1990s I worked for several years on industrial and knowledge development in a highly industrialized region in Western Norway. The local companies were small and medium-sized commodity producers that competed on the international marketplace. Our special focus was on developing a local learning and competence network (Snow and Hanssen-Bauer, 1996; Levin and Knutstad, 2003) that had as a primary goal to professionalize the local leadership cadres. The local leaders were always posing as self-confident and successful actors. An often used indigenous expression was: 'Why should we stop over in Norway's capital Oslo when we are searching global competency?' When I first heard it, I thought it was a sort of blunt joke without a deeper meaning, and I did not bother to reflect further on what it might express of a more profound understanding of regional, national and global issues. As the local leaders continued bragging about being regionalized global actors, I was forced to reflect more deeply on the importance of regional networking and global operations. First, it was obvious that local leaders viewed national boundaries as too constrained, both regarding markets for products, tools and equipment and as a border limiting where to acquire knowledge and impulses necessary to keep up with the international knowledge development. Some local companies had relationships with Norwegian universities through an action-research-based PhD program (Knutstad, 1998; Raabe, 1999), but basically they were looking for something more, or in addition to what they could get from local universities. Second, it turned out to be a mode of local operation that external impulses gave an opportunity for local meaning construction processes, shaping and disseminating insights and interpretations to a broader set of local actors. If this interpretation was correct, then regional meaning construction processes became crucial in the local knowledge developmental process. An explanation that struck my mind was that becoming global was ideologically and politically correct from the local actor's point of view, but the thrust of the argument was that regional meaning construction processes made it attainable to interact with global knowledge.

An essential question to ask is how new ideas, concepts, and tools that are acquired from the outside are rooted in the local environment. Is the interpretation of the knowledge-acquiring process of Western Norway sensible, as it indicates that transfer of knowledge and technology depends on local networking activities closely linked to making sense of impressions from the greater world? What would then be the role for a regional institution of higher education?

Knowledge and Technology – Contested Concepts – But Still the Same?

There is not one unifying concept of how technology can be interpreted. Technology is often made sense of through applying three different perspectives (MacKenzie and Wajcman, 1985; Mitcham,1994). First, technology can be understood as concrete material artefacts, that is, tools, machines, and inventions that humans can utilize for some purpose or other. This is what people usually think of when asked what characterizes technology. The second perspective implies an understanding of technology as the transformation process necessary to convert raw materials into products (artefacts). The third and final perspective interprets technology as the knowledge needed both for constructing technology and for its operation. The two latter categories focus on technology as action-oriented knowledge in the sense that it is the 'kind' of knowledge that is needed for skilful human activity, linked to either the design, creation or operation of new technology. Technology would, in the approach of this paper, be conceptualized as the concrete application of knowledge in order to create or utilize technological artefacts. It is this kind of knowledge that becomes visible through engineering activity.[1]

The conventional understanding of knowledge is grounded in its explicit forms. What can be recorded in words, numbers and figures, and thus is explicitly accessible for humans, is what counts as knowledge. In line with this understanding, knowledge is an individualistic, and a purely cognitive phenomenon that is, accordingly, quite restricted in terms of encompassing the broad field of insightful human activity. The modern debate on knowledge has added at least three important dimensions to this understanding. First, much of our knowing is tacit and expresses itself in our actions. It is not coincidental that the discussion is focused on the verb 'knowing' instead of the noun knowledge, because it underpins the point that knowledge is linked to peoples' actions.

Tacit knowing, a term usually understood to have been coined by Michael Polanyi (1966), connotes the 'hidden' understanding that guides our actions without our being able to explicitly communicate the knowledge that underpins the activity. Polanyi's argumentation is partly built on the book *The Concept of Mind* written

---

1   Technological knowledge can, according to the discussion in the later sections of this chapter, also have an explicit component. This component is what is conventionally found in textbooks and communicated through conventional lectures at universities or other educational institutions. My point in this chapter is that technological knowledge is essentially what is visible through what engineers actually do in their daily work.

by the Oxford philosopher Gilbert Ryle (1949). In fact, in my understanding Ryle created, through introducing 'knowing how' in his book, a more fruitful concept than Polanyi's 'tacit knowing'. 'Knowing how' grounds knowledge in actions, which is in fact exactly how we can identify tacit knowing. This argumentation places tacit knowing in the category of concepts that are basically redundant. The third dimension of knowledge is the inherent collective element. Work by Berger and Luckmann (1966) and Schutz (1967) on the social construction of social realities paved the way for a deeper understanding of how knowing is a socially constructed and distributed phenomenon. People working together develop and share knowledge as a collective effort. Flyvbjerg (2001) follows a different path but ends up touching upon some of the same distinctions. He refers to the work of Aristotle when making a taxonomy based on *episteme* (theoretical knowledge), *techne* (pragmatic and context-dependent practical rationality[2]), and *phronesis* (practical and context-dependent deliberation about values), which leads him to seek a solution for the future of social sciences in a closer correspondence to *phronesis* (see also Chapter 6, this volume). The argument in this chapter is that *techne* and *phronesis* make up the necessary 'know how' for regional development, for which both forms are identified as relevant. It is again interesting to notice that *episteme* (the conventional term for explicit and theoretical knowledge) is not considered as the important form of knowledge. This argument is also forcefully presented by Toulmin (1996).

The praxis-oriented knowing, which is collective, develops out of communities of practice, to use the wordings of Brown and Dugid (1991) and Wenger *et al.* (2000). This literature pinpoints how people, through working together, develop and cultivate knowledge that enables them to take the appropriate actions to achieve the tasks they are aiming for. The dominant perspectives in this picture, which is a conceptualization of knowledge as engraved in actions, are collectively developed and shared as people work together, while explicit knowledge clearly is in the background.

An interesting and important parallel to how technology was conceptualized emerges when knowing is related predominantly to people functioning as capable actors, either as individuals or in a community of practitioners. Technology, as it emerges from the discussion in this chapter, consists in the skills needed for (practical) transformation processes and the insights necessary to create new artefacts. Both forms of insight can be understood as 'knowing how', that is, knowledge linked to practical actions. This is, of course, also the essential knowing needed in regional development. Regional development does not take place inside an actor's head; it results from practical and concrete activities aimed at enhancing local economic activity. Cognitive capability is, of course, necessary, but no results will ever

---

2   *Techne* can also be interpreted as the technical rationality that is in the heads and the hands of experts. In the context of this chapter, however, it denotes the kind of knowing necessary for making skilled transformation processes and is therefore not connected to the experts' power position.

materialize unless local actors learn how to act in an appropriate and effective way. Technology and knowledge will, in my understanding, merge in an understanding of *knowing how to act* in order to reach certain desired goals. Knowledge is not a passive substantive, but emerges through actively knowing how to act.

When knowledge is *knowing how to act*, skilful actions are always situated in a certain context. It is not possible to envision action taking place in a 'generalized' environment. A person always acts in a given context, as there is, of course, no situation that is context-free. To act is to contextualize behaviour, and being able to act skilfully implies that actions are appropriate in the given context. The actor needs to make sense of the context to enable appropriate actions. Knowing how will imply knowing how in a given context; appropriate actions emerge from contextual knowing. The conventional understanding of general knowledge – that it is universally applicable – has no meaning in the perspective of this discussion. Contextualization clarifies one important regional dimension. Useful local 'knowing how' can only be effective when the actor is capable of locating the actions within, and making them appropriate to, the local frame of reference. This is an important qualification of knowledge, as it must give rise to localized 'knowing how', which, of course, is context-specific.

Transfer as Contextualization of Technology and Knowledge

Let me from the outset do away with the conventional conceptualization of transfer of knowledge. Explicit knowledge is already ruled out as an uninteresting form of knowledge for regional development.[3] Against this background, it does not create a realistic picture to envision knowledge transfer as a linear process, whereby knowledge created in universities or research institutions is diffused to practical users. Knowledge used to be basically treated as a commodity that a gatekeeper could bring through the doors of a company (Allen, 1977). Proponents of this way of thinking problematized neither what constituted knowledge nor what transfer meant (Bijker *et al.*, 1987).

In this paper, technology transfer is understood as contextualized learning and developmental processes (Levin, 1997). The transfer is basically a process of local reconstruction of meaning, accessing what has been imprinted during the 'constructor's' process of acquiring technology. Accordingly, it is a localized process of transferring 'knowing how' from one location to the other, which takes the form of a collective learning and developmental process. A dominant feature in acquiring new insights is to understand the cultural context within which they were developed, and to be able to translate that kind of knowing to the local cultural context. In this perspective, transfer of knowledge and technology is bound up with the transfer of cultural knowledge. On this view, it is easy to see that transfer is not a movement

---

3   Knowledge *of* regional development would be the explicit forms communicated in texts, while the thrust of the argument in this chapter is that knowing how to do regional development is knowledge *for* regional development.

of commodities, but involves making sense of a different culture. This implies that transfer is conceptualized in a deeper and better way when we reframe it to mean 'learning about' and transform it to a concrete application in a local context. This is, of course, exactly what we mean by transfer of technology and knowledge. Rather than being a pure movement of artefacts (either in material form as tools and machines or in explicit forms such as texts, figures and drawings), transfer is basically a local meaning-construction process transferring 'foreign' technology and knowledge to purposeful local actions.

The everyday users will be the primary actors involved in the transfer process. But limiting the understanding of the transfer in such a way that it involves only those primary groups will not shape the ground for the transfer of knowledge and technology to a region. How is it possible to envisage a process that would include the regional dimension? In other words, we need a conceptualization of the process whereby the primary actors join in for a broader regional transfer process. Which forms of regional networks support a broad diffusion of knowledge and technology? These issues will be discussed in the following section.

Regions as Contexts for Meaning Construction

Modern studies of economic development have focused on the region and given it particular prominence. In fact, regions – the broader arenas in which people interact, enabling them to bring about economic development – have almost become a mantra, repeated everywhere where development is discussed. The famous study by Brusco (1990) of regional industrial cooperation for development in Emilia Romagna, the work of Piore and Sabel (1984) on regions as stages where flexible specialization can take place, and the more recent arguments on learning regions (Asheim, 1996; Asheim and Isaksen, 1997) constitute key contributions to the modern literature of economic development. In their different ways, each of these examples shows how networks among local actors are vital factors in the development of local economies. In this chapter it is argued that the important perspective is to make sense of how regional networks function as mediators for transfer of knowledge and technology.

Flexible specialization Flexible specialization is essentially a concept that describes how local practitioners cooperate or compete with one another and how, by so doing, they create a regional community of specialized knowledge and expertise.

Cooperation and competition among actors, which are a vital feature of local economic life, are also separate variables that may very well coexist, though in a varying mixture depending on what is at stake. Professional interaction, either in the form of cooperation or competition, is very important because it creates arenas that can support a mutual development of useful knowledge. Through this process of interaction, knowledge that is initially confined to a particular locality or organization is diffused to a broader stratum of practitioners, who then form a specialized 'community' at regional level. This is why flexible specialization, in my understanding, makes a difference. It rests on a broader regional community of practice, shapes a regional knowledge platform that is shared through local interaction, and thus provides a region with a potential competitive edge.

Industrial regions   The second type of networking connections that would enhance a regional acquisition of knowledge and technology emerges through a reinterpretation of the research that followed the path of Brusco's (1990) *Industrial Regions*. The integration of marketing, design and manufacturing in a network structure creates a fertile ground for mutual learning, which again supports the regional dimension. This is an option for learning that crosses boundaries set by communities of practice. Through interaction in commercial networks, actors learn from and have an impact on each other, thus making the network a huge learning arena.

Different networks operate, of course, at the same time, creating a broad and complex web of regional economic life. Industrial networks could be viewed as the vertical knowledge chain, while communities of practitioners create a horizontal line of diffusion. The important factor that the two meaning-construction arenas discussed so far have in common is that they are linked to concrete economic activities and show how everyday business life is integrated into the wider process of regional acquisition of technology and knowledge.

Learning regions   The concept of learning regions introduces a new dynamic and developmental capability, as it pinpoints how regional networks become a fertile ground for learning and development. The learning actors (that is, the constitutive elements of the learning network) are understood as emerging from either intra-firm cooperation, inter-firm cooperation, or a more diffuse category of regional cooperation (Asheim, 1996: 391–3). The added perspective, even though very diffuse, is that the region (the collectivity of actors) as an entity is capable of collective learning. This constitutes the regional parallel to Argyris and Schön's (1978; 1996) concept of organizational learning, even though this is not recognized by Asheim (1996). Gustavsen *et al.* (2001) extend regional learning networks to include public administration and educational institutions. Their position is that regional economic development can best be achieved through creating collaboration between labour and management, enterprises, public administration and the educational system. This broader network, bridging institutions that do not interact on the basis of pure economic interests, is called a development coalition.

The regional context for meaning construction is composed of many layers of networks, some overlapping and some disconnected. All of these networks can be understood as arenas for collective learning, which again is where the local meaning construction takes place that grounds the secondary process of transferring knowledge and technology. The concepts discussed in the previous paragraphs have shown how communities of practitioners and people linked in a vertical production chain interact in the arenas where transfer of knowledge and technology takes place. But there are other important regional networks that are not part of everyday business life that might participate in the transfer process. It is not coincidental that the verb 'might participate' is used in connection with these institutions. The focus here is, of course, on higher education and public offices for the support of regional economic development.

The public sector   Public institutions and offices devoted to regional development will, naturally, play an important role. These offices control and distribute public funds and resources to support regional economic development. This can take the form of state-supported loans, business consultancy aimed at small and medium-sized companies, the development of infrastructure and so on. A characteristic of much of this activity is its often marginal connection to everyday economic life. The standard mode of operation is to negotiate support with the potential users, decide on whether to grant public sector support, then sit back and expect the desired results to show up. If the public offices operate like this, they disconnect themselves from direct and concrete learning opportunities. Gustavsen *et al.* (1997; 2001) argue for creating connectedness between actors in a regional economy, paying special attention to the importance of linking the public sector to everyday economic activity. The issue of what should be the role of the public sector in regional economic development is often a subject of political and ideological debate. This debate will be followed up on in this chapter, as its main focus is on knowledge and technology transfer for regional economic development. From this perspective, the public sector would obviously benefit immensely from participating in the networks where knowledge is contextualized for local use. The public sector would also be able to bring to this table knowledge and experiences that are complementary to other actors' insights, thus creating a broader and better contextualized 'knowing how'. It would be important to integrate the public sector in the other knowledge-acquiring networks as well, but it is beyond the scope of this paper to discuss this in further detail.

The educational system   An obvious missing element in this discussion is the educational system. The linear model of technology transfer does not seem to convey an appropriate understanding of how knowledge and technology transfer actually takes place. In the linear model, the universities hold a clear-cut and important cutting-edge role in being the institutions that create and distribute knowledge to recipient organizations. If this is not the case, what role can the university have in regional diffusion of knowledge and technology?

Local institutions of higher education could play more than one role in regional knowledge systems. If they are in the forefront of knowledge generation in a specific area, the institution will both be important internationally and potentially of utmost interest for regional activities. This potentially involves a great opportunity for the local economy given that this cutting-edge knowledge can be transformed to local economic activity. The proximity of the knowledge producer and user would certainly create a competitive advantage. On the other hand, more often the local educational system becomes the mediator of knowledge produced elsewhere. Higher education often takes on a specific role simply because academic institutions are true networkers. Academic life is just as much lived between institutions as within institutions. In a sense, academic networks were the first and are probably the only well-functioning international networks. It is a fundamental value and a prerequisite for scientific work that researchers should be able to communicate with other researchers on the cutting edge of knowledge production. The global academic conferencing system is the key engine to support this activity. With this background, a regional educational institution will have access to valuable cutting-edge insights that would potentially be important for regional development. Another important function of higher education is simply that it trains the future workforce. Through this activity, knowledge imprinted in students through their education can be transferred to the regional economic life.

The key challenge for institutions of higher education is to integrate in relevant regional meaning construction networks. It is not self-evident that this is the case. We have substantial evidence that regional universities educate students 'out' of the region, simply because they are trained in fields in which there is no local labour market.

Regional Institutions of Higher Education – Capable Networkers?

Modern universities have created an image of themselves as knowledge institutions. They are fighting to reconquer the concept 'knowledge organization' from everyday business language in which any enterprises employing professionals with a background from higher education call themselves knowledge organizations. In fact, one could be led to the false belief that business schools are the only true knowledge organizations (Fuller, 2002). Nothing could probably be further from the truth. This is a long overdue attempt by universities to reconnect themselves with the current trends and positions related to knowledge production in the larger society. The problem with many of these activities is that they are basically aimed at reinvigorating the old concept of generalizable knowledge and are thus attempting to set the clock back. In this chapter I argue that this would be a waste of time and a process that would put them fairly and squarely on the losing side.

The current devotion to explicit knowledge as the only form relevant for academic discourse will not create a platform for interaction, as networks ask for 'knowing how' related to context-bound and practical problems. This argument was presented in the introduction to this chapter, where the essence of knowledge and technology transfer was grounded in 'knowing how' to deal with regional development.

As argued in Fuller (2002), Greenwood and Levin (1998a; 1998b; 2000; 2001), Levin and Greenwood (1997; 2001), and Nowotny *et al.* (2001), among others, higher education needs a tighter link to everyday societal life. Current university activities are too much subsumed in the life world of the university and do not pay enough attention to the challenge of integrating academic work in a broader political context. Knowledge development at universities has to a very high degree become knowledge production for its own sake, and not the creation of knowledge applicable to solving important social problems. The new demand for knowledge focuses on insights that are judged according to their relevance and rigor given a broader context-based discourse (Nowotny *et al.*, 2001). In addition, knowledge should be judged according to how it can support and be developed through local actions (Greenwood and Levin, 1998b). Universities are obviously not well prepared for this transformation.

Given the current mode of operation in academic institutions, it is fairly obvious that universities at large play a minor role in regional meaning construction networks. The gap between what counts as knowledge at universities and what is useful for practitioners is too large. It is equally obvious that universities need to reach out to and integrate in regional meaning construction networks. Through this process they can ground their knowledge in the local context, which again is a prerequisite for their being able to offer the region the competence that they possess. Of course, this is a transformation that cannot and would not happen overnight. A more fundamental shift in the educational system is required.

Greenwood and Levin (1998a) deliver arguments for seeking the research topics in real-life problems. Grounding research in this way would mean that the outreach to the society was immediate, problems would emerge automatically from what actors in the society regard as important, and the solutions would have a practical relevance. The secondary effect of this research praxis, often called action research, is a democratization of knowledge production. People who 'own' the problem would become part of the network creating new knowledge. If the academic world transformed its mode of operation towards a praxis based on action research, it would be much easier to reach out to regional developmental activity. In many respects this is the same argument that is presented in Nowotny *et al.* (2001), which focuses on creating a larger 'agora' (meeting place) where academic insiders and users contextualize knowledge to make it applicable in the regional setting.

On the other hand, the arguments for a change in academic praxis are in no way arguments for reducing the universities pertinent demand for integrity, critical analysis and constructive solutions. These three factors are probably the most important virtues of academic institutions. The challenge would be to keep to these virtues alive in a situation where knowledge would be contextualized.

Institutions of higher education could become significant actors in regional development if their mode of knowledge production is transformed to meet local needs. This would imply seeking research topics that have high social relevance and that can support contextualized problem solving. In order to become such actors, the universities will be forced to change their own way of working in order to enable it to meet regional developmental challenges.

Worklife and University Cooperation in Central Norway

Over several years researchers at the Norwegian University of Science and Technology and the affiliated research institution SINTEF have cooperated with local enterprises in order to enhance enterprise development (Levin *et al.*, 1997; Elvemo *et al.*, 2001).

The main idea has been to create a development network (development coalition) preparing the ground for close cooperation between companies, researchers and public administration. The underlying purpose was to make it possible to combine resources in companies, public offices for economic development, and researchers in order to work on enterprise and regional development. This activity has been aimed both at supporting activities intended to bring about concrete changes at company level, but also at creating broader learning networks. It will often be closely linked to ongoing development activities in enterprises. Issues of common concern are, for example, leadership development, production systems, and quality of worklife. A typical mode of working is that after the first contact between researchers and enterprise actors, the parties involved seek to frame questions for research and development jointly. Different arenas can be utilized for this encounter, but the core idea is to give the actors involved a say in the discourse leading to a formulation of questions to investigate. The initial network in such a process might involve management, workers and researchers. Depending on the question under investigation and the learning process, other business actors or public offices might become involved as well. Thus, the process, if it is successful, gradually expands the network of involved actors. This is what was earlier identified as the primary transfer process, because it is closely linked to the daily operation of one specific enterprise. In the regional setting the research group developed this kind of relationship with two other companies. These contacts were pragmatic in nature; they occurred either when companies asked for advice or simply wanted a partner for their internal discussions, or when researchers took the initiative. In addition, the research team had close cooperation with companies outside the region working on enterprise development activities.

The secondary transfer process emerged as the research team created a meeting place to which enterprises cooperating with the researchers were invited. The first attempt to create a connectedness between involved companies was not particularly successful. It took place in the same city where the university was located, and the themes for discussion were chosen by the researchers involved. Not much reflection was needed from the researchers' side to see that this kind of networking would not pave the way for regional cooperation. After some restructuring, the network meetings were moved to the premises of the companies, and the topics for discussion were created through involved cooperation. This approach turned out to be quite successful, and the network continued for many years as a viable common area for transfer of knowledge and technology. In addition, the network attracted more companies and gradually expanded.

Conclusion – Discourses in Connected Networks

Regional development depends on the inhabitants' ability to act to promote economic activity. The special focus in this paper is on how transfer of knowledge and technology can support regional development. Knowledge and technology can only be successful factors when the insights can be manifested in concrete actions. Accordingly, relevant knowledge is what supports concrete actions. In this perspective, knowledge embodied in peoples' actions is the kind of knowledge that can make a difference. Both technology and knowledge for action are of the same character, as they are fundamentally embodied in peoples' actions. This 'knowing how' is actually what needs to be transferred.

There is nothing that can be understood as a generalized, skilful activity. Everything we do as human beings is in the context of the concrete lifeworld. Thus, we always act in a specific context with certain constraints and possibilities. That is the core argument for the importance of regions as the context for regional development. Knowledge and technology is transformed in the local context to skilful actions in order to enhance economic development. Whether we like the concept of the region or not, the locality (both material and social) will always be the foundation upon which all developmental activity will take place. Being global is only possible through acting locally. The important question is how regions play a part in transfer of knowledge and technology.

In a region we will find several different networks, some which are connected and some of which operate independently. These networks play a key role in the transfer of knowledge, and they shape the ground for regional meaning construction. Accessing knowledge is a social phenomenon, where social interactions and discourses create the contextual meaning. It is this contextual meaning that is crucial for economic development.

Two types of network can be understood as the primary bases for a broader regional development. Interorganizational learning and meaning construction are, of course, also very important, but as the perspective of this paper is the region, these processes are not discussed here. (See Levin, 1997 for an extensive discussion of these processes.) First, networks between local actors within the same professions are important. These networks, regional communities of practice, are created where cross-organizational learning spreads knowledge from one organization to the broader regional community. Accordingly, a potentially very broad knowledge base is created in the region. In addition it is argued that this transfer is quite effective because it will be closely linked to observable actions that occur in the regional context. The second type of network is the value-chain-based industrial network. In a region, organizations can be integrated in one specific production chain, and the diffusion of knowledge will cross boundaries, thus creating a potentially broad regional knowledge base.

Regional universities or institutions devoted to higher education can play an important role in regional transfer of knowledge and technology. In a certain but limited way, they can play a role as a channel for new insights. This supplier role will only make sense when the local institutions have (close to) cutting-edge knowledge in the field. In this situation it is obvious that regional diffusion can turn out to be a very powerful asset for the already regionalized knowledge base. A broader question is how regional universities can take part in the transfer of knowledge and technology in fields where they do not possess cutting-edge knowledge. A too simplistic answer is to limit the involvement of local universities to their only playing a role in areas where they have this knowledge. Universities have an important function; they can be integrated in regional networks, becoming active members based on their special competence, which of course will be important for the transfer process. This would imply the construction of regional knowledge networks through a broadening of the knowledge construction process to include as many of the relevant actors as possible. However, given their current understanding of what constitutes knowledge and how they interact as experts, universities are not particularly well equipped for the task. Making universities a powerful actor in regional economic development will imply that they develop a capacity to engage in Mode 2 knowledge production, which implies contextualized knowledge.[4] Mode 2 production implies a context-bound, cross-disciplinary and engaged way of creating new knowledge. From the perspective of this chapter, this would imply knowledge that is developed and verified through a broad coalition between researchers and the people in need of the knowledge.

Universities cannot reach out towards Mode 2 knowledge production unless a major internal change takes place. A reconceptualization of what counts as knowledge (from explicit knowledge to 'knowing how') and a new way of doing research is what is needed. The core argument in this paper is how an engagement in action research might create the needed bridge between universities and regional life. Action research can shape the ground for a praxis-oriented, context-bound scientific activity that can supply 'knowing how' integrated in regional life. This kind of knowledge is, of course, equally intellectually demanding as conventional explicit knowledge.

A third type of regional network involves public offices created to support economic development. It is self-evident that they should be integrated in the knowledge-procuring networks, and not be bystanders essentially creating plans for development or granting funds for economic development activities. The public actors need to learn from direct actions, and they have valuable insights to offer regional actors. Their roles have to shift towards a higher involvement in regional development.

The picture painted of regional development has a foreground of meaning-construction networks in a constant interchange. The main argument is that transfer of knowledge and technology are made sense of and contextualized through social engagement in different types of networks. The different networks should be connected to enable a broad regional knowledge coalition where different actors will take on diverse roles, making complementarity and collectivity the genuine strong points.

So let us return finally to the local leaders of Western Norway. Is it now possible to make sense of their bragging of being global actors, not particularly interested in the national dimension? They were of course quite correct in not limiting their

---

4   The Mode 2 concept is used in the same way as Gibbons *et al.* (1994) and Nowotny *et al.* (2001) use it, to identify a trans-disciplinary and context-bound type of knowledge generation.

perspective for knowledge acquisition to Norway. They have learned the lesson that regional institutions do not necessarily make a difference unless the knowledge they can support has the trademark of being contextualized to the actual region. Universities external to the region might be better capable of doing that, because they are able to convey a form of knowledge that link up with local demands.

The question will always be how to get access to the relevant knowledge, independent of location. On the other hand, what goes largely unacknowledged in the local north-western Norwegian understanding, is the importance of their own networking capabilities. Their bragging is in line with the major arguments in this paper, as they devoted much energy and resources to regional diffusion and meaning construction through their local networks.[5]

---

5   I am grateful for valuable and constructive comments from Ida Munkeby. She has been most helpful in revising the chapter.

Chapter 4

Regional Development, Universities and Strategies for Cluster Promotion

David R. Charles

Introduction

Universities and clusters have both become central in economic development fashion in recent years. Both are also closely linked with a concern for the development of new industries and new technology-based firms, although the wider implications of both in economic development terms can be simultaneously overlooked. The cluster concept in particular has become an almost obligatory element in regional economic development policies, and its application is now spreading across all scales of economic policy in both advanced and developing nations. Definitions of clusters vary greatly, but one approach that has resonance for a number of possible policy applications is that of a 'reduced scale innovation system', as used in a recent OECD study group (den Hertog, Bergman and Charles, 2001). Using this definition I focus on clusters as groups of interacting firms and agencies that collectively enhance innovation performance through acting as a system. This has some resonance with national innovation systems (Edquist, 1997), but is sectorally or technologically more focused and usually operates at a territorial scale that is less than national. Other work has also focused on clusters as communities of knowledge (Henry and Pinch, 2000).

Taking this view that clusters are primarily innovation- or knowledge-based communities, then there are obvious implications for a range of knowledge-producing bodies such as universities. Universities are increasingly being recruited by economic development agencies to underpin their aspirations to develop or enhance clusters (see, for example, Paytas *et al.*, 2004; DTI, no date), and indeed have been seen as key actors in the formation of some of the paradigmatic cases of clusters used as templates by policymakers. Universities themselves are also seeing the advantages of such an approach as a means of winning new resources to strengthen particular areas of research.

This chapter will both discuss the definition of clusters as innovation- and knowledge-based systems or communities, and examine two cases where universities are being enrolled in cluster strategies – one from the UK and one from Australia. The cases are drawn from international research on the role of universities in regional economic development, and explore both the process by which universities have become involved in cluster strategies and the forms of interaction that are emerging. The cases provide an opportunity to examine the range of possible approaches and the advantages and disadvantages of different strategies.

Clusters as Innovation Systems

The term cluster is used in a wide range of different contexts and circumstances in economic development at present, posing considerable problems for those seeking to define its meaning. In a recent paper Martin and Sunley (2001) object to such ambiguity and the lack of boundaries, either industrial or geographic, but such criticism is only partly justified. There is no possible consensus on what is a cluster, because it is a concept that is specific in place and time, and defined through the act of investigating individual clusters. Porter (1998a: 198) describes the concept as representing 'a new way of thinking about national, state, and city economies', and it is clear that he sees the cluster as a framework for thinking about how places acquire and maintain advantages or assets that affect the competitive performance of the firms located there. If we acknowledge that there are particular territories where groups of firms and industries agglomerate and benefit from external economies to the extent that they can dominate global markets, and there are of course many well-known cases, then we need means of describing and understanding such places, but without expecting a common set of processes, measurable boundaries or comparable structures. We can recognize that there may be some parallels between Silicon Valley, the City of London and the UK motorsport industry, but it is the process of understanding how different places can produce such advantages within different industries that is more important than whether one can draw boundaries that limit which firms are in or out of the cluster.

Clusters can be characterized as being networks of production of strongly interdependent firms (including specialized suppliers), knowledge-producing agents (universities, research institutes, engineering companies), bridging institutions (brokers, consultants) and customers, linked to each other in a value-adding production chain (OECD, 1999b). The cluster approach focuses on the linkages and interdependence between actors in the network of production when they are producing products and services and creating innovations. Another wording used by Porter is: 'a geographically proximate group of interconnected companies and associated institutions in a particular field, linked by commonalities and complementarities' (1998a: 199). Indeed, Porter goes on to state that the geographic scale of a cluster can range from the urban scale to even a group of countries, and can take varying forms dependent on depth and sophistication. In other words, clusters are what we define as clusters from examining the territorial embeddedness of interactions between firms and other institutions. The key question is whether we start from a pre-set view of the territorial scale and look for interactions and interdependencies within that territory, or start from a group of firms and examine the space within which a set of relationships have developed. Porter's approach is to start from the firm, although in much policy application clusters are defined for specific territories without consideration of whether they reach beyond certain administrative boundaries, or indeed whether there is any sign of critical mass, interaction or competitive advantage. This question of the boundaries of the cluster (whether sectoral or spatial) is casually treated by Porter, who suggests such definition is 'a matter of degree, and involves a creative process' (1998a: 202). Taking a social constructivist perspective it would be more appropriate to say that clusters, like other forms of network, are socially constructed through individual action, and the benefits and interactions may decay with 'distance' from the core of the network, but may never have a sharp boundary.

The idea of clusters as innovation systems should perhaps not be surprising given the common identification of competitiveness with innovation. If clusters are economic formations that enhance competitiveness, then, in the majority of cases, it is because the firms within the cluster are more innovative, and that innovativeness derives at least in part from the advantages of the cluster. The commonly described advantages of clusters in terms of rapidity of response, learning, and the accumulation of a stock of both tacit and codified knowledge, clearly underpin the innovative capacity of firms.

Recent theorization of the process of innovation stresses the importance of network building, whether through economic considerations of the role of suppliers and customers in the shaping of innovations (Lundvall, 1988), or through social constructivist and actor-network accounts (Latour, 1996). Innovations require the assembly of a diverse set of knowledges and of networks for production and consumption, and all firms must do this regardless of their location. However, empirical observation has shown that such resources related to particular industries have become more concentrated in particular places, with the consequence that firms in those locations have easier access to the tools for innovation, stimulating virtuous cycles of innovative and competitive advantage.

Another perspective focused on processes of learning stresses the importance of communities of practice within the firm: tightly knit groups of people who constantly work together, exchange knowledge and develop a shared understanding of the environment in which they work, the knowledge on which their work depends and the context in which it is used (Wenger, 1999). Whilst such communities of practice are usually confined to the firm, individuals may be connected on a wider basis through networks of practice: looser and often anonymous groups defined by a common knowledge base, but without the deeper understanding that results from regular face-to-face interaction (Brown and Duguid, 2000). Knowledge that can appear to be sticky when crossing the boundaries of such communities of practice may flow more easily across networks of practice. Clusters are thus seen by Brown and Duguid as ecologies of knowledge where firms with parallel communities of practice form an agglomeration and are connected through networks that permit knowledge to leak and quickly find complementarities. If the networks are more tightly connected by the regular movement of individuals between firms, thereby reinforcing the shared understanding, then that rate of interorganizational learning will be yet more rapid. Such ideas are central to the explanation of Silicon Valley, but also more recently to the knowledge community of the UK motorsport industry (Henry and Pinch, 2000).

This approach fits with the idea of a system of innovation, in that the term 'system' cannot be effectively defined either, but tends to refer to a set of elements or factors that interact in ways that influence the development, diffusion and use of innovations (Edquist, 1997). Brown and Duguid's ecologies of knowledge are just another form of system, although they neglect some of the economic and policy elements that tend to be the focus of much of the national innovation system work. Whatever term we use, our interest from a policy perspective is on where and how such configurations emerge and thereby present firms with competitive advantage.

Cluster Policy, Regional Innovation and Universities

What kind of policy response is appropriate to this? If clusters are innovation systems, then policymakers might wish to reinforce such systems by strengthening the knowledge base, facilitating knowledge transfer and encouraging collaboration. However, clusters have been used as an excuse for a wide variety of policies, both to strengthen existing clusters (however well developed) and to attempt to create new clusters.

In this sense there could be said to be two kinds of approaches: *policies to support clusters*, which are concerned with reinforcing the competitive advantages of existing clusters through a variety of policies tailored to the specific needs of an individual cluster, and *clustering policies*, which encourage collaboration and networking between firms in the hope that these will then become a cluster. Some policymakers even use the phrase 'to form' or 'establish a cluster', as if a cluster was some form of association that could be set up with a board of management and a set of membership rules. These policies are also developed at a variety of spatial scales: national governments such as Denmark or Netherlands have developed national cluster policies that focus on framework conditions, whilst regional development agencies internationally have cluster policies which combine infrastructure and direct business support and networking. At the micro scale many cluster initiatives are developed to support small local networks of SMEs, with a stronger focus on collaboration and the development of shared resources (OECD, 1999b; den Hertog *et al.*, 2001).

Within such cluster policies the role of knowledge institutions such as universities is frequently seen as core, especially in terms of strengthening the knowledge base of existing clusters or developing new technology-based clusters. In the latter case, the lessons of a few high technology regions where spin-off firms have played a key role tend to be adopted (Lawton Smith, 2003). The importance of the communities of practice within the firms in the cluster are thus often insufficiently appreciated, but there is clearly some role for universities in developing the core underlying knowledge base on which the firms must build.

In the UK, recent government policy statements have particularly focused on the role of higher education in underpinning economic vibrancy within a context of support for clusters and innovation. A White Paper on Enterprise, Skills and Innovation, published by the Department of Trade and Industry (DTI) and the Department for Education and Employment (DfEE) states that:

> The role of our universities in the economy is crucial. They are powerful drivers of innovation and change in science and technology, the arts, humanities, design and other creative disciplines. They produce people with knowledge and skills; they generate new knowledge and import it from diverse sources; and they apply knowledge in a range of environments. They are also the seedbed for new industries, products and services and are at the hub of business networks and industrial clusters of the knowledge economy. (Department of Trade and Industry/Department for Education and Employment, 2001)

whilst a DTI White Paper on Science and Innovation policy stresses the role of regional development agencies and of universities in clusters.

> While some elements of the framework for innovation can only be determined through national action, there are significant differences in innovation between regions, calling for different approaches. …. While all regions must participate in the economic success of the country through innovation, priorities for action within the regions differ. ….. Part of RDAs' role is to support the development of clusters, geographical concentrations of companies, specialized suppliers and associated institutions such as universities, co-located for mutual competitive advantage. (Department of Trade and Industry, 2000)

Although cluster thinking pervades the UK White Papers of 2000 and 2001, universities have been engaged in cluster-oriented activities for some time already, in some cases for decades. Clusters provide an ideal means for universities to aggregate together the demands of individual firms into research and training programmes that can endure from one year to the next (Charles and Conway, 2001). They offer the opportunity to target strategically areas of research where the university can build an international reputation and where firms can draw locally on a globally oriented knowledge base.

University cluster engagement can be either reactive, responding to the needs of an existing local cluster, or proactive, building localized expertise in the hope of stimulating cluster development. Successful regions need both forms: ongoing support for existing clusters to ensure they maintain their competitiveness, and blue skies work to provide opportunities for the entry into and exploitation of new forms of technology and market. Taking the Porter model of competitive advantage (Porter, 1990) – the 'Diamond' model – we can identify university inputs for each of the elements in the model.

Firm strategy – Universities are working with firms in a number of clusters to enhance their managerial capabilities. In addition universities contribute significantly to some regional clusters, such as biosciences in Cambridge, Manchester and Newcastle among others, through the formation of new firms.

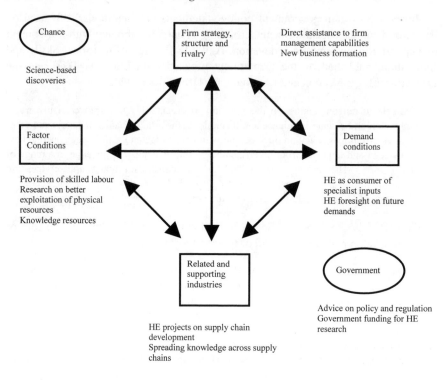

Figure 4.1   The Porter 'Diamond' model
Source: Porter, 1990

Factor conditions – Universities are a central input to knowledge-based clusters through the provision of a trained workforce and underlying technologies. In Sheffield the universities are key players in the development of a materials cluster with research and training dedicated to the needs of existing and new materials companies.

Related and supporting industries – Central to many cluster initiatives within universities is the notion of supply chain development.

Demand conditions – Universities can have an input on the demand side, and as significant research businesses they can draw through innovations, for example, in instrumentation. Again within cluster-oriented projects there is frequently a market development element.

Chance – Many clusters develop initially by chance, and one potential input to that process is the presence of a research concentration and significant new scientific discoveries. The best example of this in England is perhaps Cambridge, where developments in biosciences can be traced back to scientific developments in the University.

Government – Government has a strong role to play in the development and support for clusters, through its effect on other factors and through regulation and direct support. Universities interact with government primarily through their inputs into the policy development process, informing governments of the need for cluster policies and participating in Foresight and other consensus building exercises.

One of the dilemmas of universities when considering their commercialization strategies is how to cope with a broad diversity of knowledge. Most institutions have a wide portfolio of research interests such that commercializable ideas might come from diverse disciplines and be applicable in a wide range of industries. The nature of the knowledge required to identify and target potential users of such technologies is highly specialized, and in most cases universities have generalist technology-transfer professionals (Charles and Howells, 1992). Universities need, therefore, to try on the one hand to be responsive to the opportunities that come from the research base, but also build some specialized capabilities that enable them to maximize the benefits from particular kinds of client firm (Goddard *et al.*, 1994). Typically, this can be done through the development of specialist research centres that focus on the needs of specific industries, and increasingly such bodies are using cluster discourses to justify their actions and argue a case for resources.

Scales of University Engagement with Cluster Policies

We noted earlier that cluster policies have been developed at various different scales, from the national to the highly localized, as in the case of micro-clusters. So universities also engage with cluster policies at different scales.

National: National policies to develop particular clusters have a particular resonance with university strategies, in that such policies frequently affect resource allocation decisions for national research programmes. Specifically, such policies tend to focus on new high-technology sectors such as biotechnology or nanotechnology, but may also include strategic developments of relevance to more traditional industries such as agriculture. Typically, universities seek to orientate their activities towards these new priorities and compete to become national centres of excellence.

Regional: Universities are usually key actors within regional clusters and regional cluster policies. A number of regional-scale clusters have drawn heavily on the research and human resources of universities in the past, and new regional initiatives seek to enrol universities through access to new resources for dedicated research facilities or new courses, and through the involvement of university staff in cluster-based institutions (Benneworth, 1999; Goddard and Chatterton, 1999a).

Local/micro-clusters: Small-scale micro-cluster or networking initiatives are often developed by local business support agencies and are more modest in the resources they use, but nonetheless can involve universities in the provision of support and services. In some cases, universities have sought to develop such initiatives themselves as a means of better targeting their activities on business needs.

Internal to the university: Cluster policies may have an effect within the university as well as through its external activities. The need to address external markets orientated around clusters rather than academic disciplines can have an effect on the internal organization of either the industrial liaison functions of the university (through cluster-based business support teams for example) or through the internal organization of the academic base, especially through the development of new cross-discipline research institutes and schools that map onto identified cluster opportunities.

In the case studies that follow all of these scales of involvement will be identified, with in many cases all four being in evidence within the same institution.

Case Studies

North East England

The universities in the North East have a long history of developing initiatives to support regional industry, although with varying success (Potts, 1998). The institutions themselves are very varied in their capabilities and strengths, and in the main have sought to play to those strengths in developing outreach activities. Some of these activities are focused on specific kinds of industries and technologies, and therefore are very appropriate for cluster policies. In meeting the needs of existing firms within existing regional strengths, and seeking to reinforce and build on these, the universities fulfil two valuable functions: they provide a source of graduates and act as knowledge-producing agencies. Some specialist units have been developed to meet the needs of existing clusters, and this role in some cases encompasses the provision of pre-competitive research support for groups of local SMEs that find it difficult to invest in applied research or access public programmes at national or EU level. The region is weak in R&D in all sectors (Charles and Benneworth, 2001), including to some degree in higher education – there are some centres of excellence, but the overall level of R&D investment in the universities is one of the lowest of the UK regions. Recent programmes have seen many schemes within universities providing consultancy support to SMEs and technology awareness programmes.

The most significant development in recent years has been the formation of the regional development agency, One NorthEast (ONE), as in its regional economic strategy it has identified two priorities of relevance for this argument (One NorthEast, 1999): putting an emphasis on the universities as key agencies of change in the region, and identifying clusters as the main vehicles for economic development strategy. Both of these priorities are interrelated and translate also into funding strands within the region's Single Programming Document for the application of European Structural Funds. This opportunity for the region's universities further reinforces other opportunities arising from the national policy environment for higher education outreach and clusters.

The responses from ONE and the universities can be seen in terms of a matrix of actions and developments according to the spatial scale of the policy focus (from national to local and internal to the university) and the sectoral focus of the cluster to which the initiative is oriented. Thus, from a university perspective, we see a variety of initiatives around specific clusters combining funding from a variety of sources with a variety of spatial scales of operation.

Taking the national policy scale, central government departments have been supporting cluster-oriented initiatives focused on centres of excellence that can interact with firms within a cluster at a national or sub-national scale. Such schemes include the University Innovation Centres, launched with the 2001 White Paper on Skills, Enterprise and Innovation, in which Newcastle and Durham Universities are collaborating around a new centre for nanotechnology based in Newcastle. Another such initiative, this time involving the Department of Health and the DTI, subsidizes the Genetics Knowledge Parks to develop health-related post-genomic technologies, and, here again, Newcastle is leading a consortium that has won one of these awards. Although nationally funded, and not restricted to local collaborations, these national awards are being linked with specific regional initiatives in collaboration with ONE.

At the regional scale, ONE has been seeking to enrol the support of the region's universities in its emerging cluster strategies. Altogether ONE has at various times identified around fifteen 'clusters', although their status is highly variable (some are genuinely strong and internationally known while others remain aspirational), and not all are currently receiving support. Different universities are developing projects that fit within these clusters, but, more significantly, ONE has identified the need, with the assistance of a review of the science base (Arthur D. Little Ltd, 2001), for five Centres of Excellence, which are intended to underpin the development of the clusters: in life sciences, nanotechnology, digital technologies, process industries and renewable energy. The universities are central players in four of these at least, and these link also to the two national initiatives described above. The Centres of Excellence also link with a new North East Science and Industry Council, which has been established to help develop the region's science base.

On a smaller and more local scale, individual universities have developed links with smaller groupings of firms around specific research and technology centres, often with a 'cluster' focus in that collaboration and multifaceted support are involved. Sunderland University, for example, has been developing a Digital Media Network of small firms, and the Resource Centre for Innovation and Design at Newcastle has been working with a cluster of engineering companies, encouraging interactive learning.

Finally, within the universities themselves, there have been a number of developments reflecting the cluster focus. In the University of Newcastle, the Higher Education Reach out to Business and the Community (HEROBC) programme, a Higher Education Funding Council for England (HEFCE) funded initiative, has financed the formation of a new business development team to support cluster-oriented developments. Each of the newly appointed business development managers was assigned to a specific 'cluster', mapping onto the strengths of the University and the cluster priorities of One NorthEast. As a consequence, a number of cluster-oriented initiatives are being developed with the active assistance of the business development managers, notably in the biosciences but also in information and communication technologies, environmental sciences and renewable energy. One example of the re-orienting of the University has been highlighting the need to restructure research activities around such cluster themes as part of a wider university restructuring, such as in the formation of a new environment institute.

However, it is perhaps more interesting to look at how various initiatives are coming together across these different policy scales to address the needs of particular clusters.

Biotechnology or life sciences is perhaps the best example from the North East where the examples already mentioned are supplemented by a number of other developments.

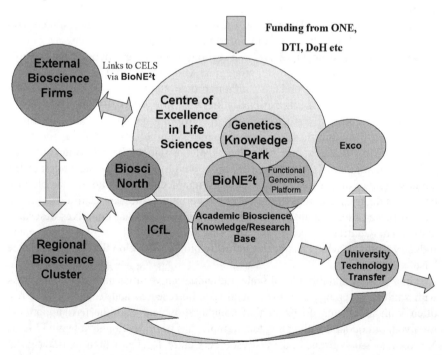

Figure 4.2   The North East biotechnology support cluster

In the diagram we see a representation of a number of initiatives. The core regional development is the Centre of Excellence in Life Sciences (CELS), a regional technology promotion and exploitation organization to coordinate activities on behalf of the regional cluster, and to underpin with resources from ONE and the European Regional Development Fund (ERDF) the research base in the region's universities (although primarily the research-intensive universities of Newcastle and Durham). The Centre of Excellence builds on the foundation of the Genetics Knowledge Park (funded by the Department of Health and the Department of Trade and Industry), one of the regional hubs of a national initiative to develop post-genomic technologies for the health sector. The Genetics Knowledge Park funds specific research to support innovation in healthcare, but also links with a programme of public understanding through the International Centre for Life, which is described below. Associated with the Genetics Knowledge Park is a Functional Genomics Platform, which is a network of technologies and researchers that support genetics research. A fourth component of the cluster research infrastructure is BioNE²t an Engineering and Physical Sciences Research Council (EPSRC) funded post-genomic regional research network which supports scientific networking activities, expertise databases, symposia etc, and develops linkages to businesses regionally and internationally. These national and regionally funded activities all support and enhance research in the academic departments of the region's universities, and notably Newcastle University's medical school.

CELS also absorbed the former Bio Sci North, an ERDF-supported biotech support agency.

The final core element is the International Centre for Life (IcfL), a localized development in Newcastle city centre that was initially promoted by the old Tyne and Wear Development Corporation, with funding from the Millennium Lottery Fund and ERDF. IcfL combines, on one site, research laboratories for Newcastle University's Institute for Human Genetics, an incubator for biosciences companies, a visitor attraction on the subject of genetics technology, and a small research centre in the sociology and ethics of genetics technology, which also has a strong public outreach function. IcfL also hosts CELS offices and the Genetics Knowledge Park.

Each of the universities involved in these various initiatives takes responsibility for the commercialization of the technologies emerging, although there are currently discussions about a joint agency being established, with the collaboration of ONE, to oversee commercialization in conjunction with the five Centres for Excellence.

The significance of these developments is threefold.

First, the universities are being enrolled by the regional development agency and national bodies in a set of cluster-based initiatives that require them to collaborate both with business and with each other on a scale that has never before been seen before, within this region at least. At the same time the universities are actively shaping the agenda to ensure that these developments help reinforce their research strengths.

Second, whether they are aware of it or not, university staff are entrepreneurially assembling funds from a variety of sources to develop networked initiatives that bear many of the hallmarks of clusters themselves – for example, interdependent networks of funding, researchers and businesses which offer the prospects of competitive advantage.

Third, regional agencies have been convinced of the importance of university research to the success of clusters to an unprecedented degree, and we see the beginnings of a regionally coordinated university system, but with goals of international excellence.

South East Queensland, Australia

The second case study takes a different national context. Australia also has been tentatively adopting the cluster discourse for its national strategic innovation policy, although the more conservative Commonwealth Government has taken a less interventionist stance. However, at the state level, the predominantly Labor governments have tended to take a different approach. Queensland has been perhaps the most interventionist state government in recent times, a massive shift in what was formerly the most conservative of states.

Again the most significant policy development has been the development of subnational policies that have sought to prioritize investment in key growth clusters, although the term 'sector' still tends to be used in Australia. This has, however, been paralleled by a prioritization of certain technologies nationally, with the Australian Research Council for the first time this year earmarking a proportion of funds for key technologies.

In Queensland, what is being termed the 'Smart State' strategy is a comprehensive state development strategy covering almost all aspects of public services. The innovation and economic development aspect has tended to focus on biotechnology and information and communication technologies, although with other more niche-oriented clusters such as tourism, and sustainable mining. Most recently a consultation or issues paper has been issued on an R&D strategy for the state (Queensland Government, 2002). This notes that:

> The Government is also funding initiatives to position Queensland as a world centre for critical enabling technologies and new R&D areas such as information and communication technology, biotechnology, nanotechnology, light metals, "new era" foods and advanced mining technologies. The providers of this research are predominantly Queensland's universities, medical research institutes, co-operative research centres and State Government departments.

At a more local level, specific local authorities have identified small-scale cluster initiatives such as aerospace in Ipswich, west of Brisbane, a variety of local clusters in Logan, south of Brisbane, and pleasure boat building on the Gold Coast.

Universities in Australia are keenly embracing these kinds of opportunities given the increasing reliance on private sector and state government funding and the decline in the core grant from the Commonwealth education ministry. Without the equivalent of a Research Assessment Exercise, there is also less of a conflict between academic and industrial research than perhaps is the case in the UK. In

Queensland the universities are following this trajectory, with the active assistance of a state government that is more interventionist than others.

Table 4.1 Queensland support for biotechnology provided in 2000/01

- providing AUS$ 5.5M towards the establishment of the AUS$100M Institute for Molecular Bioscience (IMB) at the University of Queensland, as well as dedicating AUS$77.5M over ten years to support the IMB in attracting key researchers and developing strategic research programs

- providing AUS$4.5M towards the establishment of a Centre for Biomolecular Science and Drug Discovery and an associated research commercialization centre at Griffith University's Gold Coast campus

- providing AUS$0.5M towards the AUS$3M fit-out of laboratory facilities for the Centre for Immunology and Cancer Research at Princess Alexandra Hospital

- establishing BioStart, an initiative designed to encourage and support start-ups in bringing the intellectual property developed in their research activities to an investment ready position

- establishing a networking programme (BioLink) that facilitates the development of a tight-knit, supportive environment within which biotechnology will prosper

- participating in and supporting Queensland biotechnology missions to major biotechnology conferences including BioJapan 2000 and Bio2001 in San Diego, USA

- supporting international biopartnering initiatives that facilitate the commercial development of Queensland's bioindustries by increasing global competitiveness

- establishing a Government-wide mechanism to help to identify the key priorities for research and development spending and provide a clear policy basis upon which to assess individual R&D projects

---

Source: Queensland Department of Innovation and Information Economy 2001 Annual Report.

Again, as in the North East of England, biotechnology is an important element in the state strategy, and within the universities. Queensland has established a Bioindustries Taskforce within the Department of Innovation and Information Economy and is working particularly with the three universities in Brisbane to support the development of the cluster, by developing significant new research infrastructures, new degree courses, support for spin-off firms and other networking and promotional activities.

Employment, although small, is growing rapidly from just over 1225 jobs in October 1999 to an estimated 2700 currently, of which the majority are in research institutes.

Particular initiatives include the development of a new Bachelor of Biotechnology Innovation degree with Queensland University of Technology – an interesting move as undergraduate teaching funds are normally provided by the Commonwealth Government. The primary research developments have been with the University of Queensland, focused on an Institute for Molecular Bioscience, but another research centre is being developed in Griffith University.

Table 4.1 illustrates some recent developments.

As an aside, just south of the Queensland border in New South Wales, Southern Cross University has been developing a strategy also based on biodiversity, but in this case on the exploitation of plant resources for alternative therapies etc. In a development labelled Cellulose Valley Technology Park, the University is seeking to develop a commercial base to exploit the knowledge of a host of university-based research and training activities focused on natural and herbal treatments, and associated agriculture (Davis, 1999).

At a more local scale Brisbane has been developing a strategy for the cultural and creative industries over many years now despite a former reputation as something of an overblown country town. With a population of around 1.5 million and growing quite rapidly, Brisbane lacks the scale and perhaps the style of Sydney or Melbourne, but has nonetheless in recent years been able to develop a cosmopolitan ambience and a rapidly expanding cultural cluster, both in the publicly subsidized sector and increasingly in the private sector.

As the capital city of the state of Queensland, Brisbane has benefited from state investment in a set of core cultural facilities – State Museum and Art Gallery, Performing Arts Centre and so on – but the city has pursued a more aggressive strategy since the 1980s to raise its profile internationally through culture, sport and tourism. In the 1980s the Commonwealth Games (1982) and Expo 88, both signalled a major shift in external profile and also a shift in perceptions within the city. The Expo in particular was highly popular, regenerating a ribbon site along the South Bank of the River Brisbane opposite the city centre, leaving a legacy of a high-quality linear riverside park with the State Library, Art Gallery, Museum, and Performing Arts Centre at one end, and an exhibition and convention centre, IMAX and Maritime Museum strung along the site. Also adjacent is Griffith University's Queensland Conservatorium, a further education college and another new campus of Griffith University, the Queensland College of Arts. Across the river in the city centre Queensland University of Technology (QUT) has a central city campus with a gallery and theatre alongside the city's old Botanical Gardens. A new pedestrian bridge links the QUT cultural precinct with South Bank.

Building on this physical concentration of cultural activities in the city is the new creative industries precinct north of the city centre adjacent to another campus of QUT at Kelvin Grove. Here the emphasis is on linking the University with the commercial activities of the creative industries as part of a new urban village. The 16-hectare site was a former army barracks which has been linked with adjacent derelict land, low-quality open space and under-used housing. QUT's Kelvin Grove campus lies to the rear of the site, with poor access, and a joint-planning framework has been drawn up with the Queensland Department of Housing to include a new QUT Creative Industries faculty, around 700 housing units, a 'town centre' with retail and commercial property, and other community amenities.

The initiative has developed alongside restructuring within the University to bring together a range of creative industries into a new 2500-student integrated faculty that seeks to break down the boundaries between performance, production, writing and design disciplines. The Creative Industries Precinct combines these teaching facilities with wired interactive exhibition space, black box performance space, an art house cinema, a Creative Industries Enterprise Centre, the Creative Industries Research and Applications Centre (CIRAC), and studios for computer design and animation, computer-aided design, performance and music, visual arts, film and TV and set/props construction. The studios will be available for use by QUT staff and students as well as private sector partners. The first phase, comprising AUS$60 million of university and studio facilities, attracted a AUS$15m subsidy from the Queensland government and was opened in May 2004.

The creative industries strategy that is now developing is recognized by the City Council as part of a knowledge-based industry strategy, and is considered within its 'emerging industries' brief. In support of this, the City is working with CIRAC to develop a long-term creative industries cluster mapping activity that will operate over a four-year period. The initial elements have been studies on the Popular Music cluster and on Indigenous Peoples' Creative Industries.

Throughout this activity the emphasis is on creative industries as private-sector-based, non-subsidized, new economy activities based on intellectual property arising from creative arts. The strategy recognizes the foundations that have been laid through investment in cultural activities and facilities, but is focused on building on this to develop new employment- and wealth-generating activities. Current opportunities lie in film and TV production, software and music production, each of which is growing strongly in the city. Overall, cultural goods and services in Queensland are growing at 7 per cent per annum, with a 285 per cent increase to gross state product over 10 years, and an employment increase of 42 per cent between 1995 and 1999. The overall current size of the industry is estimated as being in excess of AUS$5 billion.

Conclusion

One problem with attempts by universities to collaborate with industry in the past has been their fragmentation into small projects and initiatives, across a wide range of technologies, and the cluster approach would suggest a greater consolidation into those areas where growth potential lies. Current university funding mechanisms do not support such a strategic approach, and so additional resources are needed to ensure that regional needs are being met. To be successful, cluster-oriented initiatives should bring together collaborative research, technology extension and upgrading, skills development, and graduate placement and enterprise, all under the same framework. The focus should not be on the volume of firms assisted, but on the quality of assistance and the maximization of impact in terms of firm development and jobs created.

A second focus for the universities lies in the realization of future opportunities. A central weakness of a region such as North East England has been its inability to foster new industries based on new technologies. Regional strategies have typically focused on the attraction of mature industries to the region. Universities have been encouraged to work with existing industries, and there have been relatively few start-ups in emerging sectors. Consequently, by the time the region discovers a new opportunity, it is usually too late and other regions have already built critical mass.

Such regions do, however, have universities that are successful research-based institutions with considerable involvement in international research networks. Such research strengths can be the focus of new economic activities as has been seen elsewhere, as in Cambridge and Grenoble (Lawton Smith, 2003), although it must be clear that it is real research strengths measured by very large R&D investments that are likely to lead to such advantages.

New investment opportunities could be identified by a process of regional foresight, drawing on the expertise of the leading scientists in the universities and industrialists from science-based companies. These could then used to identify highly selective areas within the universities for support in novel applied science and associated business development. The role of regional development agencies, the Structural Funds and the like would be to provide some pump priming and facilitate the business development process, whilst other sources such as Framework Programme and Research Councils could be targeted for the main research support. Such an approach would have a higher level of risk than conventional forms of intervention, although job creation within the higher education sector and leverage of other funding into the region would be at least as much as most other forms of assistance. However, the long-term benefits of a successful intervention would be greater than almost all other forms of assistance, taking into account deadweight and the short-term nature of most impacts.

The ultimate objective of all of these policies has to be the creation of a different notion of success for a region, measured not by its ability to attract individual firms, or by the creation of jobs in individual firms, but by the creation of successful clusters. Another way of viewing a cluster from that normally presented is as a collection of knowledge assets that constantly reinvents itself, successfully attracts investment, and delivers jobs and wealth for its region. In such successful clusters the survival of individual firms does not matter, as new firms constantly emerge to absorb any surplus labour, and indeed the regular death and birth of firms is a sign of dynamism and creativity. Such a vision requires a new way of looking at the economy, a new way of considering the role of clusters and a stronger role for knowledge-based institutions such as universities.

Chapter 5

The International Network University of the Future and Its Local and Regional Impacts

Huib Ernste

Introduction

Universities are often seen as very important knowledge producers and nodes for knowledge transfer (Rutten *et al.*, 2003). Traditional university research is still a major producer of new knowledge. At the same time, universities collect and provide access to literally 'worlds' of knowledge produced elsewhere. This knowledge is transferred to other realms of society and the economy through their educational programmes and through consultancy and cooperation with external partners. Finally, this knowledge also 'travels' with university researchers who take up careers outside universities.

In this way, universities play a crucial role in the local economy. The role of such knowledge providers becomes even more important as the competitive edge of the economy is increasingly being determined by the ability to compile, share and apply relevant knowledge in world-spanning networks. This explains the vast amount of research that is focused on the impact of universities on local and regional economies. This research often takes existing university locations as a starting point in order to deal with their knowledge-providing role for the region involved. Most of it does not deal with the dynamics of university locations, or of the spatial organization of these universities, and regards universities as given entities. The locations of universities themselves are hardly ever seriously questioned. The founding and location of new universities has only been an issue in the context of certain regional development programmes. This can well be understood, if one takes into account that universities, especially in the European context, often have long traditions. Furthermore, as largely state-dependent organizations, universities have often been thought to be only indirectly affected by the dynamics of the market or by any other societal forces. And any effects these forces do have hardly ever bring substantial locational or spatial consequences. Locational and spatial decisions are thus not routinely made at universities. In contrast, in private industry location decisions are much more common, and the locational structure seems to be much more volatile.

However, this situation is changing quickly, and more and more new forms of spatial organization for universities appear to be evolving; sometimes as a deliberate policy, but more often as an implicit consequence of other policy decisions. Obviously, it no longer suffices to take existing university locations as a starting point for research into the impact of universities on local and regional economies anymore. The spatial dynamics of the university organization itself need to be taken more and more into account. Therefore, I would like to focus on precisely this issue. Drawing mainly on the Dutch case, I will first describe how most universities were originally regionally based. I will then show how changing economic, societal and institutional contexts have forced universities to develop a new perspective, and how this in turn has led to an organizational response in the form of the 'network-university'. This is likely to have substantial repercussions on our idea of what a 'university' is and will be in future. Finally, I shall elaborate on the lessons that can be learned from these developments.

The Regionalization of a Universal Institution

In an article on current changes taking place in many universities, Philip Altbach (2004: 4) notes that almost all of today's universities have the same historical roots, namely, the medieval European university (Figure 5.1). And to emphasize the persistent influence of these roots, he quotes the former chancellor and president of the University of California at Berkeley, Clark Kerr, who once said (2001: 115) that 'of the institutions that had been established in the Western world by 1520, 85 still exist – the Roman Catholic Church, the British Parliament, several Swiss cantons, and some 70 universities'.

Needless to say, a long-term perspective is required in order to obtain an idea of the current changes taking place in the spatial organization of universities. Before the emergence of the modern nation-state, universities in Europe were highly international and formed a network that spanned many different countries. Students were not educated in the framework of formalized curricula, as is mostly the case nowadays. In those days, lecturers and students were highly mobile; they often only spent a limited time at one institution to teach or attend specific lectures. Students came from all over Europe. In the 'Low Countries', the first university was founded in Louvain in 1425 and the second in Douai in 1559. The first university in the Netherlands was founded in Leiden in 1575, because the Eighty Year War against Spain cut the Netherlands off from the predominantly Catholic universities in other places in Europe. As this example also shows, the reason why a university was founded in the first place was not so much to provide sufficient education for the population, but rather to serve the needs of the state, the church and the ruling elite (Baggen, 1998: 21–2). As the first humanistic university in Europe, Leiden grew to become one of the most important, holding a very international position, in which, for example, 44 per cent of the population of students and faculty were foreigners.

Until the late eighteenth century, most university foundations were mainly geared towards contributing to the power, influence and prestige of local territorial authorities (Müller, 1962; Mayr, 1979). This was particularly the case in the Netherlands because, there as elsewhere, before the emergence of the nation-state university education was mainly a matter for provinces and cities. Neither people's needs for educational services, nor economic considerations played a role in deciding where a university should be established (Meusburger, 1998: 439). All over Europe, universities were mainly located in capital cities or other centres of (local) power. If universities were founded in other locations, the main reason was often a wish to expand worldly or confessional influence in these areas, which also is reflected in the founding of the University of Leiden. The example of Leiden was soon followed by the other Dutch provinces, which also sought to have their own 'cadre school' (Franeker, 1585; Groningen, 1614; Utrecht, 1636; Harderwijk, 1648; Nijmegen, 1655), creating one of the highest densities of universities in Europe, a situation that would last until almost the end of the eighteenth century (Baggen, 1998: 25).

Figure 5.1   Medieval universities
Source: Shepherd, 1923: 100

We can thus observe a close link between universities and local powers. In this sense, universities clearly had a local and regional function. But because most scholastic, and to a lesser degree also humanistic, universities were in those days based on a conception of the university in which pure scientific metaphysical contemplation *scientia* (faculty of theology) dominated over the more applied *prudentia* (faculty of law) and finally over *ars* (faculty of arts), university teaching was mainly focused on broad erudition and on the knowledge obtained from 'the classics'. Teaching took place in Latin, which was the academic *lingua franca* in those days. Therefore, in this respect universities offered a very general and abstract kind of knowledge, which was expected to be applicable in the same way all over the world. A direct relationship to local professions and labour markets was hence almost absent (Baggen, 1998: 31). All in all, universities in the seventeenth and eighteenth centuries were much more international and mutually compatible than university systems nowadays.

The humanist concept of a university was the first step towards a continuous process of secularization and modernization. First of all, so-called 'academies of sciences' were established in most countries during the second half of the seventeenth century and the first half of the eighteenth.[1] Most of these were voluntary associations of scientists; but others, such as in the Netherlands, were direct instruments of the ruling government. They all focused on research in sciences outside the traditional university faculties. They tended towards more worldly and rationalistic forms of knowledge. Science did not have to prove itself in relation to the classical authorities, but through rational argumentation. The subjects they dealt with were topical issues in government, education, medicine, agriculture, etc., and as such were much more related to practical problems in society. For some time, their view of science was in opposition to that of the traditional universities, and a certain division of labour developed. Later the universities increasingly adopted the academic perspective. Because there was a lack of a central authority in the Netherlands, a national academy of this kind was founded rather late (1808) and no such division of labour could emerge. Hence, the Dutch universities introduced the academic style of doing science themselves within their own realm at a very early stage. It was not until the second half of the eighteenth century that regional scientific associations emerged in the Netherlands.[2] These universities established a new style; they focused increasingly on a kind of knowledge that had much more direct practical value for local society

---

1   The first was the *Accademia Secretorum Naturae* (1560) in Naples, followed by the *Accademia dei Lincei* (1603) in Rome, the *Accademia del Cimento* (1657) in Florence and, north of the Alps, the *Academia Naturae Curiosorum* (1652) in Schweinfurt. Other well-known examples are: the Royal Society of London for the Advancement of Natural Knowledge (1662) and the *Académie Royale des Sciences* (1666) in Paris (Baggen, 1998: 33). In the Dutch republic of united provinces such an academy was founded rather late in 1808 as Royal Institute of Sciences, Philology, and Arts (*Koninklijk Instituut van Wetenschappen, Letterkunde en Schoone Kunsten*) (KNAW, 2004).

2   For example, the *Hollandsche Maatschappij der Wetenschappen* (1752) Haarlem; *Zeeuwsch Genootschap der Wetenschappen* (1769) Vlissingen; *Bataafsch Genootschap der Proefondervindelijke Wijsbegeerte* (1769) Rotterdam; *Teylers Tweede Genootschap*, (1773)

and that was oriented towards progress and improvement rather than towards the timeless authority conferred by studying the classics.

A further step in the secularization of universities was brought about by the development of what was called 'realistic education' at secondary level, which was focused on specialized expertise and practical professional skills. As soon as these curricula developed, the division of labour between humanistic education at universities and realistic education in non-university institutions deepened, and the number of students studying at traditional universities drastically declined. Those who still attended university were, to a substantial degree, from the highest classes in society. But even these students progressively studied at university in more formalized curricula in order to obtain an official degree, which qualified them for certain professions and with which they could enter the labour market. Even though universities at first kept emphasizing a general education as opposed to professional training, they gradually also integrated *realia* in their programmes. This entailed the universities becoming less and less involved with the local authorities and more and more concerned with providing real educational services to the population. This tendency was amplified by the nationalization of most educational institutions after 1795 and 1807, following the founding of the Batavian Republic in the post-Napoleonic era, in which the power of the Dutch provinces and cities crumbled. As a consequence of all these tendencies, the international status of universities slowly but surely gave way. Their spatial distribution became progressively linked to local markets for education and labour, and only three of the five universities survived this shake-out (Leiden, Groningen and Utrecht). Generally speaking, the same development can be observed in Europe as a whole. Several more peripheral university locations were closed down and, in the main, central cities were chosen or kept as important university locations. Moreover, for the first time economic criteria and the demand for educational services from the local population became important locational factors (Meusburger, 1998: 440).

At the beginning of the nineteenth century Dutch universities were integrated in a nationwide three-tiered educational structure. They initially remained focused on a very general curriculum based on an encyclopaedic orientation covering a full spectrum of different scientific disciplines[3] (Huizinga, 1951, quoted in Baggen, 1998: 69; Wachelder, 1992: 204–30). The tendency for universities to offer curricula and conduct research in a very broad spectrum of different scientific fields continues until the present day. In the nineteenth century, however, not only the universities, but also the regional scientific associations were in decline. The latter were being replaced more and more by national disciplinary associations for the various sciences. The medical associations in particular initiated a new model for the disciplinary organization of scientific activities, in which the differentiation between academic and non-academic sciences disappeared. This system was quickly

---

Haarlem; *Provinciaal Utrechts Genootschap van Kunsten en Wetenschappen*, 1778, Utrecht (Baggen, 1998: 39).

3 Royal decree concerning higher education, 1815, Art. 53.

adopted by many Dutch universities, a process that was further amplified by the fact
that the initial encyclopaedic approach had soon reached its limits because of the
explosive increase in knowledge in the different fields of study. The curricula had to
be split into different disciplines. Here we find the organizational roots of the current
university system, which is organized around a still very broad spectrum of highly
specialized disciplines, combining theoretical (academic) knowledge with empirical
(practical) knowledge.

This more practical orientation was enhanced by the abolition of the guilds in
1818, which strengthened the grip of the national government on the professions
and on professional education. Consecutively, different branches of professional
education were institutionalized and nationalized. For example, the former military
(technical) academies,[4] educating technicians for service to the state, were combined
to form a full-fledged technical university in Delft, educating both state *and* industrial
engineers.[5] In general, at this stage a large number of the newly founded universities
in Europe were regarded as more praxis-oriented technical universities or economic
universities (Meusburger, 1998: 440).[6]

As previously stated, as a direct effect of the institutionalization of the more
practically oriented education and the traditional, more generally oriented universities,
theoretical (academic) knowledge and empirical (practical) knowledge were soon
combined. This also resulted in the enhancement of the traditional university
curricula with more practically oriented subjects. For the first time the integration of
'industrial schools' and 'pedagogical schools' with the universities was discussed.[7]
This development continued until the first quarter of the twentieth century, in which
even more new faculties and inter-faculties were created.[8] At the same time, the

---

4   The Royal Military Academy, Breda, founded in 1828 and the Royal Naval Institute,
in Medemblik, founded in 1829.

5   The historical links between this new technical university and government needs for
highly educated technical scientists, still finds its expression in what is called the 'historical
factor' in the allocation of state funding for universities, through which Delft still receives
substantially more funding per student than any other Dutch university. The same is true
for Leiden, since it was the first Dutch university originally established for governmental
purposes.

6   In the Netherlands, the Netherlands School of Commerce (now Erasmus University
Rotterdam) was founded in 1913; the Catholic Economic Institute for Higher Education (now
University of Tilburg) in 1927; the Delft Institute of Technology (now Technical University
Delft) was founded in 1905, and succeeded the Royal Academy of Civil Engineers in Delft
from 1842. The State Academy of Agriculture, Horticulture and Forestry (now Wageningen
University and Research Centre) was founded in 1904 as successor to the Wageningen
Municipal School of Agriculture in 1876. The Technical Institute for Higher Education in
Eindhoven (now University of Eindhoven) was founded in 1957.

7   In the current debate, mergers between the traditional general universities and the
professional universities and polytechnics has become highly topical again.

8   For example the united faculty of law and arts and the united faculty of mathematics
and arts. The latter, by the way, housed the new curriculum for human and physical geography,
which is also the discipline in which this contribution is written.

traditional comprehensive university structure with its five faculties was dissolved, and universities with fewer faculties, serving specialized needs, appeared. The technical and economic universities mentioned before were typical examples of this development, but so also were the newly founded confessional universities, such as the protestant Free University of Amsterdam (1880) and the Catholic University of Nijmegen (1923). These 'special' universities often served special needs, which were not covered in the same way by other universities in the country, and as such they provided themselves with a 'national' mission. Nevertheless, their location was often clearly chosen in such a way as to give them a more or less a central position for serving their main recruitment area.

In addition, the full entitlement of the graduates of the 'higher civil school'[9] to enter university without having had any education in Latin or Greek (1917), accelerated the development towards more secular and practically oriented universities. Because of this development, the number of university students increased again, and, at the same time, the humanistic academic ideal further fell by the wayside. A great number of new curricula ranging from sociology, musicology, sports, Byzantine language, to technical physics, etc., were introduced. Increasingly, the graduates of universities found jobs not simply in the traditional academic professions, for example, as physicians, priests, teachers, lawyers or civil servants, but also in manufacturing, banking, agriculture and trade. From that point onward, universities became less exclusive and therefore more embedded in local society.

In the final stages of the nineteenth century and the first phase of the twentieth century, applied and fundamental research started making its great advance at Dutch universities and was established as a more and more important and independent branch within universities. This development mirrors the accelerated technological development during this time. Moreover, many universities expanded their activities into new fields and infrastructure (laboratories), and their personnel structure as well as their organizational form underwent fundamental changes. The location structure, however, was not fundamentally affected by this development – or only at the micro level, in that many new university structures appeared at several locations within the same city.

Again we see the relationship between universities and local needs for professional skills strengthening. Although this never seemed to be a deliberate policy issue for universities or for the responsible state agencies, it did have its effects on the areas where universities recruited their students and on ties with the labour markets where their graduates found jobs. Thus, step by step, universities became less 'universal', in reference to both the content of their educational programmes and their external relationships. They also became more and more locally/regionally/nationally embedded. Of course, all these developments are closely related to general societal trends. All things considered, this step-by-step development has been consistent with the growth of an enlightened and modernistic conception of science and university.

---

9   Hogere Burgerschool (HBS).

After the Second World War, the universities were confronted by high-birth-rate generations and, accordingly, most universities grew quickly. This also led to the founding of a few new universities (the Technical University of Twente, in Enschede, 1961; the State University of Limburg (now University of Maastricht), 1976; the University of Eindhoven, 1956). Just as in most of the other European countries, during this phase of expansion spatial policy and sociopolitical location factors gained importance for the first time. Some of these new universities were deliberately founded in economically depressed and peripheral areas, such as the former textile region Twente and the former mining area of South-Limburg. They were intended, on the one hand, to relieve the other universities from some of the expansion pressure, and, on the other hand, they were expected to stimulate regional development in these areas. Meusburger (1998: 440) notes that at that time the quality and specific profiles of universities only played a minor role. The spirit of the time was focused on quantitative effects and on societal manipulability. Only in this framework can one understand how in Germany the idea arose of finding the

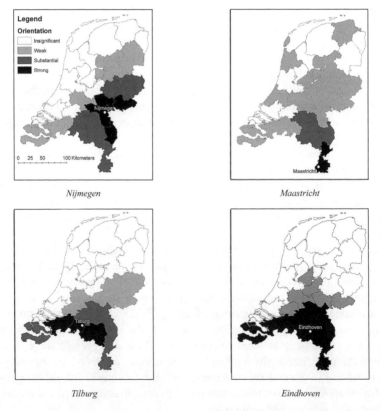

Nijmegen   *Maastricht*

Tilburg   *Eindhoven*

Figure 5.2   Student recruitment areas of the four southern universities in the Netherlands

Source: Buursink & Vaessen, 2003: 33

optimal locations of universities through a linear programming model based on the minimization of travel-time to university (Bahrenberg, 1974).

Throughout the post-war period in the Netherlands, a strong welfare state was set up, which also emphasized the egalitarian approach to universities. University education lost its former aura of academic status and elitism and became 'just' a daily service for 'all'. University education went from being a 'privilege' to a 'right'. The disenchantment of academia would appear to have been complete. Universities had almost become mere 'outlets' of standardized educational services. As a consequence, if students did not have a very good reason for going to a specific university, they would usually choose the university closest to their homes. As Figure 5.2 shows, this was to a large degree still the case at the end of the twentieth century.

Viewing these developments, we can conclude that universities were originally constituted to be 'universal' institutions, based on a universalistic ideal of knowledge. These classic universities were closely linked to local authorities, but the link with local society was rather weak, so that the student population itself was very international. The location of universities was mainly determined by the strategic considerations made by the ruling authorities in order to increase their influence and power. Over the centuries, this ideal of knowledge changed. A much more pragmatic, specialized and empirically based concept of knowledge, which was of practical use in society, took its place. This meant that the relationship between universities and the immediate community grew and that universities were increasingly serving local markets by providing educational services to the people. Along with this development, the student population became less international in comparison with the classical universities. Since the beginning of the twentieth century, applied and fundamental research activities have also been firmly established at universities. This has enhanced their importance to the local economy. As their ties with the local economy were strengthened in various ways, it became important for universities to be located at central places serving these markets. In the 1970s and 1980s, new university locations were often selected on the basis of regional policy objectives. Although during times of expansion many universities increased the number of their locations in their hometown, a more fundamental spatial reorganization of the university system was hardly ever considered. In the last few years, however, under the influence of changing circumstances, a more fundamental reordering is quite likely to happen.

In the following section, I will first focus on the developments in society that are responsible for this upcoming spatial restructuring, before looking at the spatial organization of the university in the future.

Universities in a Globalizing World

As we have seen in the previous section, universities have gone through all kinds of organizational changes with respect ot educational paradigms. Notwithstanding the fact that these developments clearly strengthened local ties, there hardly was any substantial rethinking of the traditional university locations in space. However, '[d]uring the last decade, technology, globalization, and competition have caused the ground to shift under higher education worldwide, defying national borders and calling into question honored traditions, sacred myths, and previously unquestioned assumptions' (Green *et al.*, 2002: 7). So, what was seen for so long as quite a stable organization, at least with respect to its spatial configuration, is now being seriously questioned. What has happened, so that, suddenly, the spatial organization of the university system is being rethought?

First of all, we should note that science and technology are increasingly determining the course of society. Today's universities are not simply affected by this societal trend, they are also responsible for carrying it forward. Indeed, it is part of their success. Universities have become crucial knowledge producers, and knowledge and information are gaining quickly in importance, for the economy and for society in general. The competitive edge of companies, regions and countries is becoming determined by their ability to retrieve, compile, share and apply relevant knowledge in world-spanning networks (Castells, 1996; Dunning, 1997). The pace at which new technological developments appear and diffuse has drastically grown. But also organizational and institutional changes are quickly following one another (Florida, 2002). The volatility of today's society is dwindling. Under these circumstances, fast and flexible adaptation becomes decisive.

In addition to this more general role of science, technology and knowledge in our society, new technological developments also have a much more direct and specific effect on university operations. The most dramatic impact is probably the enabling of 'distributed learning'. Distributed learning comprises a whole spectrum of different forms of learning, ranging from full-fledged distance learning, which involves full- or part-time students who may be separated in time and space from their peers and instructors, via a mixture of online and campus-based courses, or courses which embrace both elements, to fully campus-based courses, which make use of a electronic course support systems, with electronic distribution lists, chat-boxes, digital drop-boxes, online testing and course evaluation, and so on to foster active and group learning both in and out of the classroom. In most high-standard universities, all course information and course materials are made available, or at least are documented, through electronic networks. Therefore, the forms in which knowledge is transferred and communicated in university education is experiencing a phase of profound change, notwithstanding the fact that these innovation processes in practice often take much longer than forecast, because they also involve organizational adaptations, the development of technical skills, and, most of all, a reshaping of teaching and didactics.

New technologies play an increasingly important role not only in teaching itself, but also in all the accompanying communication and data-retrieval processes, such as library use, internet searches, the downloading of e-publications and website presentation – not to mention the role of these information technologies for all the research-related activities of university staff. All of these developments have made the whole market for the products of higher education much more transparent, both for providers and for consumers. For example, today it is simply a matter of course that, if one has to develop a new course or curriculum, one should at least also check out the set-up of similar courses through a quick-scan internet search, instead of reinventing the wheel from scratch. Moreover, students can much more easily compare different offers and choose accordingly.

Second, since knowledge and knowledge production have become a core issue for the economy and for society, many more producers of scientific knowledge have entered onto the scene in addition to the traditional universities. Private industry has taken up applied, and sometimes even also fundamental research activities, and even state authorities have set up a number of independent research institutions separate from universities. In addition, many private research and consultancy companies today conduct a substantial part of research. As a result, universities lost their monopoly on the production of scientific knowledge quite some time ago. The same is true for scientific education, even though in Europe, with its dominant system of publicly supported universities and centralized policies, inter-institutional competition to recruit students was suppressed for a long time. Now that knowledge is much more short-lived, it has become necessary to organize 'life long learning', and many new educators have entered this lucrative part of the market. Universities are now increasingly competing with other knowledge providers. Many companies have developed separate instructional divisions for their own employees, but they increasingly also market them to other corporations, resulting in what in the United States are called 'corporate universities'. There are other markets as well, where universities will meet fierce competition, such as the labour market for talented scholars and faculty, since demographic development will bring shortages and new generations will also have more choices. Finally, many universities will face a tough fight to obtain funding, to gain prestige and to receive other resources.

Third, we can observe a strong tendency towards a liberalization of markets and the privatization of many former responsibilities of government. State intervention is more and more reduced, which also has its effects on the traditional government task of providing higher educational services. Direct government funding for universities is under high pressure and has been made a subject of all kinds of market performance criteria, not to mention the number of students who are attracted. This is emphasized by a general attitude, which is rather critical towards the supposed usefulness of elitist institutions such as universities. Universities have been requested to leave the 'ivory tower' of academia and prove their worth by generating their own funding. In combination with typical Dutch pragmatism, this has led to a financial austerity policy by the Dutch government in respect to universities. Direct public funding as a percentage of the gross domestic product was reduced from about 1.2% in 1990

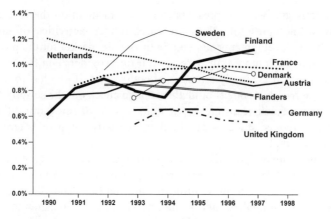

Figure 5.3   State spending on education as percentage of GDP
Source: Boezerooy & Kaiser, 2001: 44

to less then 0.9% in 1997,[10] whereas in most other European countries it has been kept more or less constant or has been raised (Figure 5.3). These tendencies are not unique to the Netherlands, although the Dutch are traditionally quite fast in adopting and implementing these policies. For example, Green, Eckel and Barblan (2002: 14) quote James Duderstadt, an American university president who joked about his institution's shrinking reliance on public funding: 'At first, his university was a "state institution", which then became a "state-supported", then "state-assisted" institution. A short time later, it was simply "state-located". Now, he describes it as "state-annoyed", to convey public officials' demand for accountability, yet their unwillingness to provide sufficient funding' (see also Duderstadt, 2000).

Figure 5.4 also shows that in the Netherlands priorities in state funding have clearly moved away from the university sector. This tendency has continued since then. We can observe a continuation of the shift in perspective on scientific research and education, which had its beginnings in the nineteenth century, but nowadays seems to have had substantial influence on the direct financing of universities.

Fourth, the previously mentioned tendencies, in combination with others, add up to a trend towards achieving a globalized world. Technology, particularly information technology, enables the compression of the world (Harvey, 1989; Cairncross, 1997) and lets us directly feel the hot breath of our competitors. Liberalization of the markets in a borderless world does the rest. Globalization in this context implies that goods, services, people and ideas will flow almost freely around the globe. On the other hand, globalization is often associated with the hegemony of capitalism and the domination of the economically rich, the loss of regional differences, national identities and culture and finally, also

---

10 For technical reasons, the corresponding data of the OECD seem to have come up with slightly higher estimates, but this does not change the tendencies.

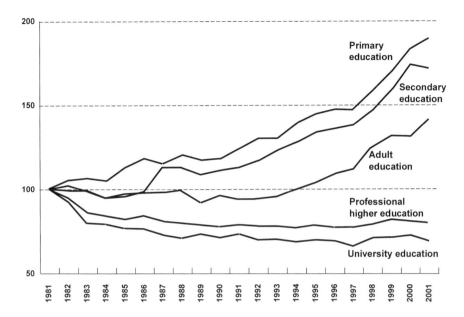

Figure 5.4   State spending on education per student (1981 = 100)
Source: VSNU, 2002: 59)

the loss of control. These tendencies are further enhanced by the increasing dominance of English as the *lingua franca* of the academic world and by the Bologna Declaration of 1999 and the subsequent Prague (2001), and Berlin Communiqués (2003) in which the objectives for the development of a common European Higher Education [Market] Area by 2010 were formulated. These have set the agenda for restructuring the European university landscape and for making educational products comparable and compatible. Similarly, the European Councils in Lisbon (2000) and Barcelona (2002) defined a programme to make Europe 'the most competitive and dynamic knowledge-based economy in the world'. It is also indicative that a debate was initiated on the role of the General Agreement on Trade in Services (GATS) for international trade in higher education services (Knight, 2002; 2003). Because of the diminishing relevance of national borders to educational markets, universities are entering a new stage of re-structuring. With great haste they are forced to change their roles from local knowledge providers to 'global' players on an international education market (van der Wende, 2001).

It is certain that much will change, but what difference do these trends really make for the way universities organize themselves and for their spatial configuration in particular? And how are the Dutch universities responding? How will the changing spatial configuration of the university of the future affect the research done on the role of universities in regions? In the final concluding section of this contribution, I will try to address these issues.

University Response and Spatial Consequences

In general all of these changes are amplifying the competition between universities for students, funds and fame. Particularly, the competition to recruit students has made many Dutch universities re-think their location strategy.

Expansion to Other Regions

To gain access to other regional markets of higher educational services, the opening of branch campuses was envisioned. Some universities, such as the Free University of Amsterdam and the State University of Groningen, systematically looked for regions where the participation of the population in higher education was below average, thus indicating a market development potential. The University of Groningen opened a branch campus in Leeuwarden. The Technical University of Twente, as well as the (agricultural) University of Wageningen, are both operating branch campuses there, and all three have successively combined into one joint three-university branch campus. The Free University of Amsterdam opened a branch campus in Zwolle in the eastern part of the Netherlands. Other universities have selected the location of their branch campuses on the basis of other criteria, often related to the specific kind of curricula offered at these locations. The University of Amsterdam, for example, created a new location for its university in the booming new town called Almere, in one of the IJselmeerpolders, while the University of Utrecht created a branch of their international honours college, called the Roosevelt Academy, in the rather remote town of Middelburg. A similar initiative has just been taken by the University of Nijmegen, which is going to establish a short version of its honours programme in the form of summer schools at the location of their international partners. The University of Leiden founded a new campus in The Hague, the seat of the national government, and the University of Maastricht finally created a branch called the 'Transnational University Limburg', in collaboration with the 'Limburgs Universitair Centrum', at Hasselt and Diepenbeek in Belgium.

Of course, these new locations are not 'new university locations' in the true sense that they offer the full spectrum of university education services. Most of the time they are confined to just a few disciplines, or just to a specific stage, for example, the introductory propaedeutic year of the total (bachelor) programme. In the latter case, they are thought of as 'intake locations', the final goal being to facilitate the stream of students from that particular region to the main location. In other cases, such as the Roosevelt Academy in Middelburg or the Transnational University Limburg, the new campuses are conceived as being special-purpose

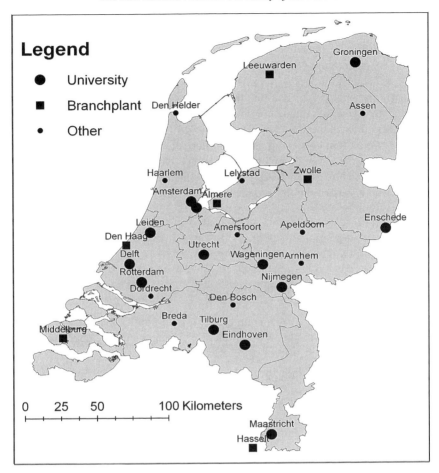

Figure 5.5   Main Dutch universities and university branch campuses

branches, for activities which are not offered at the main location, or for which the new location represents a special added value in itself, and is not seen as just another outlet point like the others.

Obviously, there are different strategies and recipes involved, but still the bottom line is that many Dutch universities are gradually and deliberately moving away from their implicit and *de facto* regionality, towards being universities which serve a much broader regional, or even national, and in certain respects even international market. They cannot only be seen as being located at their original 'natural' locations, but they are more or less aggressively also penetrating other regional, national and international markets.

Internationalization

With the current European harmonization of higher education and the graduation
system, an expanding grant system for student exchanges and the spread of
English as language of instruction, it is to be expected that this tendency will not
stop at the national border and that the number of international branch campuses
will increase. Actually, this is not a new phenomenon; the same phenomenon has
been observable in the English-speaking world (Davis, 2004). These branches,
however, were often conceived as small international centres dedicated to short-
stay arrangements for study in a foreign country. Nevertheless, a model similar to
the Dutch one is being increasingly used, in which international branch campuses
are concerned primarily with local recruitment (Observatory on Borderless Higher
Education, 2002).

   These international branch campuses play an important role in what is called
'programme and institution mobility', and they are often enhanced by different
modes of distance learning (OECD, 2003: 10–15). Distance learning is a form
of programme mobility. Students enrol in the distance-learning programmes of
foreign universities, but often these programmes are supplemented by face-to-face
teaching or tutoring provided by local partners or small centres operated by the
institution in the student's' own country. This often implies institutional mobility
or franchising arrangements. With franchise arrangements a local provider is
licensed by a foreign institution to use external courseware, or even to offer a
foreign degree under certain contractual conditions. Then no institutional mobility
is involved.

   A comparable arrangement is found in so-called 'twinning programmes', where
students take courses partly at home and partly abroad, but both parts are an integral
part of the official curriculum, which means that even the parts taken abroad are
regarded as part of the home curriculum. Often these cooperative arrangements
are reciprocal, which means that the same is true for students who do it the other
way around. In some cases, this also leads to double degrees for the students
involved. These kinds of arrangements involve both student and programme
mobility.[11] Thus, what we see is that it becomes ever more difficult to localize
higher education service provision. The university appears to have dissolved into
a network of flows, in which students, faculty and programmes are highly mobile.
In the framework of these different modes of geographical extension of service
provision, we recognize a phenomenon that Castells (1996) aptly calls 'the space
of flows'.

---

   11 It is very difficult to document precisely the extent of these new types of 'de-
territorialized' education provision, because they tend to fall outside standard data-gathering
systems (OECD, 2003: 11). Even in the interviews with representatives of the university
directorial boards of the Dutch universities conducted for this contribution, no exhaustive
picture could be drawn, although the phenomenon was generally recognized.

Specialization

Closely related to these developments is a reconsideration of and reflection on the specific profile, competitive edge and core competences of each university. Each university must now find out how it differs from others and what it should specialize in. This is a rather new phenomenon, since all of the Dutch universities are subject to the same funding regime and the same regulations, and, as long as they conceive themselves to be comprehensive universities, they cannot expect to differ much. The increasing pressure to do more with less, however, is a strong drive to specialize, and concentrate on just a few core fields.

At the same time, there is not just competition from other comprehensive universities, but also from the institutes for higher vocational education such as 'professional universities' and polytechnics. Consistent with the long-term trend away from the traditional academic universities towards the more applied sciences, these institutes have been increasingly better funded and the number of their students has risen. To avoid this competition, some universities have merged, or started cooperating, with the local institute for higher vocational education. A number of the newly created university branch campuses are actually satellites of local institutes for higher vocational education.

Other universities meet the competition by returning to their academic tradition to strengthen their specific scientific profile. The Roosevelt Academy and the University of Nijmegen, for example, both clearly share this ambition.

What is true for all Dutch universities in general is that that they are forced to make choices and specialize. This is also clearly illustrated by the newly created branch campuses and by the intensified cooperation with institutes abroad and at home. In order to specialize without narrowing their end product and without losing too much of the market, but also in order to enhance their existing supply of educational services with the specialities of other universities, thus strengthening their market position, universities are cooperating more and more within the framework of bilateral partnerships and multilateral alliances and consortia. Appendix 1 lists a number of well-known examples from the English-speaking world, but many more could be mentioned.

Often universities are involved in a multitude of such networks. Some are more discipline-oriented whereas others involve the university in a more comprehensive way. There are different reasons for creating these kinds of consortia and cooperative networks, which often go hand-in-hand. One is that the partners are engaged in similar activities, and by co-operating they can increase economies of scale, mutually strengthen their image and exposure, and increase their market area. Another is that they enhance each other's programmes in such a way that they can each deepen their specialization, while they can both keep up the full scope of their educational services. Through the latter kind of cooperative networks, universities can thus practise a flexible global sourcing strategy for the provision of educational services. This also implies that universities will conduct some activities on their own, whereas for other purposes they might decide to collaborate with other partners in different cooperative frameworks.

Reconsidering University Locations

Although the micro-location of university establishments was not the original focus of this chapter,[12] all the tendencies discussed so far do have micro-locational repercussions. Whereas 'the' location of a university as a whole could in future very well dissolve in a kind of network of flows, each activity still needs its 'place'. In the past – and this is certainly the case in the Netherlands, where regional markets were more or less taken for granted – university locations were merely a collection of the university facilities needed for research and education. In these locations the spatial arrangement of university facilities only played a very minor role. By contrast, finding a place for different university activities will entail a much more strategic decision in future. As a consequence, university policy makers will have to consider carefully where and within which node in the network a certain activity should be based, and how the spatial setting specifically contributes to the quality, esteem and marketability of the activity in question.

For example, for certain field-work activities, a locational base off campus might prove to be the right one, while for academic contemplation and intensive exchange a retreat in splendid solitude might be a more suitable location. For attending daily classes and meeting fellow students, a compact campus or conveniently arranged, not too expensive, medium-sized university town might be the best bet, whereas for international exchanges far and exotic places might be the most attractive. The 'The Hague' campus of the University of Leiden is, for example, praised for its proximity to the national political and polity centre. It comprises the Grotius Centre for International Legal Studies, the Centre for Government Studies, as well as providing evening classes in political science and part-time education in law. The Roosevelt Academy in Middelburg targets international students, and offers a typically broad but small-scale academic bachelor programme, where the location away from the big centres may be purely be functional.

University policy makers will not be the only ones who will probably make more use of the new degrees of locational freedom of the network university; students and researchers as well will make more conscious decisions concerning where to conduct their studies and research. Therefore, on the one hand, the traditional location of universities might disappear in network structures. On the other hand, the locational ties of specific university activities will probably increase and become of greater strategic importance.

Winners and Losers

In this intensified struggle for market shares and strategic locations, there are not just going to be winners. It can be expected that there will be a shake-out and that

---

12 See, for more general elaborations on the micro-location of universities, also Mayr, (1979: 63ff.), or for more recent work on this issue e.g. Judith Elbe: http://www.zit.tu-darmstadt.de/campus

universities will undergo fundamental organizational changes. Even today one can recognize, for example, that with the realization of the European Higher Education Area there is much more at stake than just creating an internationally compatible educational architecture for universities. It is the outset for a general and sweeping restructuring of the whole university landscape. Many European governments are seeking to make their university system fit for the global future, so that they will be able to stand the challenges of fierce competition. If we look at the USA as an example, we can expect that in Europe too there an Ivy League of universities will develop with a large number of lower-ranked universities around them. To stick with the network analogy, it is probably better to speak of 'hubs' and 'spokes'. The question is still open as to how many university hubs Europe can support and how many universities, in the long run, will only play a secondary role.

The Massachusetts Institute of Technology (MIT) with its Open Knowledge and Open Course Ware initiative, in this respect, made an interesting move, a move that reminds us of Microsoft's strategy for market dominance. MIT's policy of freely sharing its educational material, philosophy and modes of teaching, in combination with its renown, has made it a standard and reference point, which might very well result in a situation in which it determines how 'science and technology' should look in these fields. The MIT label will then be all over the place. No better advertisement could exist, and it gives them a head start in new developments. As a senior strategist of the MIT stated in an interview, the real business is then done through the conjunction of the content, a faculty member, and the students 'in an environment that supports inquiry and provides facilities to support the pursuit of knowledge'.[13] Of course, there are many strategies that might lead to market leadership, but even with this initiative we notice the strategic value of where the real learning is supposed to take place.

In contrast, Dutch universities, which are known to be rather dynamic, seem less inspired to take great strategic leaps forward. Many of the developments referred to in this chapter were more or less the unintended consequences of other decisions made in the past. In a number of explorative interviews with representatives of the central boards of the Dutch universities, the Dutch Association of Universities (VSNU), the Netherlands Organization for International Cooperation in Higher Education (Nuffic) and the Advisory Council for Science and Technology Policy, I have tried to confirm the main argument of this chapter. Most of them were very well aware of these tendencies, and partly of their consequences. Without exception, they confirmed that these kinds of developments have indeed been observed for some time now. However, hardly anyone has seriously included these aspects in their vision for the future, and they seemed to be rather preoccupied with short-term policy issues, of which there does not appear to be a shortage in the Netherlands. A few exceptions can be made. The Free University of Amsterdam and the University of Maastricht seemed to be highly sensitive to these developments and both have

---

13 Gilbert, S.W. and P. Long in Commentary, March/April 2002: http://ts.mivu.org/default.asp?show=article&id=979.

had explicit strategic responses on hand – perhaps because the former has never conceived itself as being a 'regional' university and because the latter's peripheral location within the Netherlands near the border has logically led it to pursue a strong internationalization policy. It is uncertain, however, if one of the Dutch universities will be able to be one of the future knowledge hubs.

To proceed further with this argument, the winners will probably be those universities that manage to build strong national and international alliances and to specialize in a few strong core fields in a very efficient way. This also implies that they develop a location strategy and that they must develop their locations in such a way that they are able to contribute directly to the quality and esteem of the activities which take place there. This will also delineate the future relationship between the university and the region in which it is located.

Conclusions

Although the tendencies that I have tried to explore in this chapter may be rather tentative, one can indeed see how throughout the centuries Dutch universities have gradually grown to be regionally bound and increasingly community-serving. As such, they have become more and more market-oriented and also market-dependent. The latest developments towards globalizing markets for higher education form a continuation of these tendencies, except for the fact that the university as a localized organization is increasingly dissolving into a flexible and fluid network organization. This ever more footloose organization thus seems to have lost its regional footing. This also implies that, in much of the economic geographic research which focuses on the knowledge transfer from universities to their regions, all of a sudden, the university, taken for granted as the object of this research, seems to have disappeared. At the same time, specific educational and research activities within these networks have for the first time become subject to spatial strategies. Their locational settings are perfectly capable of developing to real 'selling points' in global competition. Their regional boundedness has thus increased. With respect to their role in the knowledge transfer process, we should be much more specific and explicit when referring to the various kinds of activities involved and to the relationships with other locations, nodes and flows.

Appendix: Examples of university consortia

Consortium	Partners	URL
Cambridge-MIT-Institute	University of Cambridge and MIT	www.cambridge-mit.org/cgi-bin/default.pl?SID=7
Cluster	Technical University of Catalonia, Barcelona, Technische Universität Darmstadt, Technische Universiteit Eindhoven, Institut National Polytechnique de Grenoble, Universität (T.H) Karlsruhe, Ecole Polytechnique Fédérale de Lausanne, Imperial College London, Université Catholique de Louvain, Kungl Tekniska Högskolan, Stockholm, Politecnico di Torino. Associate Member: Indian Institute of Technology, Delhi	www.cluster.org/
Cardean University	Stanford University, University of Chicago, Carnegie Mellon, Columbia Business School, London School of Economics	www.cardean.edu
Great Plains Interactive Distance Education Alliance	North Dakota State University, South Dakota State University, University of Minnesota, University of Nebraska, Iowa State University, Kansas State University, University of Missouri, Oklahoma State University, Texas Tech University	www.okstate.edu/hes/gpdc/
Colorado Community College Online	Arapahoe Community College, Colorado Northwestern Community College, Community College of Aurora, Community College of Denver, Dawson Community College, Front Range Community College, Lamar Community College, Morgan Community College, Northeastern Junior College, Northwest Missouri State University, Otero Junior College, Pikes Peak Community College, Pueblo Community College, Red Rocks Community College, Trinidad State Junior College	www.ccconline.org/
Pennsylvania Virtual Community College	Bucks County Community College, Butler County Community College, Cambria County Area Community College, Community College of Allegheny County, Community, College of Beaver County, Community College of Philadelphia, Delaware County Community College, Harrisburg Area Community College, Lehigh Carbon Community College, Luzerne County Community College, Montgomery County Community College, Northampton Community College, Northwest Pennsylvania Technical Institute, Reading Area Community College, Westmoreland County Community College	www.pavcc.org/

Southern Regional Electronic Campus	This consortium includes upwards of one hundred participating institutions. Several examples are listed below; for a more complete listing, go to the URL: Auburn University, University of Arkansas, Delaware Technical & Community College, Florida State University, Georgia Institute of Technology, Western Kentucky University, University of North Carolina at Chapel Hill, University of North Carolina at Wilmington	www.srec.sreb.org/
SUNY Learning Network	This consortium includes upwards of one hundred participating institutions. Several examples are listed below; for a more complete listing go to the URL: State University of New York, University at Buffalo, Binghamton University, SUNY Old Westbury, SUNY Brockport, SUNY Empire State College, University at Albany, SUNY Plattsburgh, Adirondack Community College, SUNY New Paltz, SUNY Purchase, SUNY Cortland, Clinton Community	sln.suny.edu/ admin/sln/original.nsf
Western Governors University	Several examples of participating universities are listed below; for a more complete listing visit the URL: ComputerPREP, Magellan University, Northern Arizona University, Brigham Young University, Texas Tech University, University of Guam, University of Hawaii, Idaho State University	www.wgu.edu/wgu/ab out/educators_instituti ons.html
Universitas 21	McGill University, University of British Columbia, University of Toronto, University of Michigan, University of Birmingham, University of Edinburgh, University of Glasgow, University of Nottingham, Lund University, Albert-Ludwigs University Freiburg, Fudan University, Peking University, The University of Hong Kong, National University of Singapore, The University of Melbourne, University of New South Wales, University of Queensland, University of Auckland	www.universitas.edu. au/members.html
OntarioLearn. com	Algonquin College, Canadore College, Cambrian College, Centennial College, Conestoga College, Confederation College, Durham College, Fanshawe College, George Brown College, Georgian College, Humber College, Lambton College, Loyalist College, Mohawk College, Niagara College, Northern College, Sault College, Seneca College, Sheridan College, Sir Sandford Fleming College, St. Lawrence College	www.ontariolearn.com

African Virtual University	Anglophone Universities: Addis Ababa University, University of Accra, University of Cape Coast, University of Science and Technology, Egerton University, Kenyatta University, University of Namibia, Technikon Southern Africa, University of Pretoria, The Open University of Tanzania, The University of Dar Es Salaam, Makerere University, Uganda Martyrs University, Uganda Polytechnic, National University of Science and Technology, University of Zimbabwe. Francophone Universities: Université nationale du Bénin, Université d'Ouagadougou, UVA Notre Dame de Tendresse, Université de Nouakchott, Université de Niamey, Universite Nationale du Rwanda, University of Kigali, Université Gaston Berger, Université de Dakar	www.avu.org/
EuroPace	Several examples of participating universities are listed below; for a more complete listing visit the URL: University of Brussels, Helsinki University of Technology, University College Dublin, University of Bologna, Warsaw University of Technology, Kazan State University, University of Castilla- La Mancha, Asian Institute of Technology, University of Ljubljana	www.europace .be/
American Distance Education Consortium	Several examples of participating universities are listed below; for a more complete listing visit the URL: University of Arizona, University of Arkansas, Clemson University, Cornell University, Texas A&M, Michigan State University, University of Minnesota, University of Florida, University of Georgia, Utah State University	www.adec.edu/about. html
Scottish Knowledge	Below several examples are listed of participating universities; for a more complete listing visit the URL: Fife College of Further & Higher Education, Glasgow Caledonian University, Heriot-Watt University, Napier University, Queen Margaret College, Royal Scottish Academy of Music & Drama, The Edinburgh College of Art	www.scottishknowled ge.co.uk/ home.cfm
National Technological University	Below several examples are listed of participating universities: for a more complete listing visit the URL: Auburn University, Boston University, Clemson University, Colorado State University, Columbia University, Florida Gulf Coast University, George Washington University, The Georgia Institute of Technology, Illinois Institute of Technology, Iowa State University, Kansas State University	www.distancelearn.ab out.com

| **Fathom** | Columbia University, London School of Economics and Political Science, Cambridge University Press, The British Library, The New York Public Library, The University of Chicago, University of Michigan, American Film Institute, RAND, Woods Hole Oceanographic Inst., The Natural History Museum, Victoria and Albert Museum, Science Museum | www.fathom.com/index.jhtml |
| **Jesuit Distance Education Network** | Several examples of participating universities are listed below: Boston College, Canisius College, College of the Holy Cross, Creighton University, Fairfield University, Fordham University, Georgetown University, Loyola Marymount University, Rockhurst University, Saint Joseph's University, Saint Louis University | virtual.wju.edu/ jnet/ |

Source: The Futures Project, 2000

PART 2
Knowledge Production, Management and the Academic Role
§1: University Governance: Actors and Identities

Chapter 6

Who Are the Real 'Problem Owners'? On the Social Embeddedness of Universities

Davydd J. Greenwood

Introduction

For whom do universities exist? In this chapter, I provide a framework for thinking through this question by reviewing the constituencies that universities putatively serve in order to see which are being supported effectively, which are not, and why. This analysis makes clear that regions generally are among the least attended-to constituencies of universities. This is not a pessimist's conclusion. I will make the case that significant improvements are possible, necessary, and can help revitalize universities. There are examples of universities that serve their regions and localities well and that have gained much from these relationships. However, the lesson of such cases is that significant overall institutional changes will be necessary for most public universities[1] to become important contributors to the well-being of their regions and localities.

Gaining perspective on these issues requires a review of the political economies of universities – of both the broad political economies they operate in and of their own internal political economies. These forces tell us a good deal about whom universities do and/or must serve in order to survive. This review also enables us to think about why certain legitimate constituencies for universities are likely to be ignored, among them the localities and regions where universities are located.

Numerous diatribes and reports, both political and private, refer to the failure of universities to serve their constituencies well and provide a variety of recipes for reform, ranging from full entrepreneurialization of universities to moral renewal and civic commitment (Boyte and Kari, 1996; Rhoads, 1997; Ehrlich, 2000; Ruch, 2001). Unfortunately, many of these critiques and recommendations are based on oversimplified views of the complex and contradictory missions, internal dynamics and sources of support for universities. Few address the localities and regions where universities are located in systematic terms.

Perhaps the central issue any analysis of this sort must deal with is the 'corporatization' of universities. Corporate management strategies in US universities

---

1   That is, publicly funded universities, whether at national or sub-national level.

and around the world increasingly treat universities as fee-for-service providers, students and research contractors as clients or customers, and faculty as wage labourers. This way of understanding universities' relationship to their surrounding society and markets is not just a matter of rhetoric; it is the far-reaching result of a sea change in the political economy of higher education. Pursuing it has already fundamentally altered the relations among the problem owners universities serve.

These management changes must be understood in more than polemical terms. My particular conclusion in this chapter is that, under these changing conditions, the role of universities in regional and community development is not favoured, indeed it may weaken even more. Effective regional and local development strategies involving public universities as key partners will not emerge spontaneously from the increasingly corporate management strategies being applied to universities. Intentional redesign of structures and relationships is required to make regional development an important university focus. Such intentional design requires analysis, hence this chapter.

Context

The Political Economy of Higher Education

The necessary point of departure is an understanding of the political economy of higher education. I cannot develop such an analysis in a brief chapter and so present here what basically is a checklist of the relevant elements in order to problematize the relationship between universities and regional development.

1. *Types of institutions*: Higher education worldwide is a highly complex and differentiated system, undergoing rapid growth/proliferation almost everywhere. Many types of institutions are involved, ranging from large and small public universities, universities that are research-centred with a somewhat subordinate teaching function, universities that cater to national, international, and/or regional constituencies, large and small private universities, secular and religious universities, private colleges of a wide variety of orientations, professional training institutions, for-profit corporate universities that either operate in the open market or are subsidiaries of the firms whose name they carry, and a host of vocational/technical schools. Here I shall concentrate only on public universities, because these constitute the most relevant case in Europe in general and because public universities presumably exist to serve the public, thus raising the very issues I am concentrating on.

2. *The problem owners[2] of public universities*: There are a wide variety of types of problem owners in public universities. Among the economic problem

---

2   I use the term 'problem owners' rather than 'stakeholders' because the notion of the legitimate owners of the problem, those directly affected by it and having a right to intervene

owners are those internal to the university, including students, university staff, faculty, and administrators. External problem owners include suppliers of goods and services consumed by the university, including contractors for construction, lawyers and notaries, national overseers including education ministries and national accounting offices. There are also the private sector and public sector consumers of graduates and of university research. And there are the taxpayers whose funds support the universities and the regional and national economies affected by the universities' presence and actions. Among the social problem owners in public universities, we find the political system that is responsible for the national public university system, the upwardly mobile citizens and international students and their families for whom a university career improves job and income possibilities, and the local and regional communities affected by university presence.

I have drawn up this list because one of the defects of the literature on change in universities is the tendency to identify universities with only one or two of these problem owners and, thus, to build analysis on too narrow a base. Whatever we ultimately decide to do about universities, we must take account of the impacts on all the legitimate problem owners.

The Affirmative Strategies toward Corporatization of Universities

No change in universities occurs in a neutral or depoliticized environment. There can be very little doubt that the predominant issue in the development of public universities at this point in history is the debate about the degree to which universities are like, or should be like, private sector corporations. This is not the central focus of this paper so I again will be brief.

Two of the most comprehensive and persuasive analyses of these problems, based on strong empirical work, are Marginson and Considine's *The Enterprise University* (2000) and Slaughter and Leslie's *Academic Capitalism* (1997). Through comparative studies of countries and institutions, they document carefully the increasing momentum toward viewing universities as if they were private-sector corporations, the imposition of increasingly hierarchical forms of administration under the guise of corporate discipline, the reconceptualization of students and research funders as customers and faculty as a labour force, and the view of teaching and research products as forms of intellectual property to be bought and sold, etc. One of the most striking features of these processes is the degree to which this rush to corporatize universities is a worldwide phenomenon. Another is the hegemony of the economic rhetoric of 'markets' and rational choice as the principal languages of the increasingly large groups of professional university administrators.

---

in dealing with it, is much clearer in my mind than the concept of a stakeholder who might simply be a distant investor or someone with a passing interest in the problem.

Reviewing these works, looking at the checklist of university problem owners, and thinking about my 37 years at a public university, 15 of which have been spent in a variety of academic administrative positions, I find the dis-analogies between public universities and conventional corporations striking. Unlike private corporations, driven by market tests of profitability of particular goods and services, universities are composed of a mixed, confusing and even contradictory set of activities. They are expected to promote respect for the past, to pass on the values and understandings that make for good citizenship, to provide job training, to advance the frontiers of knowledge on all fronts and to serve the public. Nothing in this package of missions guarantees or even suggests university economic self-sufficiency or profitability. What constitutes a market test for any of these activities is a matter of debate and, until recently, the notion of such market tests would have been considered silly. This is why universities, until recently, have been, and were expected to be, heavily subsidized by both the public and private sectors.

Universities are generally non-taxable institutions, apart from the taxes on the income of the faculty and staff and on the incomes of those who supply them with goods and services. In many places, university real estate is not taxed either. Further, universities are directly tax-subsidized through nationally provided operating budgets and through public and private funds for research, scholarships, etc. Universities, particularly public universities, for all these reasons, have historically not been expected to earn money.

This does not mean, however, that the public has no legitimate interest in how they are run. This non-pecuniary focus of universities creates public expectations about governmental oversight and social accountability. It also, quite reasonably, creates the expectation that, in return for so much tax support, universities 'owe' something to the public, though it is by no means clear just what the 'public' means in this context or how we should identify and value what they 'owe'. Many professors and administrators appear to have forgotten this debt to the public and consider the flow of tax money in their direction as a fundamental, pre-political right.

It seems to me that the corporatization of universities is, in part, a public reaction to this disconnection of universities from a sense of obligation and service to the public. The imposition of public oversight and the general climate of hostility towards universities as places of waste and laziness has been quite a shock to university administrators and faculties; their response to these challenges so far has been less than impressive, save in a few instances. Defensive arrogance generally prevails in the responses and it has been markedly ineffective.

One way to think about this is to realize that universities, in the 'public mind', now appear to fall loosely into the category of public utilities, like power companies, telephone companies and railway systems. We know that these public utilities are subject to constant political and public attitude swings about their mode of operation. Since the creation of public utilities, the ongoing debate has been about whether they should be treated more like private companies or like public goods functioning according to a non-market logic. We are living in an era when the pendulum has swung hard toward the 'privatization' of all public utilities. I personally think the corporatization of universities is the academic expression of this process and that administrators and faculty members who continue to insist on understanding what is happening to them merely as the result of stupid ideas in the heads of a few politicians and cynical university administrators are failing to understand this sea change.

The Internal Dynamics of Public Universities

All large institutions are complex and have their own peculiar dynamics. Universities are no exception. To organize my thinking about this, I find it useful to use Slaughter and Leslie's distinction between market behaviour and market-like behaviour (Slaughter and Leslie, 1997: 11). The meaning of market behaviour is self-evident. 'Market-like' behaviour, for Slaughter and Leslie, involves competition for external funding sources. I prefer to amplify their notion of market-like behaviour to include sociopolitically motivated competitive behaviour masquerading under the rhetoric of rational choice and meeting market requirements. In this way, it can be understood both as an ideological cover and as the result of general confusion about how to make sensible decisions about complex matters in which there are powerful winners and losers.

Market-like behaviours   Among the market-like behaviours of universities, we find the competitive seeking and execution of research grants and patenting of discoveries, which are major activities in some public universities. Universities are also constantly subjected to a wide variety of competitive ranking systems; they undergo general ranking as teaching and research institutions, and their various schools and faculties may be ranked as well. These rankings increasingly have budgetary consequences in terms of student matriculation, research grants won, and so on. Universities also engage in competitive service contracting, advertising to attract students, and similar activities.

But there are other 'market-like' behaviours whose status is more complex. Treating students and families as clients or customers has a market-like sound to it, but a thorough application of this logic would reduce universities to fee-for-service providers with courses only offered in areas of high demand. Following this line necessarily results in the proletarianization of the faculty and the reduction of the curriculum to only what the customers are willing to pay for at any given moment. An educational institution of this kind may be successful and useful, but it hardly qualifies as a university.

A very popular management idea these days in many university systems is to treat some academic units as 'tubs on their own bottoms'. That is, the academic units are permitted to collect their own revenues and have to pay the university for all services they receive. Though, to my knowledge, comprehensive studies of this process do not yet exist, my experience is that this model is less about market rationality than it is about centralizing university administrative control, lowering fixed costs, and converting the faculty into a contract-based workforce. The complexity of this particular notion is particularly evident in American universities, where the same university treats some units as tubs and others as subsidized loss centres creating a decision-making morass of Herculean proportions.

The use of a wide variety of reputational and performance rankings, including universities' role in attracting student and research 'customers', is increasing every year. The underlying premise of these ranking systems, to the extent that anything other than the politics of reputation is involved, has to be that clear numerical criteria for ranking university performance are possible and that the summary of these criteria yields a point system tantamount to a rational ranking of universities. Of these ranking systems, Britain's Quality Assurance (in both teaching and research) within the higher education system is one of the most comprehensive. The influence of the US National Research Council rankings on the internal administration of many universities is also immense.

While some of the elements that go into these rankings are sensibly rendered in numbers (for example, research monies acquired, research outputs achieved, faculty/ student ratios), many are not. The summation of all these elements into an overall ranking is an epistemological impossibility that masquerades as a simple market measure. This is a direct analogy to the impossibility of the interpersonal comparison of utilities, which makes cost–benefit analysis a political process masquerading as rational economic analysis (Harsanyi, 1955).

Non-market behaviours   Many European university faculty members are still career civil servants, not wage labourers. Market behaviour with a significant workforce that cannot be fired is impossible. Of course, corporate ideologies in academic administration are mounting a gradual and quite successful attack on the insulated employment situation of university faculty members, either by attacking the faculty employment system directly or by replacing regular faculty with a growing number of part-time or short-term teachers and researchers.

Students in public universities, whatever else they are, are not very usefully understood as customers. They do not pay the full cost of their education, they do not usually have a completely free choice of universities and fields of study, and they often make profoundly uninformed decisions on the basis of very little in the way of economic analysis. While this may not distinguish them from the typical buyers in any economic market, readjusting the offerings of universities in response this demonstrably false analysis can produce nearly random outcomes. If calling students customers makes universities more attentive to them, that is fine, but the same students do not behave at MacDonald's, at an auto dealership, or when choosing a disco to frequent in the same way that they do when choosing a university and a course of study. What students need and deserve is important. Calling them customers does not enhance their well-being, but it is certainly increases the power of university administrators and education ministers who claim to be able to express the will of their student 'customers'. When administrators project themselves as the sole interpreters of what the student 'customers' need, they gain a relatively free hand in forcing the faculty to meet demands that only the administrators themselves have actually articulated. And it is clear that relatively little analysis of the 'academic' demands of these 'customers' is actually ever done.

Universities all have internal redistributive resource systems based on non-economic notions of curriculum requirements and other non-market considerations. There are many 'public goods' in a university, including expensive libraries, low-enrolment courses and even whole faculties with low student demand but high academic prestige. However, based on my private sector experiences, it is not clear to me that universities are more economically irrational than big private corporations. I have had the opportunity to observe firsthand the huge expenses private corporations incur in building elegant corporate headquarters, adopting new logos, placing fine art objects in their facilities, buying expensive office furniture, and paying senior executives astronomical salaries that are nearly impossible to justify economically. Apparently, these behaviours in the private sector are accepted as market behaviour but, when university corporatizers see them on university campuses, they view them as non-economic behaviour to be eliminated. So the corporate model being applied to universities is not exactly the corporate model from the business world, another example of market-like behaviour in a university setting masking a variety of other agendas.

There are major cross-subsidies within most disciplines. At the sub-disciplinary level, there are some activities that bring in many students and/or lots of research resources and others that do neither, for example, philosophy courses on medical ethics as opposed to courses on advanced symbolic logic. The music department with few students and lots of infrastructure requirements is *de facto* subsidized by the physics or chemistry department through the mediating political economic work of deans and university financial officers. A university that only offers the courses that are demanded or only does the research that is externally financed ends up without many of the departments and sub-disciplines that have been associated historically with university life and becomes a vocational school. Implementing an acceptable scope of disciplines and sub-disciplines at a university requires internal redistributions from the haves to the have-nots, and these are a typical feature of academic life.

Tubs on their own bottoms notwithstanding, university financial authority is generally quite centralized. Interestingly, this centralization appears to be increasing, precisely when many private sector corporations are pushing decision-making and economic responsibility as far down toward the site of production as they can. In this regard, the corporate model of universities is much more like mid-twentieth-century US manufacturing corporations than twenty-first-century global, multi-sited corporations. There are, as always, some exceptions to this general model: a variety of enrolment and research accounting schemes exist that create some lower-level economic power in a few public university systems, for example, those of the Netherlands and Denmark.

Conclusions for the First Part

What should capture our attention is that so far in this exposition, I have made no mention of the regions and communities in which universities reside. I have shown public universities to be a complex mix of market and market-like behaviours with complex and internally inconsistent missions. They are principally financed with public monies. They do compete with each other in a delocalized space for students, governmental support and faculty, but this competition is modulated by complex political, spatial, social and cultural forces. Universities can be engines of economic development through research and through training, but this role mainly responds to national and international markets, even if there is some modest local wealth creation due to the university's presence.

Little in the political economy of public universities directly obligates them to their regional environment. In many senses, universities are within regions and communities, but not of them. Many public universities seem to me analogous to enclave tourism developments where some job creation and other economic activities are created locally but most of the funds come from outside the region and most of the wealth generated leaves the local area, even the country. Thus, thinking about universities in the context of regional development and promoting this role requires major changes in orientation, management, funding, and even in the conception of what and whom a public university is for.

The Social Functions of Universities

Though public universities putatively exist to serve society, it is not so clear what society means in this context. Generally speaking, universities are said to enhance national economic competitiveness through education and research, to improve the qualities of citizenship in their students, and to provide social class mobility through educational attainment and the consequent income improvements.

In this view, universities are upholders of tradition, sources of innovation, locations of social critique, and sources of direct support for the well-being of their 'societies'. The mechanisms that are used to accomplish these ends are university research, assistance in policy design and evaluation, training of political and managerial elites and the creation of more informed citizens.

What should stand out here is that the 'society' being served is an abstraction. There is no clarity about what 'society' means or about who the legitimate problem owners are. Historically, since the Humboldt reforms, society usually has meant the national society. Public universities were a direct product of national intervention and are still principally directed at the national level. If the national society is the focus, then universities are more or less meeting problem owner needs, notwithstanding the typical host of complaints about inefficiency, bad management, poor teaching, and so on.

On the other hand, if 'society' is treated as a more concrete concept that includes a more local/regional referent, then university service to society is less clear. In my experience, most public universities are not motors of regional social and economic development, except circumstantially. They were not constructed to be such development engines and they are rarely managed with this in mind. However,

I have no doubt that they could serve usefully in the role of agents of regional development and I personally think they should do so – for the academic, practical and moral reasons that I will take up below. However, the political economic and social analysis I have offered so far shows that, for universities to become important in regional development, significant change at all levels of university administration is required because nearly all the characteristics of the current system orient universities everywhere but toward their immediate surroundings.

The economic problem owners in universities, internal and external, generally get something of value. As regards the economic effect on students, outcomes vary from country to country – but, certainly, in the US more higher education results in higher salaries (Washington Research Council, 1999). The situation of faculty members likewise varies from country to country – but, certainly, being a faculty member with the status of a civil servant, as in some European contexts, was a desirable and secure occupation. University administration is a growth industry with ballooning administrations nearly everywhere. The same can be said for middle-level university staff members, as the administrative functions and requirements of universities multiply. Universities also clearly benefit suppliers of goods and services as their campuses grow in size and complexity.

Similarly, for the overseers of the national systems, universities are the source of their employment, and for education ministries universities are an element in national politics. For the national accounting offices and accrediting services, universities provide the object that creates their activity. For the private and public employers of university graduates, universities provide a steady supply of supposedly qualified candidates. For consumers of university research, the matter varies greatly by university; nevertheless, active research universities apparently remain attractive partners for private sector corporations and for national funders of research. For the social problem owners, depending on the national system, university graduates may be a principal source of political leadership. For the students themselves, a university education has been a key institutional source of mobility other than direct entrepreneurship.

And what do the local and regional communities affected by university presence gain? Some purchases of goods and services and some expansion of the local job market, an occasional university business park, and some spin-off businesses.

Responses to the Non-localization of Universities

It should be clear that, though this is a complex and varied picture that needs to be specified on an institution-by-institution basis, the regional link is quite possibly the weakest of all. The disconnection between universities and regions that I have been articulating is not news, and there have been some attempts to deal with this issue in the past. University industrial parks are one of the preferred solutions, though their net effect on the regional economy is little studied. A number of universities have created various kinds of extension services (the largest being the land grant extension service in the US). There have also been some cases where universities have made general commitments to local sourcing of goods and services where possible. All in all, this is not a very impressive effort and it leaves the general political economy and internal dynamics of most universities more or less untouched.

Normative Change in Support of a Richer Academic Life

Perhaps the proper response to this dilemma is to ignore it. After all, universities are national creations, have been primarily national in orientation, and are notoriously hard to change. However, I think there are normative, political, and academic reasons to press the issue of the intelligent regionalization of public universities.

It seems to me that it is difficult to sustain the position that public universities are 'in' but not 'of' the communities where they are located. The tax subsidies they receive come in two forms. The direct subsidies from the national treasury include tax monies provided by local community members. Though they are not the principal source of these tax monies, normatively they have as much right to service from the institution as any other taxpayers. To think otherwise is to argue that those who pay the most taxes should get the most service, a kind of neo-liberal fee-for-service notion incompatible with the supposedly redistributive meaning of taxation in a political democracy.

Equally important is the fact that, in many countries, the properties and internal activities of public universities are tax-exempt. This takes both real estate and economic activities out of the local tax system creating a *de facto* local tax subsidy. In return for this local subsidy, university administrations regularly argue that their local presence is a spur to the local economy. While this is undoubtedly true in some general sense, universities can also be a burden on the local economy. The legendary tensions between university people and local townspeople, tensions that university people often view as caused by status and educational differences with their local social inferiors, seem to me to stem just as much from local people's sense that they are doing a great deal to support universities and that the universities do not reciprocate their support sufficiently.

Thinking politically, there are a number of reasons why building stronger regional connections makes sense. For national politicians, a strong network of regional universities can, if well handled, be an element in regional development and population de-concentration strategies that all industrialized countries are interested in (Goddard *et al.*, 1994; Goddard, 1997; Goddard *et al.*, 1997). For regional and local politicians, strong alliances and support from regional universities can add high-cost expertise and labour to local and regional development initiatives. For the universities, under increasing scrutiny and with fewer and fewer friends in national politics, building a strong base of regional support can provide political leverage at the national level for university agendas and resource acquisition.

Beyond these normative and political reasons, I believe there are very strong academic reasons to press for stronger integration of universities into their regions and localities. The complex, multifaceted problems involved in creating regional economic and social development provide a superb environment for the joint practice of many academic disciplines and for setting knowledge creation agendas for the academy that are more intelligently 'socialized' than those set by national and international markets, by national political priorities and by academic disciplinary and professional associations. I will expand this point below, but to anticipate a counter argument, I am not suggesting that universities simply become consultants for local economic development. Rather, I think sustained engagement in local development can make fundamental contributions to knowledge development and student training in very nearly all the disciplines taught in universities.

What are the Obstacles to Service to Regional Constituencies?

Given the above arguments, it seems hard to understand why universities are not already major forces in regional development. Under current institutional mechanisms, public universities are mainly subject to national and international markets, ranked by national and international ranking systems, and under the direct control of national level management of university budgets. Regional authorities rarely have a clear statutory role in most public university systems. But these are not laws of nature; they are the results of the history of public universities as national institutions. These conditions can be changed.

Another important source of disconnection is university *autopoesis*. University scholars are members of disciplines and professions with strong national and international professional structures, ranking systems, and recruitment and promotion practices. Many analysts note that university professors show more loyalty to their disciplines than they do to their universities. Individual prestige is much more associated with national and international grants and publications than with local service, even in high administrative positions. And, of course, in continental Europe, most professors are national or provincial *civil servants*, not regional *employees*. There are also more than a few academics who genuinely dislike the complex, demanding and even confusing world of direct social engagement. For these 'scholars', the ideal university is a place of refuge from society. While this is understandable, as holders of tax-supported positions in public universities, their preferences for such a life are morally questionable, and their behaviour lends legitimacy to the strategies of those senior managers seeking to turn universities into corporations.

For those professors whose interests include direct engagement in matters of regional/local importance, the path to this kind of work is not easy. Hierarchical, authoritarian administrative structures – from department heads to deans to vice chancellors or rectors – make horizontal collaborations within the university and between university professors, students, and local institutions and actors difficult, though not impossible. Put briefly, the Fordist division of labour in universities is inimical to collaboration both inside and outside the university.

These dynamics also respond to an internal politics in universities in which each unit competes for budget, respect and power with every other unit on its same structural level. Collaboration across units is seen by many faculty members as 'trading with the enemy'. For many senior administrators, such cross-unit collaborations are as unwelcome as labour union mobilization because they potentially upset their own carefully managed systems of political control. Multidisciplinary efforts seldom prosper for long in public universities, as everyone knows.

Finally, the everyday structures of academic work life strongly discourage external engagements of a sustained sort. Most public universities do permit faculty a certain number of days per month of private consulting, and a fair number of faculty take advantage of these provisions. However, the ground-level reality of professorial activity is that teaching, research supervision, faculty meetings, committee assignments and professional service at the national and international level cut the academic work week into shreds. While a one-day-a-week consulting assignment with an external organization is sustainable, work with a multidisciplinary team comprising ten to fifteen faculty members and ten to fifteen community members cannot be fitted into the single day and these available days are unlikely to coincide across disciplines either.

These are powerful structural disincentives to external engagement but they are not laws of nature. Just as they were created by actions based on a cloistered and Fordist conception of a public university, they can be altered by conscious actions designed to encourage and reward local/regional engagement.

How Disconnection from the Local Context is Destructive to the Institution in General and to the Social Sciences and the Humanities in Particular

At this point, I wish to leave aside the moral and political arguments for regional engagement and focus on the state of health of the sciences, engineering and medicine, the social sciences, and the humanities and on how regional engagement might improve their situation. The same story cannot be told for all these broadly different areas of knowledge. Each has their particular struggles to deal with and so, again, here I have to be brief.

The sciences, engineering, and medicine   The literature on the sciences, engineering, and medicine has, for years, been replete with a profound tension between basic and applied science. We need to leave aside the inadvisability of making too clear a distinction between these variants of scientific activity because research with an applied focus has often resulted in unexpected discoveries in basic science and vice versa. While a great many professors are genuinely interested in applied scientific problems, most are aware of the value of so-called basic science, that is, science that is not done opportunistically to solve practical problems but that is done to extend the frontiers of knowledge. However, in the past two decades, national governments have decreased their willingness to fund basic science. Neo-liberal models of the university, taken to extremes, demand that all science be demonstrably applicable – a position that, if it could ever be put fully into practice, would have made a great many of the scientific discoveries that have improved our lives impossible.

Under these conditions, it should be no surprise that university scientists would view pressures to be engaged with local and regional problems on a sustained basis as simply one more effort to achieve the extinction of basic scientific research funded by the public. To engage scientists whose research does not have a direct regional application would require major administrative change at the national level, perhaps on a quid pro quo basis of support for basic science in return for demonstrated commitment to regional and local work.

On the positive side, while some of the sciences are learned and practised in laboratories, many areas of science, for example, geology, meteorology, ethology, ecology, structural engineering and medicine, involve direct field research and hands-on experience. Students have to learn how to conduct such research, both a scientific and an organizational problem. You cannot learn teamwork in a book.

Public universities are notoriously weak in this kind of training (Schön, 1983). Furthermore, a great many university graduates will not become university scientists but will end up joining the labour force in small and large businesses and public authorities where their ability to carry out team-based research and to collaborate with people very much unlike them on practical and immediate problems is important. The critical literature on university training in the basic and applied sciences is filled with references to the poor practical training of graduates in these fields. Engagement in sustained university-locality-region multidisciplinary research projects with visible outcomes is an excellent way to overcome this long-standing deficiency in university training of scientists and engineers.

It is also evident that these experiences might also lead to local/regional job placements for university graduates. Regional development initiatives of this sort could well enhance the employment market, particularly for students who already have learned the skills of local collaboration. For those students already with families and who reside in the region, the increase in jobs matched to their training is also desirable.

The social sciences Here, it is necessary to distinguish between the older conventional social sciences of economics, sociology, political science, psychology and anthropology and the younger 'new' social sciences such as business administration, human resource management, organizational development, planning, and program evaluation. The latter are growing rapidly at the expense of the conventional social sciences, and this process bears an interesting relationship to issues of regional engagement.

The conventional social sciences are, in my view, the expression of academically self-regarding behaviour carried to an extreme. Nowhere else in the university do we find such hermetic, discipline-dominated and self-regarding behaviour as in the conventional social sciences. Frederick Winslow Taylor would have loved these fields, in which disciplinary expertise and management by experts trump all other considerations. As my colleague Morten Levin and I have written in a number of papers (Greenwood, 1995; 1996; 1999; Greenwood and Levin, 1998; 1999; 2000a; 2000b; 2001; 2002), this is a situation that the conventional social sciences have managed to create over nearly a century and a half. Beginning as a single field, political economy, from the late 1800s on the social sciences began to separate, first into economics and politics and then into the conventional social science fields now known. In all their founding documents, these new fields of social inquiry justified their existence in terms of creating expertise and research that would be of value for the welfare of society as a whole.

Though a few social scientists attempt to live up to this goal, it is quite clear that the conventional social sciences are mainly cartel-like organizations that consume their own products and promote their own interests, usually in a language unintelligible even to a well-educated person. Mono-disciplinarity and highly territorial behaviour are hallmarks of these fields, except among the most prominent and respected practitioners like Anthony Giddens, James Scott, Pierre Bourdieu, Clifford Geertz, Amartya Sen, and Albert Hirschman. Not surprisingly, under the pressures of corporatization, the social value of these fields is increasingly questioned and the lack of an intelligent response from the conventional social sciences has harmed their situation a great deal.

The new social sciences Predictably, the new social sciences of business management, planning, program evaluation, public policy analysis and so on have taken many of the resources that used to go to the conventional social sciences and been growing rapidly at the latter's expense. These new fields are multidisciplinary, problem-oriented, productivity-oriented and competitive-minded. Extra-university experience is highly valued, faculty compete in terms of the scope and importance of their external engagements, and teaching regularly includes complex cases brought to the classroom from faculty experience in the private and public sectors. In this sense, these fields are ideally constituted to serve as a point of integration for the kinds of multidisciplinary university-locality-region collaborations I have mentioned.

But before we become too enthusiastic about this, we should note that the same dynamics that gradually made the conventional social sciences socially irrelevant have appeared in the new social sciences. Many of these fields show growing signs of valuing abstract theorization over practical knowledge, of over-privileging the judgements of professional peers about what constitutes an important problem and a valuable solution, and of the other pathologies I have referred to above. In addition, the status hierarchy inherited from the conventional social sciences with economics at the top and anthropology at the bottom, appears to be reproduced increasingly within the new multidisciplinary social sciences. It seems to me only a matter of time before they become as autopoetic as their predecessors.

Public support for the conventional social sciences is heading toward an all-time low. At this point, such support for the new social sciences is stronger, based on the belief that their orientation is more toward solutions to practical problems of social welfare. But the conventional social sciences, with all the institutional arrangements and sunken costs involved, have a chance to salvage some part of themselves by becoming directly engaged, as team collaborators, in the study of real local and regional problems and the generation of solutions to them. Not only could this redirect the efforts of faculty members, but it could provide students with the kinds of practical experiences needed to alter the autopoetic trajectories of these fields.

Under these conditions, the new social sciences could also be helped to arrest the trend toward self-regarding isolationism, and the consequent loss of public support, by reinforcing their commitment to multidisciplinary, team-based problem solving in extra-university environments.

The humanities Far from being a haven of irrelevance, in the past quarter century the humanities have remade themselves, realigning disciplines, engaging in multidisciplinary development of discourses about modernity, post-modernity, gender, positionality, subalterity, power, and social change, and invading the territory of the conventional social sciences with abandon. The enormous development of the both social scientific and humanistic field of 'cultural studies' shows that, when competently practised, these combinations can be a powerful source of insight and constructive cultural critique.

While the humanities also remain as self-referential and prestige-oriented as ever, their intellectual agendas are now much more 'engaged' with problems that people outside the university understand to be important. Of course, they are also havens of irrelevance, egotistical work, incomprehensible jargonizing, and status competition, but it is too easy to tell negative stories about them. As they struggle with the dual dynamics of disciplinarity and social relevance, engagement in local/ regional initiatives can provide an anchor for the better practice of cultural studies, public philosophy, and moral debate.

What Kinds of Problems are Important to Regions

Typical local/regional problems centre on economic development and job creation, improved social services, the problems of youth, migration, social incorporation and the like. These are what Russell Ackoff calls complex multidisciplinary 'messes' (Ackoff, 1999: 99–101). Examples might be the amelioration of groundwater contamination caused by industrial and agricultural pollution, urban and regional planning, the assimilation of immigrant populations into local communities, the inability of regions to get resources and attention from national governments or the European Union, work redesign and worker safety, and freedom of dress or religious practice in public schools. These are complex, dynamic, multidisciplinary problems that have scientific, technical, social scientific and humanistic dimensions. They do not yield to typical disciplinary nostrums and they do not map onto the current Tayloristic division of labour in universities. Yet these are precisely the kinds of problem that graduates of universities will face in their work lives and that local, regional and national governments consider to be urgent.

Trying to address such problems without altering the current Tayloristic organization of universities, through the typical ruse of creating multidisciplinary centres and institutes, has proved inadequate. Such centres are always vulnerable: often under administrative attack, and the first to be sacrificed when there is a financial crisis. To deal with such problems, the needed collaborators come from the three broad areas of knowledge that, in university politics, engage each other primarily in internal competition for resources at each other's expense. Their students, generally, are 'disciplined' to be narrow in focus and to be 'experts', and the university administrators largely either operate by promoting this disciplinary competition as a mechanism of control or feel impotent in the face of the hegemony of the departments, disciplinary associations and professors.

Another strategy has been to do a certain amount of 'public' work to appease regional and national constituencies, an approach that rests on a discipline focus and on a separation of 'academic' from 'applied' work with all the academic prestige and rewards still going to the 'academic' work. That is, public universities devote a token amount of resources to public service programmes and voluntary activities by the faculty and students in service of the local community, the so-called service-learning movement. These efforts are rarely sustained enough or well enough supervised by the problem owners to be successful in any but a palliative way.

So the difficulty with local/regional problems is that they are too complex for the current knowledge-generation organization of universities to handle. The Tayloristic response cannot work, as most successfully competitive manufacturing businesses have learned. A serious imitation in universities of current corporate models would place a premium on multidisciplinary, team-based efforts tied directly to financial and social rewards, and to flattening hierarchies. This is what the private sector is doing but, in universities, the result of ignoring these needed organizational changes is the great difficulty they have in articulating meaningful, comprehensive relationships with regions. The costs of this difficulty are the loss of public support for universities and the inadequate training of students for their future work lives and their civic duties as community members.

In my view, this is the core of the crisis of public universities. Failing to respond comprehensively in a more intelligent way will result in further pressures for neo-liberal 'corporatization'. This will continue to weaken universities and will worsen further the public dissatisfaction with universities. And there is no reason to think that the 'lean and mean' entrepreneurial university will be likely to take on complex and demanding public problems affecting regions. The money is not there and the incentives that mainly matter in corporate universities are to chase the money.

Moving On

Why Public University Involvement in Regional Development is First and Foremost an Intellectual Problem

It is important to identify the problems being dealt with in a proper way. A central problem of regions and nation-states is globalization, which undermines the economic and social structure of particular regions and which seems to be an uncontrollable force. Yet we know from many examples ranging from political mobilizations, NGO activities, to regional development initiatives that intentional regionalization can achieve a level of protection for regional societies/economies from some of the depredations of floating on world markets. Innovative work practices, product designs and finding competitive advantage where none was seen before are all part of this story. Knowledge and organization are central to these efforts. Indeed, John Goddard has coined the term 'learning regions' to describe this situation (Goddard, 1997).

Universities are large stores of publicly financed knowledge and labour power. Not to mobilize them to support regional development is to waste the resources already allocated. To be forced to pay again for additional knowledge resources to be used as a substitute for university involvement is to force regions to pay twice for the same service. So the issue is how to bring university resources to bear on the problem, not whether it is a good, morally defensible idea.

Though it may appear counterintuitive, I believe the core of the problem is an intellectual one. To achieve serious university engagement in local and regional communities is not merely a political or ethical matter, as most literatures and reformers suggest. It requires a significant intellectual reorientation of the university that recalibrates the relationship between three forms of knowledge distinguished by Aristotle in 350 BC.

The Aristotelian distinctions I refer to are those between *episteme*, *techne* and *phronesis*, terms that have been brought back into active use principally by the British philosopher and historian of science, Stephen Toulmin, the Norwegian social theorist and action researcher, Björn Gustavsen (Toulmin and Gustavsen, 1996), the Norwegian philosopher and action researcher, Olav Eikeland (Eikeland, 2006), and the Danish sociologist/planner, Bent Flyvbjerg (Flyvbjerg, 2001).[3] The three-part distinction, familiar already to many, centres on distinguishing three kinds of knowledge. No one is superior to the others; all are valid forms of knowing in particular contexts. The key here is the context.

Episteme *Episteme* centres fundamentally on contemplative ways of knowing aimed at understanding the eternal and unchangeable operations of the world. The sources of *episteme* are multiple: speculative, analytical, logical and experiential, but the focus is always on eternal truths beyond their materialization in concrete situations. Typically, the kinds of complexity found in *episteme* take the form of definitional statements, logical connections, building of models and analogies and so forth. *Episteme* is highly self-contained because it is deployed mainly in theoretical discourses themselves. While *episteme* obviously is not a self-contained activity, it aims to remove as many concrete empirical referents as possible in order to achieve the status of general truth. The evaluation of *episteme* is done by intellectual peers who examine the definitional structures and logic of arguments and who seek to develop additional elements and connections among the parts. Therefore the typical form of engagement in work centring on *episteme* is with a group of like-minded theorists who are similarly situated socially. These like-minded theories are, for whatever

---

3   This part of the discussion was developed in a paper delivered at a recent conference in Spain (Greenwood, forthcoming).

reasons, interested in the same problems and can provide critical commentary and analysis.

Techne   If this meaning of *episteme* accords rather closely to everyday usage, this is not the case with *techne* and *phronesis*. *Techne* is one of two other kinds of knowledge beyond *episteme*. *Techne* arises from Aristotle's poetical episteme. It is a form of knowledge that inherently action-oriented, inherently productive. *Techne* engages in the analysis of what should be done in the world in order to increase human happiness.

The sources of *techne* are multiple. They necessarily involve sufficient experiential engagement in the world to permit the analysis of 'what should be done'. This means that *techne* is not properly translated as mere 'technique' and it most certainly cannot be understood as the mindless application of theoretical knowledge. *Techne* centres on the production of happiness in the world in accordance with moral/ethical/social designs and preferences. It is a mode of knowing and acting of its own. To quote Flyvbjerg: '*Techne* is thus craft and art, and as an activity it is concrete, variable, and context-dependent. The objective of *techne* is application of technical knowledge and skills according to a pragmatic instrumental rationality, what Foucault calls "a practical rationality governed by a conscious goal"' (Flyvbjerg, 2001: 111).

The development of *techne* involves, first and foremost, the creation of that conscious goal, the generation of ideas of better designs for living that will increase human happiness. The types of complexity involved in *techne* arise around the debate among ideal ends, the complex contextualization of these ends, and the instrumental design of activities to enhance the human condition. *Techne* is not the application of *episteme* and, indeed, its link to *episteme* is tenuous in many situations. *Techne* arises from its own sources in moral/ethical debate and visions of an ideal society.

Techne is deployed in the political process, in social service programmes and in any other activity designed to improve the human condition. *Techne* is the realm of professional experts who set the ideal goals for an activity, who putatively have the expertise necessary to design instrumental actions that lead to greater human happiness, and who are capable of learning from other expert practitioners. *Techne* is evaluated primarily by impact measures developed by the professional experts themselves, who decide whether or not their projects have enhanced human happiness and, if not, why not. Practitioners of *techne* do engage with local problem owners, power holders, and other experts, often being contracted by those in power to attempt to achieve positive social changes. Their relationship to the subjects of their work is often close and collaborative but they are first and foremost professional experts who do things 'for' not 'with' the local problem owners. They bring general designs and habits of work to the local case and privilege their own knowledge over that of the local problem owners.

Phronesis   *Phronesis* is not a well-known term because contemporary social science has crushed the world of Aristotelian distinctions to a dualistic and intellectually indefensible theory/practice or theory/application distinction. *Phronesis* is a complex idea. Formally defined by Aristotle as internally consistent reasoning that deals with all possible particulars, *phronesis* is best understood as the design of action through collaborative knowledge construction with the legitimate owners of a problem.

The sources of *phronesis* are collaborative arenas for knowledge development in which the professional researcher's knowledge is combined with the complex and deep local knowledge of the problem owners in defining the problem to be addressed. Together, they design and implement the research that needs to be done to understand the problem. They then design the actions to improve the situation together and they evaluate the adequacy of what was done. If they are not satisfied, they recycle the process until the results are satisfactory to all the parties.

The types of complexity involved in *phronesis* are at once intellectual, contextual and social, as *phronesis* involves the creation of a new space for collaborative reflection, the contrast and integration of many kinds of knowledge systems, the linking of the general and the particular through action and analysis and the collaborative design of both the goals and the actions aimed at achieving them.

Phronesis is a practice that is deployed in groups in which all the problem owners, research experts and local collaborators, have legitimate knowledge claims and rights to determine the outcome. It is evaluated by the collaborators diversely according to their interests, but all share an interest the adequacy of the outcomes achieved in relation to the goals they collaboratively developed. Thus, *phronesis* involves an egalitarian engagement across knowledge systems and diverse experiences.

It should be clear that two of these three forms of knowledge generation are authoritarian and autopoetic: *episteme* and *techne*. *Phronesis*, by contrast, is a combined theory-action framework that necessarily implies linking all the relevant problem owners in the knowledge-generation arenas where the agenda for research and action is collaboratively set and the actions are collaboratively taken. The extra-university problem owners are essential partners in the process. *Phronesis* matches the complexity of life in the everyday world where no one has all the necessary knowledge and skill and where complex problems can only be dealt with by combinations of knowledge and action in an egalitarian arena where all of society's knowledge and effort is needed. All three forms of knowledge generation produce valid results but, of the three, only *phronesis* involves the agenda of extra-university problem owners directly. So the question becomes how to promote *phronesis* in universities.

Phronesis does not grant unilateral authority to university experts, but it also does not deny the potential value of their expertise, when utilized in collaboration with extra-university problem owners. *Phronesis* is a highly pragmatic activity, using theories and methods from any and all fields, as they appear relevant to a particular set of problems. Thus *phronesis* routinely builds on insights gained from the practice of *episteme* and *techne*, even if the mode of operation in *phronesis* is fundamentally different. The difficulty is that many university professors, students and administrators, used to thinking of a university education and job as a validation of their superiority over other citizens, find that this more collaborative model is hard to learn. Authoritarianism is a difficult behaviour to overcome.

I believe that more university activities based on *phronesis* would dramatically change the political climate universities operate in. The attacks on universities and their inefficiency, the calls for more businesslike management would evaporate if universities were operating in an authentically collaborative mode with extra-university problem owners, who, after all, are taxpayers and voters. Instead of a defensive and/or arrogant university reaction to these pressures and instead of handing the university over to a group of accountants, a more intelligent response would be to evaluate the depth of the crisis universities find themselves in and to engage in a public process of redesigning university work life together with the legitimate problem owners, including those within the regions.

This kind of organizational redesign is commonplace in the private sector, and it includes dealing with problem owners outside of the organization. It involves developing criteria for salary improvement, job acquisition, promotion that rewards *phronesis*-based activities and evaluation of the activities by all the legitimate problem owners. This means a reallocation of resources to support *phronesis*, while understanding that successful *phronesis* is often based on excellent work in *episteme* and *techne*. That is, it does not mean undermining other non-*phronesis* dimensions of university life, but making them accessible to and responsive to major university *phronesis*-based efforts.

At many universities, applied work and public service are treated as marginal activities or even as a shallow public relations effort. These activities would be transformed as well, not merely by proliferation of more marginal activities but by the reconceptualization of the university's relationship with the local and regional community as a cooperative, egalitarian one in which the setting of agendas respects both the community's and the university's interests.

Needless to say, the curricula would have to be substantially redesigned so that students in all fields would gain direct experience in *phronesis*-based work as a key element in their training in any subject. And, of course, there would have to be teeth in the reforms, including punishments for non-compliance, for example, resource deprivation, closing of units or elimination of programs. This is no less hard-headed than the pseudo-corporatization currently taking place, but it is a reconfiguration of public universities that puts universities at the service of all the taxpayers. Pseudo-corporatization puts universities at the service of the wealthiest private sector interests and high-level national politicians only.

Is this Impossible?

I have no patience for useless schemes, having participated in too many during my academic career. Elements of what I am describing are being carried out in some places but a good, general conceptualization of these issues is lacking and very few universities have made this kind of work a central focus. Still, as a Cornell University colleague of mine, Alan McAdams, is fond of saying, 'If it is happening somewhere, it must be possible.' In any case, the alternative to working through these issues seriously is university corporatization with the elimination of as many *episteme* and *techne*-based activities as possible, the conversion of students and funders into customers and the proletarianization of the faculty. If faculty, students and administrators cannot bring themselves to change their behaviour in the face of such challenges then I personally do not care what happens to them.

A more likely scenario is that *phronesis*-based activities will become popular as a few smart universities respond intelligently to increasing external pressures and the less nimble universities lose their resources and public support. There are a variety of examples of institutions large and small that are meeting the needs of at least some of their major regional problem owners more effectively through *phronesis*-based activities and there is reason to think that the careful evaluation of these experiences can lead to innovative initiatives elsewhere.

Example – the land grant university system in the US   The US system of public land grant universities was a creation of the Morrill Act of 1862, which sold public lands in return for the creation of public universities dedicated to research, teaching and extension to the community. Historically, the formal extension service was a much later creation and it functioned primarily in support of rural and agricultural communities in the state where the university was located. Over the years, the system has deteriorated into a division of labour in which most faculty do no extension work. Rather, extension is carried out by low-academic-status professionals. And there are many cases, perhaps the majority, where *techne*, not *phronesis* is the mode of operation.

However, this is a large and complex system and some valuable activities happen within it. In the case of the state of New York, Cornell Cooperative Extension is funded 50 per cent by the county where the services are delivered. This gives county officials some real control over the selection and direction of activities. My colleague, Scott Peters, is engaged in a long-term project doing profiles of professors and extension professionals and their ideas of civic responsibility. These profiles show that, within a larger system that is heavily authoritarian, there are still many professionals, including scientists, for whom extension is a truly *phronesis*-based activity (Peters, 2000; 2001; 2002a; 2002b; 2003; Peters *et al.*, 2003;2005). The dilemma here is how to reorganize the administrative structures of the land grant system to privilege such work rather than continuing to have *phronesis*-based work be the exception.

The United Kingdom   The quite fundamental and basically neo-liberal reforms of higher education initiated by Margaret Thatcher have resulted in a major shake-up in the system and the creation of a variety of metrics for measuring how well universities are meeting nationally set goals. Within this context, there has been a good deal of debate about the regional links of universities. One of the most consistent voices on this subject is John Goddard of Newcastle upon Tyne.

Regarding the National Committee of Inquiry into Higher Education Report of 1997 (also known as the *Dearing Report*), Goddard (1997) points out that the role of higher education in regional development is rather prominent. The Dearing Report made clear, among many other things, that national funding strategies discourage regional development initiatives, that the unsystematic location of universities over the geography of the United Kingdom makes rational policy hard to build, that more and more students are choosing to stay in their regions for their higher education, that there is a lack of good career counselling with regard to regional employment opportunities, and that the national research assessment exercise fails to include regional research collaboration as an element.

In response to these dilemmas, Goddard and his colleagues at the Newcastle upon Tyne Centre for Urban and Regional Development have devoted a good deal of effort to the development of a conceptual framework that builds a stronger regional framework into higher education. Conceptually, they have developed the idea of the 'learning region' as a way of conceptualizing the university-region partnerships that would promote *phronesis*-based activities, all as a counterweight to the corporativizing reforms being imposed centrally (Goddard *et al.*, 1994; 1997).

Southern Cross University, Australia   Created in 1992 through the fusion of older special-purpose higher-education institutions, Southern Cross University privileges regional development and internationalization as its core strategic objectives. Among its most interesting features is a very powerful commitment to action research as a major work modality, that is, to *phronesis*. A look at the webpage maintained by Bob Dick at Southern Cross there shows one of the most comprehensive collections of action research materials found anywhere (*http://www.uq.net.au/action_research/arhome.html*).

The Southern Cross Institute for Action Research contains a mix of university professors and action research professionals. Their mission statement prominently includes a commitment to 'provide a world class service in the use of action research to practitioners, organisations and communities…[and to] engage with communities where the campuses of the University are situated to promote action research for the benefit of the community'.

The Centre for Working Life Development, University of Halmstad   Created in 1988 as a research unit at Halmstad University, Sweden, the Centre's focus is working life. It has a staff of approximately 25 from a wide variety of fields. The method employed is action research.

The 'Innovative Networks' project of the Centre describes the Centre's approach as follows:

> The approach taken by CAU [the Centre] is based on the mutuality of research and development. The Centre is engaged in the development and improvement of social systems through studying their process of change, i.e. action research. In action research, researcher and practitioner work in close collaboration and are jointly involved in generating new knowledge whilst achieving practical results. Methods such as the 'search-conference' and participative design have proved to be very effective tools for the initiation of a process of change; they achieve broad participation and commitment from all those involved, allowing them all to participate in the development of their

organisation. Innovative Networks is an action research project. Action research means solving practical problems in a real life situation. This is done in a democratic process, where researchers and companies act on equal terms in a joint learning process. The point is to both solve practical problems and develop new knowledge. (*http://www.hh.se/work/ old/cau_sv/projekt/innonet/Innonet_eng.htm*)

This Centre is one of the main sources of regional development expertise and assistance for the Halmstad region and its operations have made this relatively new university a well-respected regional partner that enjoys public and political support.

Many more initiatives could be described: Harry Boyte's 'Public Achievement' program at the University of Minnesota, Minneapolis, The Center for Community Partnerships of the University of Pennsylvania, The Campus Compact, and the wide variety of democratizing interventions by people like Ira Schor and Stanley Aronowitz, but the above provide a flavour of what is happening in different places. These are initiatives that work, that have an impact, that improve the quality of life.

These initiatives, however, will not proliferate by themselves; action is needed. To paraphrase Chris Argyris, *phronesis*-based work is the effort to 'increase the likelihood of unlikely but liberating outcomes' (Argyris *et al.*, 1985: xii). To regionalize public universities and to promote *phronesis*-based collaborative research and teaching based on partnerships with the local/regional problem owners can be such a 'liberating outcome'. It is an unlikely one. Making it more likely is our job. The alternative is unacceptable.

Chapter 7

Regulation, Engagement and Academic Production

Tim May

Introduction

This chapter[1] examines the issues that inform the relationship between academic modes of production and the knowledge economy. It is not content for this examination to take place against the background of presuppositions that the knowledge economy is a distinct subsystem, or even the dominant system, informing the development of capitalism, or that it has self-evident implications for the direction of higher education. Nor is it content to invoke outdated notions of academic freedom, or join those voices that speak of the 'academic' as if it had no relevance to contemporary issues. Therefore, it exists in a place that is in the process of becoming, but is not yet fully developed as the site of public debate concerning the role and place of higher education in the future.

I wish to examine some current issues that relate, specifically, to the institutional context of knowledge production in universities. In the process questions will be raised about claims within academia, as well as those made in relation to environmental 'imperatives'. Only after some of these issues have been properly examined, as opposed to regurgitated as supposed truisms, can the future, and so potential, role of universities be properly assessed. No claim to exhausting any such possibilities is made here; this is simply one contribution to a set of possibilities and what is hoped to be a productive assessment of the basis for developments.

Universities: Change, Choice and Conflict

In this section I turn to issues informing knowledge production. Without an understanding of the dynamics of context – which implies a context sensitivity that collapses into neither relativism nor abstract objectivism – in relation to what is produced, exchanged and disseminated, the consequences and possibilities that come with the knowledge economy will not be fully understood. What we find is a variable response to the knowledge economy: from assumptions concerning its evident existence and the need for wholesale change in its image, through implications for

---

1   My thanks to Beth Perry for her helpful comments on an earlier draft of this chapter.

engagement and development, to acts of detached criticism and the idea of having to slow down time for the purposes of academic production. This is a contribution to engagement, challenge and development.

There is a consensus of opinion that the knowledge economy, in relation to its growth and form, represents a significant development for the future of universities as a whole (Braun and Merrien, 1999; Delanty, 2001). At one level this is nothing new. E.P. Thompson, for example, protested against the University of Warwick forming itself in the image of industry. This protest was not born out of Thompson being 'against' a relationship between industry and higher education: 'In the conflict it became apparent that what was wrong was not a close relationship with "industry" but a particular kind of subordinate relationship with industrial capitalism' (Thompson, 1970: 17). As the conclusion to the book, which was a collective enterprise written in a week, put it: 'These events have given more relevance and importance than ever before in Britain to the international conflict as to the role of a university in a modern capitalist society' (Thompson, 1970: 165). Similarly, in his history of universities and business in the US Christopher Newfield writes: 'the research university was created to serve a newly corporate form of capitalism's educational and technological needs, and this service involved adapting to the economic values of that society and creating a large number of cooperative employees to make it work' (2003: 218).

What has altered is the scale and intensity of transformations (de Weert, 1999; Bryson *et al.*, 2000; Marginson and Considine, 2000), leading to a qualitatively different set of circumstances in which academic production takes place (Hill and Turpin, 1995; Smith and Webster, 1997). Responses vary according to how the consequences of these transformations are perceived for academic knowledge production: as threats to its critical capacity and impartiality due to an increasing instrumentalism, at one end of the scale, but as positive developments that enable universities to take advantage of their centrality in the production, distribution and exchange of knowledge, at the other (Brint, 2002; Robins and Webster, 2002; Pels, 2003). At the core of these debates lies the importance of being in an organization that is seen to embody a certain set of values that are taken to be exemplified in practice and so distinctive from other sites of knowledge production.

In Search of Distinctiveness

Arguments for the distinctiveness of the university as a site of knowledge production often hinge on a context that is regarded as core to a means of providing a distance from the type of short-term necessity driven by narrow economic criteria. Calls for 'relative autonomy' (Pels, 2003) for the university centre upon an alignment between disposition and institutional position. Its distinctiveness then centres upon affording a working context that is denied to those immersed in the everyday business of the economy where knowledge is a commodity subject to the exigencies of market forces. So the university can be seen as providing a context in which a 'point of view on points of view' (Bourdieu, 2000), combined with a long-term exposure to a body of knowledge, turns the subjects of research into objects of analysis in a process that is not replicable in other sites of knowledge production. A combination of gaze and position is thus the basis upon which the uniqueness and viability of the university is so often defended (Filmer, 1997).

This is understandable. Any claim to scientific knowledge requires grounds upon which to validate its practices, and this is held to reach a more mature state when the justification for such grounds becomes an object of its practitioner's considerations. Knowledge in universities is then demarcated according to its belonging to identified persons with common sets of educational experiences working in contexts whose culture is conducive to those activities and values. When it comes to those whose knowledge is derived from outside the university setting, the applicability of academic knowledge can be readily dismissed as irrelevant. The resultant spaces of practice then become what Elliot Freidson (1994) calls 'shelters': that is, places of relative autonomy in which the macro realities of political economy are connected with micro experiences and activities to create particular kinds of labour market segments.

The operation of this boundary closure is part of the claim to expertise, along with the exceptionality of the educational experiences and qualities of practitioners (Parkin, 1974). Clear differences in orientation may then be constructed between those who lie within the boundaries of disciplines and share a common set of experiences and those who remain on the outside. Accompanied by a sufficient degree of stability in such environments, a disciplinary orientation can then emerge which, when combined with organizational context, creates positions that enable particular practices to occur.

Without these conditions and acts of reflections in place, accompanied by a clear defence of a value to society as a whole, the realm of professional justification can easily become the province of those who lie outside of the disciplinary and more general, organizational context. Not only can this undermine distinctiveness, but it may also affect a defence of the basis upon which its legitimacy rests in the public realm. If anyone can practise its inner workings, and its standards are open to variable interpretations, it can no longer claim a privileged position for itself. If those positions from which the discipline is practised are so multiple that they no longer provide uniqueness in relation to the process and product of knowledge, then its forms of understanding are also readily understood by non-professionals and the situation changes. Its ways of working are not esoteric and the boundaries through which its practices are maintained are not closed, but permeable and open to varying interpretations. As a result, the authority for its findings and the basis for its practices are then diminished (Turner, 2003).

In looking towards the future of the university, there must be something different about working in those contexts and, as a result, something different in the knowledge it produces. Without this in place, what is its likely future? The attractions of private-sector-financed research can lie in financial rewards and improved conditions of service. The university, therefore, needs to offer something else. As noted, for some this is a different culture in which the necessities that apparently drive the knowledge economy are apparent, but are not determining of practice. It has also been recognized that, in the knowledge economy, the free circulation of knowledge contains no incentives for production and so a 'social unit', such as government or the university, must act as a site of production (Bell, 1980).

Does such a claim take sufficient account of changing contexts and modes of academic production, as well as the realities of organizational life in universities? Daniel Bell's observations, for example, are based on a Fordist, rather than post-Fordist regime. If not, they are nothing more than a resort to unrealistic possibilities, or indicative of a form of autonomy whose conditions, if they ever existed, have long gone. Disciplines, after all, are practised within university contexts in which there have long been threats to integrity – where integrity means having a clearly defined and bounded set of practices governed by professional ethics. If justifications for the uniqueness of the academic mode of production do not take account of such circumstances, as well as the form, content and effects of change, their success is inevitably diminished. One of those changing dynamics relates to the demand for 'relevant knowledge'.

Relevance and Imagined Worlds

In practice, as opposed to second-order reflections upon practice, the realm of professional justification can easily move into different sites of knowledge application. Knowledge is required to be produced with ever greater speed, according to the varying needs of those who fund research. Concerns about validity and reliability are seen by academics to be comprised by an increase in speed of production and the narrowness of the interests of those who fund research with the result that political, rather than intellectual, values can end up informing the process of knowledge production itself (see Hammersley, 1995).

In those situations where the boundaries between distinct forms of practice have become blurred, those who revert to particular forms of justification for knowledge production may find their practices characterized as falling somewhere between luxury and indulgence. They will appear to have 'too great' a distance from necessity, and their work may be deemed irrelevant. Knowledge in these instances can easily become 'what works' and conditioned by those with the power to determine the criterion of relevance for its evaluation. Findings will be then be expected to confirm proposed solutions and/or pre-existing prejudices.

In these instances the articulation of prior assumptions is often absent from initial negotiations between parties in the research process. What we end up with is imagined and unarticulated expectations in relation to both process and product. Yet, whilst often not articulated by either the producers or the funders, these are readily activated when encountering a disconfirming instance during the production process itself. What might these instances be? Examples include the following: the production of research in the form of findings and reports that do not accord with prejudices; preliminary or final results being seen as additions to problematizations without accompanying solutions; changes in the research brief itself during the process with a resulting ambiguity in terms of its aims and value. From a professional disciplinary point of view, to change this relation according to an anticipation of these forces would undermine the integrity of practice: 'in addition to the requirements for personal integrity in general, individuals who practise or profess an academic subject are also constrained by the integrity of their subject' (Noble, 1999: 173).

Relevance is an old and frequent visitor to universities whose intensity increases and decreases at various points in time. As with all similar demands, it works through unexamined assumptions that are placed beyond question and thus never subject to explicit challenge, or which are placed beyond challenge through fear of the consequences of such action. Its power thereby resides in the inability to question apparent self-evidence: it is a discourse rooted in naturalized presupposition. 'What do you mean by relevant?' There are times when this question cannot even be asked because it betrays the very symptoms that are the object of attack by those whose claim to speak in the name of self-evidence. These are dispositions so deeply held that they lie beyond question. Only those who do not understand this unarticulated self-evidence, bolstered by claims made on behalf of necessity, could possibly pose it in the first instance. In the very asking, a distance from those 'necessities' is betrayed that should not be the object of reflexive problematization among a community of scholars, but of practical intervention for the purpose of obtaining solutions to problems. In the process it is the needs of the economy that are so frequently the referent for relevance.

In the face of unarticulated self-evidence stand claims to professionalism in which engagement of the type expected is antithetical to notions of value freedom. The debates over value freedom are long and detailed (Williams and May, 1996). A simple separation between facts and values, however, is not sustainable and such claims are best seen as strategic, rather that strictly methodological (Scott, A., 1995). Thus, if practices do not take account of the relations between such claims and the context of knowledge production, they can easily be identified as weaknesses manifest in what appears to be indulgent and irrelevant questioning, accompanied by an evident failure to grasp what is taken to be the important, immediate and necessary.

Struggles for Difference and Distinctiveness

In examining these dynamics, the issue of difference between forms of academic work arises. Academic professionalism, like all claims to expertise, can be both enabling and constraining. Here we see a degree of alignment between Michel Foucault (1984) and Jürgen Habermas (1992) with respect to the colonization of the life world by expertise and the relationship between knowledge and power, respectively. When dealing with expertise we see ambivalence in which respect mixes with fear and even hatred (Merton, 1976).

This is precisely the same type of ambivalence expressed by academics. At one moment their Department may provide the basis for resistance against the encroachments of external influences, whilst at another, casualization of work, rivalries and hierarchies produce differentiations leading to uncertainty and retreat. Therefore, when dealing with the issue of engagement between the university and its environments, we are not simply dealing with the potential for unimaginative and passive regurgitations of limited understandings from those paid to run universities. We are also examining the tendency for academics to exercise idealized defences of their professionalism from positions that do not live up to these claims.

Whilst there are those who allude to critical distance without due reference to the conditions of knowledge production, there are also those who regard critical distance as a luxury in the face of apparent 'necessity'. For this latter group we might reserve the term 'doxosophers'. These are the: 'technicians of opinion who think themselves wise' and who 'pose the problems of politics in the very same terms in which they are posed by businessmen, politicians and political journalists...' (Bourdieu, 1998: 7). Those who refuse to grant self-evidence to existing states of affairs are viewed by such persons as guilty of a naivety or bias in their 'refusal to grant the profoundly political submission implied in the unconscious acceptance of commonplaces' (Bourdieu, 1998: 8).

To illuminate the reasons for this state of affairs, we find a striving for distinction (Bourdieu, 1986) informing the activities of those who contribute to knowledge production. Fields of production are constituted by distributions of capital that inform the struggles that take place within them and are exemplified by particular expressions of inclusion and exclusion (a field being constituted by positions and relations among participants and characterized by the distributions of capital mobilized in the struggles that take [or have taken] place within them. See Bourdieu, 1993: chapter 9). We can see this in, for example, routine references to 'junior' and 'senior' members of staff among academics. Such terms exemplify the struggles for distinction that are part of the professional ethos in which a tacit knowledge of the mode of operation of the field, including its stakes and interests, is implied in its practices and positions.

As opposed to a more general focus upon the conditions that afford knowledge production in the first instances, concern then focuses upon the conservation or subversion of the structure of the capital within the field, as opposed to a consideration of the potentiality for its reconstitution and the consequences of that for knowledge production. All have a stake and a place within such relations and cannot but contribute to its reproduction at some level. However, to what different degrees and with what consequence?

Those who benefit from current arrangements will seek to defend orthodoxy when it speaks in their name. History, including their own biographical trajectories and positions in the field, may be displaced in a process in which forgetting becomes more important than memory. Yet if the resultant strategies and tactics (May, 1999) fail to take account of the reconstitution of fields according to new forms of control and knowledge production, misrecognition will result from the operation of what is a presentist empiricism in which the past and the future evaporate in a focus upon a narrowly constituted immediacy.

We find this in universities and those organizations that regard themselves as part of the knowledge economy in which what is traded is ideas about ideas without concern for context. Consequentially, this will serve to reproduce those distinctions that are indifferent to an explanation of the institutional conditions that enable them to take place. Any overall disjuncture, rather than being an object of reflection that is taken forward in action, can then be neutralized by the hierarchies and logics constituted by limited understandings of the changing conditions of knowledge production.

What we then find is an alignment between those who castigate others for questioning the self-evident and those for whom the limits of critical questioning arise when it comes to an examination of the positions from which their pronouncements are made. As Pierre Bourdieu puts it: 'efforts to find, in the specifically linguistic logic of different forms of argumentation, rhetoric and style, the source of their symbolic efficacy are destined to fail as long as they do not establish the relationship between the properties of discourses, the properties of the person who pronounces them and the properties of the institution which authorizes him to pronounce them' (1992: 111). A relational dimension evaporates. Knowledge is divorced from context and packaged for resale as a commodity, or as part of the constitution of cultural capital on the conference circuit.

In terms of the relationship between this specificity, organizational position and a reflexive attitude towards relationships (May, 2000), the relational dimension varies in universities, with those reliant upon the next contract tending to have less latitude given the need for the next grant in sites of production that rely on so-called 'soft' monies. Yet an absence of compliance or questioning cannot be assumed as a result of such circumstances. Others, by default, may invoke their position as a guarantor of distance from these implications, casting disdainful glances at those whose existence is dependent upon a more direct relation to external partners and income generation. This mixes with those academics turned managers who, in these individualistic cultures, find capitulation to a self-evident managerialism driven by environmental necessities a matter of fate, rather than choice. Past knowledge then becomes useless in the face of new necessities, and that knowledge can then be retrospectively justified as unrealistic (Prichard, 2000).

Narratives from academics tend to draw upon issues associated with being adaptive, and those in managerial positions will say that they seek a balance between managerial and academic values. Yet we are dealing with stratified professions where the capability to maintain degrees of control is differentially distributed (Henkel, 2000). In the face of such strains, universities become diversified sites of knowledge production in which instrumental forms of knowledge production mix with the critical and reflexive forms. This leads to institutional uncertainty in the face of a diversity of practices. If universities are everything to everybody, they also run the risk of being nothing to all. Calls for understanding in these circumstances are deafening in their silence in contexts where the self-evident mixes with varying degrees of distance from what is constructed as 'necessity'. Here, in the extreme, knowledge production may be deemed irrelevant when it fails to inform particular and frequently unarticulated ends. The idea of the university as a meeting place of challenge, learning, potential change, mutual understanding and dialogue, evaporates in the process.

Management: Control, Organizational Forms and Values

If within academic professional communities we find an absence of concern with the past and future, it is also apparent in universities as a whole in the forms deployed to control work and extract accountability. Output measures, including research articles, have often been referred to as 'deliverables'. A deliverable in the context of the university is also the volume of research income.

The very term connotes that which is beyond question as an 'objective' means to judge the effectiveness of performance. It either is, or is not, attained as a performance goal. Faced with these demands in situations where obtaining funding for research becomes core to performance, the modus operandi may easily become 'give them what they want'. There are benefits to this course of action because a large part of organizational practice is then validated against this background. Here, however, practices accord with the same attitude that drives the deliverable. Process and context evaporate in an abstraction that is held to be self-evident and measured accordingly.

Allusions to the 'deliverable' are shorthand demands by those technicians of organizational transformation (May, 1994) who frame it within narrowly conceived administrative imperatives. It is seen to work because it relieves people of the need to question their presuppositions and because an information-gathering exercise informs its practice as if it were a technical matter, rather than one of choice in the face of alternatives. The power of these systems of internal audit then lies in their construction of performance in their own image (Power, 1997). The opportunity to understand why and how different forms of knowledge production exist, often in the same institution, is thereby dispensed with as a result of the existence of such forms of control. A resulting bureaucracy is indifferent to difference and becomes externalized within internal administrative systems that flatten and sideline its existence (Herzfeld, 1992).

Moving beyond the operational to the strategic level, universities often find themselves subjected to restructuring due to ambiguities in their command and control functions around 'internal' issues associated with accountability, costs, quality and effectiveness. Equally, the 'inside' of the university may be reconfigured in the name of the 'outside', as if any boundaries did not exist at all or any differences between them derive from an academic idealism. E.P.Thompson was taking aim at this tendency, for it is particularly selective in what it regards as 'necessity'. As a result the spaces to discuss and act upon matters of purpose, value and overall effects shrink as internal systems of audit are held to represent, with no apparent interpretive mediation, environmental necessities. Within universities these discussions are then so easily held to be symptomatic of speculative indulgence. The result is that, at an institutional level, contingency collapses into necessity. In situations where there is no apparent choice, only one way forward is possible and information gathering is the slave of this one-dimensionality. Yet, in this process, what of academics turned managers and their values in these processes of change?

Academics often find incentives in new positions that reinforce the passive message of change and end up producing the very ossifications that were the target of the original transformations. Culturally speaking, what is argued to be, at the level of second-order justification, a critical, reflexive but supportive role for the institution in relation to the economy ends up as nothing more than a 'normalization' of narrowly defined assumptions. In practice, particular issues are focused upon to the exclusion of those that may lead to more imaginative possibilities, particularly when these come too close to treasured assumptions concerning autonomy.

Individually speaking, past utterances and actions, particularly among academics turned managers, are easily accommodated via cognitive dissonance. Past knowledge can be rendered idealistic in a distance from a new set of necessities that are never subject to the same critical faculties that were once exercised by those same individuals. It thus becomes the case that those who once represented such knowledge are the same who now dismiss it as irrelevant to their new situations. Equally, the phenomenon of 'gate fever' (the experience of prisoners as they near the end of their sentence) can also alleviate a situation, as when people occupy a temporary managerial position in return for a sabbatical at the end of the period of office.

There is also the ability to apparently attend to different knowledges at the same time, the implications of whose differences never meet in practice. The exemplar of this would be those who regard themselves as 'critical' scholars whose day-to-day managerial practices are no different from all those that went before. There is at least solace in the belief that praxis never did make perfect! So we may see the publication of critical texts on management alongside a managerial practice that is conventional. This is hardly unheard of in academic life. It becomes something else when used to inform those who appear to embody contrary forms of knowledge that their practices are not sustainable in the 'real world' with its evident imperatives. Again, there is no shortage of attempts to bolster this distinction in relation to market-driven initiatives (see, for example, Martin, 1999; Amit, 2000).

Overall, mixtures of audit, bureaucracy and an academic professionalism saturated with tactics of differentiation that lead towards individualization, render universities sites of bewilderment to those in other sectors (whose organizations, it should be added, are equally bewildering to others). Therefore, seeking a minimal basis upon which to constitute purpose, beyond empty statements of 'vision', is problematic, since anything that appears as a pragmatic compromise is seen as a threat to a narrowly constituted professional autonomy, or to managerial prerogatives.

To this we have to add the observation that an absence of engagement equally occurs through the existence of inappropriate organizational forms, leading to studies around the relationship between university structures and socioeconomic environments (Sporn, 1999). In terms of the norms and cognitive aspects of academic professionalism, we would expect an ad hoc organization in which the environment is complex and dynamic thereby requiring continual mutual adjustment. Instead, we find prime coordinating mechanisms occurring through standardization, which itself assumes a large and stable environment. These then mix with professional bureaucratic elements that require particular skills, but within complex and stable environments (Mintzberg, 1979)!

All in all, the organizational structures of universities are a peculiar mixture of elements that are not sensitive to the differences that exist within them, nor often to the opportunities they posses to engage with and shape the worlds of which they are a part. For some, this makes them wholly unsuitable for many aspects of emerging academic practice. In particular, the need for flexibility within those environments that are rapidly changing is hardly enabled by laborious and mechanical bureaucratic structures. Whilst strategic managers may argue that their existence has been constituted by the organizational issues noted above, a very restricted set of parameters so often informs their restructuring that they often work to prevent the emergence of new practices.

When engagement does occur and new practices emerge, which happens on a regular basis, as universities are also sites of innovative work, it is because of the existence of rationalities that exist despite attempts to normalize them through formal mechanisms of control. In the face of such practices a simple question arises for strategic management: is this *despite*, or *because of*, the existence of current organizational structures? In the evident silence that surrounds this question – leaving exceptional practices to be once again individualized – what is once again lost is that relation between context and practice and so, overall, the value of universities in society.

Context, Contrasts and Distinctiveness

Many of the answers to the earlier question about distinctiveness have been in the form of defences or attacks on universities from liberal, free-market and left wing perspectives, as well as by the religious colleges for whom knowledge is founded upon faith. In addition, debates have taken place in relation to the role of legitimacy in knowledge production giving way to power and self-referential language games (Lyotard, 1984; Habermas, 1992). My argument is that silence exists around the actual processes and practices that inform knowledge production and the expectations that people have of the university as a place of work.

Instead of having this discussion, two apparent opposites combine to produce an overall effect. The doxosopher's view aligns with an audit culture and those who do not submit their academic positionality and its implications for the production of knowledge to critical examination. As a result, contingency becomes necessity by default and there is no productive challenge to existing states of affairs and the means of production is left to reflect an apparent environmental urgency with differential consequences for those in the academic hierarchy.

Academics often maintain that they are challenging current trends. However, they stubbornly refuse to submit to critical examination the relations between their position, knowledge production and its consequences for understanding organizational action. Instead, a narrowly based professional ideal separates what is produced from its context in an act that apparently creates the possibility of generalizable and transferable knowledge (May 2005). All of these perspectives end up denying context, but from different points of view and, in so doing, empty out the possibility for constituting the difference of the university from other sites of knowledge production.

As Paul Rabinow puts it in an essay on academia, representations, modernity, postmodernity and social facts: 'What we share as a condition of existence, heightened today by our ability, and at times our eagerness, to obliterate one another, is a specificity of historical experience and place, however complex and contestable they may be, and a worldwide macro-interdependency encompassing any local particularity' (1996: 56). Instead, in universities we so often find an idealism whose tensions and contradictions are easily passed down to individual practitioners, as opposed to being matters of larger communities of debate and support. Hierarchies and uncertainties manifested in frustrated ambitions are the order of the day, with the consequences of such ways of working being variable according to the different positions in the occupational hierarchy and the varying levels of material securities enjoyed by different practitioners.

So here we find an alignment that is not the usual subject of writings on the university: that between the professional attitude and the institutional context. The limits to the professional attitude, despite all the writings on reflexivity (Schön, 1983) inhere in an understanding of the relations that exist between local identities, organizational conditions of knowledge production and claims to expertise. Academics are frequently indifferent to these relations and instead, when reflexive, adhere to a justification for the existence of their practices that is narrow and unsustainable in contemporary conditions. This completely misses out on what is needed in terms of a broader understanding of the role and place of universities in society.

From an audit point of view, to examine context for those predisposed to narrow views of organizational action reproduces the very reasons for intervention in the first instance: the consequences of the exercise of professional discretion. For academics, an admission of organizational position reproduces a context-dependence that denies professionalism as nothing more than relativist knowledge. In both, the limits to reflexivity reside in the asking of uncomfortable questions about the processes of production and their organization and management. Overall, therefore, there is good reason to: 'doubt the reality of a resistance which ignores the resistance of reality' (Bourdieu, 2000: 108). How is this to be explained in order that we can move beyond these limited ways of seeing and being?

Knowledge management gurus and academics travel the globe and make calls upon their time in order to display their wares to different audiences. Each time they must produce a claim to distinction in order to be part of the markets in which they operate. They display knowledge that is assumed to be empowering. However, the empowering notion of knowledge derives from the idea that knowledge meets the criterion of substitutability: that is, 'The more ways there are to embody the same piece of knowledge, the less opportunity there is to use that knowledge as an instrument of power, since it becomes accountable to a wide range of standards. Does this mean that genuine knowledge *is* disempowering? Not exactly, since each knowledgeable agent is indirectly empowered by being immunized against certain power relationships that are based on corresponding forms of ignorance or lack of access' (Fuller, 2002: 67).

Yet this is exactly what so often does not occur. As noted, past knowledge is castigated in the name of necessity and even opportunity, but not shared through recognition of diversity. Instead it becomes translated as the circulation of ideas according to needs that are not the subject of debate in terms of their feasibility, desirability and sustainability. Where this occurs, the call for relevance is the substitute in the service of the knowledge economy without a concern for the relations between what is produced, in terms of context and consequences, and what is received in terms of its implications for actions and understandings. Hierarchies forged in networks of connections and accumulations provide for critique within strictly defined parameters and thus provide for an epistemic superiority assumed to be beyond question. The result is self-referential and self-justifying.

As a result we see an inability to submit the relations between the present, past and possible futures, in terms of the constitution of the field of analysis, to investigation. Instead, we find allusion to 'ruptures', 'breaks' and changes in modes and contexts of production in relation to justification and application. Organizational change is not something with purpose, but instead is the demonstration of action in the name of necessity. Importantly, what is then lost is historical critique, as forgetting becomes more important than memory (Bauman, 1997), and with that the potential 'to free thought from the constraints exerted on it'. Instead, by default, we see a surrender 'to the routines of the automaton' and a treating of 'reified historical constructs as things' (Bourdieu, 2000: 182). The knowledge economy and the university are two such 'things'.

Reactions to this state of affairs are frequently exemplified through tactics of individualization. Here we witness general issues being reduced to the assumed peculiarities of persons – often accompanied by the assumption that anything else would be too political, idealistic or even unprofessional. Forms of life world boundaries, which are part of social life and provide for the conditions of production of knowledge about that life, are not subject to comparative investigation in order to analyse their implications for understanding. When our everyday life in the world consists in oscillating between being caught in the headlights of routine and our idea of ourselves as individuals who shape that life and are afforded recognition and redistribution as a result, are the sites from which knowledge is produced about that world so different in practice? The assumption must be that they afford difference in some way, but exactly how?

Within the field of academic production, an apparent ability to rise above the particularity of established ways of seeing is a reason to be accorded higher status, reproducing the idea that individual characteristics are solely responsible for innovation (which is not to say that 'character' is not a component). The vantage point from which innovations are produced is via numerous texts that seek to reorientate by shattering habitual modes through which social reality is constituted. A willingness to consider and engage with ideas separates out those capable of epistemic insight from those left in the wake of new ways of seeing. Those pre-reflexive assumptions that were required to practise research in the first place (action could not include continual reflections as that would lead to a paralysis of actions) find themselves subjected to detailed scrutiny and then deconstructed in order to expose the fallacious reasoning informing the assumptions that enabled engagement in the first place.

Critiques may derive from those 'outside' disciplinary practices, but also from 'insiders'. Yet in a culture where displays of knowledge set each producer apart from one another, resultant texts add to the process of accumulation that, in turn, relates to degrees of recognition afforded by those positioned as the judges of worthiness. In the process, connections and capacities blur with the result that it is not what someone knows which is at stake, but who they know. Further, as ideas are imported from other fields and disconnected from those that have emerged with their own histories, novelty can be claimed adding to the process of accumulation and recognition for the knowledge worker.

With the search for new ways of seeing and new ways of constituting knowledge as part of the process of innovation, history can easily be condemned as misinformed or even dubious and dangerous. Whilst we hope to learn from the past, mistakes can be easily replicated in such instances. A subsequent generation may be able to enjoy a distance from the immediacy of the current to see error, but doing so without a sensitivity to context (which implies neither relativism nor excuse) is more likely to repeat error.

Summary

As the above conditions shape the production and flow of knowledge, the basis of justification is argued to move from universities and groups of academics judging each other's work to contexts of application (Gibbons *et al.*, 1994; Nowotny *et al.*, 2001). However, I have also suggested that sensitivity to context is precisely the element that is missing in the knowledge economy, as well as among academics and managers. Whilst networks of individuals, working together around particular issues, can bolster activity according to resources and contacts at their disposal, the sustainability of such activities is dependent upon the level and durability of resourcing. Increasingly, this is informed by ideas of the relevance of knowledge from what are unstated and unexamined points of view in relation to social, economic and political ends. How that happens, under what circumstances and with what effects, is central to an understanding of the relationship between universities and the knowledge economy.

There is a current failure to recognize that '[t]he chances of translating knowledge for action into knowledge in action are immeasurably improved once it is recognized that the probability to realize knowledge is dependent on context-specific social, political and economic conditions' (Stehr, 1992: 121). In addition, the struggles of the past in producing a distinctive set of practices according to a common purpose are seen as a luxury in the face of the constructed 'necessities' of the present. The future then evaporates and, with that, opportunities for productive development and engagement that is not a passive, but an active and transformative undertaking.

Instead of understanding that can be born in practice between universities and the knowledge economy, we find an oscillation between the revenge of empiricism and the denial of position. In one, we have the denouncement of doubt in the name of order and certainty; in the other, the abandonment of understanding leaving the terrain to those who are not so reserved when it comes to speaking in the name of order divorced from context. Both commit the fallacy of universal certainty – but from totally different points of view.

My point here is not to overdraw similarities, nor to underestimate them. At present, assumptions are made both about academic knowledge and the flow and production of knowledge in the economy. Without greater clarity, as opposed to unexamined assumptions, the productive potential that comes from engagement and an understanding of differences and similarities, is lost.

Policy-makers and academics too easily fail to see the relationship in these terms. What we often find is a polarization between the fetish for knowledge in the service of the deliverable as a self-evident property and outcome, and critique conducted in the name of forms of justification that are unreflexive concerning the implications of changing conditions for the future of universities. Changing the way we view this relationship enables not only a better understanding of the conditions that inform knowledge production and reception, but also how we can achieve a better understanding of the ways in which universities can inform, shape and be shaped by, the direction of the knowledge economy.

Chapter 8

Narrating the University: Values across Disciplines

Dolores Byrnes

Research into the production of knowledge within universities and specific disciplines has yielded numerous interesting accounts.[1] Scholars addressing the management, reform and future of universities have, however, noted a relative lack of interview-based, reflexive and ethnographic data about the complex workings inside the 'black box' of the university itself. In this chapter, I summarize research results that constitute a partial glimpse of these internal workings as regards disciplinary distinctions expressed through language and communicated to undergraduate students. The data also suggest interesting metaphor shifts in contemporary knowledge production.

My research, which is described in more detail below, provides examples of educators' stated aims across academic disciplines and university sites. One marked pattern was that, in answering open-ended questions about departmental or educational goals and communications with students, interviewees tended to assume a dichotomy which was expressed on the one hand through an emphasis on 'relevance', and on the other hand in terms of an apparently oppositional emphasis on the aesthetics of knowledge, as for example in the beauty or wonder of learning, or awe in the face of the unknown. In a sense, this distinction may seem to date comfortably back to Aristotle's separation of knowledge into the theoretical, practical, and productive or poetic. But in contemporary contexts this juxtaposition of relevance to aesthetics has some rather sobering implications. For, as Eric Gould asks in his study of university culture: 'to what extent is the aesthetic ideological?' (2003: 213).

Where relevance was taken to be invisible or at least implicit and unexamined, as in the natural sciences, a different emphasis emerged instead, depending upon the level of expertise. Communicating the precise boundaries between 'what science is, and what science is not', was key at the undergraduate level, whereas for practitioners and graduate students, the fun, aesthetics and play of scientific investigation, discovery and knowledge production were more marked.

---

1   Abbott, 1988; 2001; Anderson and Valente, 2002; Anderson, 2003; Bok, 2003; Burawoy, 2005; Clark, 1998; Friedson, 1986; Fuller, 1993; Greenwood and Levin, 2000; Gulbenkian Commission, 1996; Kirp, 2003; Krause. 1996; Messer-Davidow *et al.*, 1993; Newfield, 2003; Ross, 1992; 1994; Sil and Doherty, 2000; Strathern, 2000; Veysey, 1970, to name a few.

I elaborate upon this relevance/aesthetics distinction below in order to suggest that it indexes privilege within the political economy of the university. It is not surprising that some disciplines have more status than others, or that some universities have more status than others. Indeed, the privileging of scientific research and 'Big Science' is 'nothing new', as one faculty member observed to me. But it is the *terms* of self-definition among the relatively less privileged that demand our attention, if they indicate that institutional imperatives are producing an impoverished or reduced sense of disciplinary mission and identity in certain fields.

My research also suggests a cross-disciplinary sense of language 'play' (following on this concept as developed by Ludwig Wittgenstein and Jacques Derrida, among others) in the face of the profound unknowability of the object(s) of research, yet it seems that the sense of freedom and fun in this play varied according to power, status and money within the political economy of the university. These dynamics may reflect the phenomenon of 'science as sport' suggested many years ago by Larry Owens (1985). As an indicator of priorities within the United States, these dynamics are important for many reasons, not the least of which is that they shape the language which is used to communicate with students, and thus in part determine students' decisions about which majors and career paths are 'best'.

In sum, the data indicate a vocabulary in the natural sciences in which basic, pragmatic relevance is not only assumed or taken for granted, but in which a privileged claim is also asserted over the realms of human knowledge associated with the unknown, the uncertain and playful, the truly awe-inspiring – claims which, in the past, were at least *shared* by those representing the humanities and the social sciences. These latter fields have, moreover, historically provided the kinds of analysis: reflexive, critical, historical, literary and/or systematic, which are not normative in the physical sciences. If those in the 'softer' fields are increasingly forced to define their mission in terms of its relevance, we may be seeing an example of the process Tim May refers to, in which 'relevance' comes to be synonymous with 'the needs of the economy'. He notes that the unexamined usage of 'relevance' glosses over both the historical past and the potential for action, while contributing to a 'denouncement of doubt' (Chapter 7, this volume: 132).

My research results indicate that there is some range in the connotations for relevance, possibly related to institutional and departmental contexts. The meanings for relevance that emerged in interviews were: utility (primarily through critical analytical skills) for students facing a tight job market, resonance with student experiences and realities, a critical tool for those interested in problems of social justice, and a timely focus on current events in a complex world.

It is clear that how we metaphorize the processes of knowledge production matters deeply, a point which Thomas Kuhn first explored in depth (1970 [1962]). The directions from which new and valuable insights will emerge are unpredictable, thus an institutional and societal-level openness to new and/or subordinated metaphors, paradigms and perspectives is important; such openness is a key to the distinctiveness of the university setting. Eric Gould captures this moral value of the university when he writes of its role in making students aware of the multiple claims or 'working propositions' made to and about 'truth' and the importance of allowing multiple meanings for the pursuit of truth (2003: 158). A professor of political science noted during an interview that the ontological and epistemological distinctions within the social sciences are 'basically one big fight... it is the disunity, these disagreements, that constitute the social sciences'. This insight about the social sciences can be applied to the ongoing tension, or what Gould advocates as 'a deeply symbiotic relationship', between the three current, loosely defined realms of humanities, natural and social sciences, to allow us to see that each realm needs the metaphors and methods that the others employ (*ibid*.: 213). While cross-disciplinary openness and learning may be hindered or precluded by many factors within the university, they are crucial to the continuing value and role of universities.

Research Contexts

The rhetoric of the lifelong learning model, e-universities and the knowledge economy suggests that learning occurs everywhere. Universities do, however, continue to both signify and to constitute the primary physical site where the discourse and practice subsumed under the concept of 'higher education' occur. Yet, the processes within the black box of the university are rarely examined reflexively. These factors contributed to my decision to conduct in-depth research at specific university sites. I focused on Binghamton University, LeMoyne College and Cornell University, all of which are located in central New York State, each with a uniquely defined educational mission (described below). In an effort to understand some of the specific workings of discourse in actual cases of communication to students, and because language is the key means used within academic disciplines to produce scholarly knowledge, literally shaping the contours of what is perceived, deemed of value and studied, I chose to explore the vocabularies used across the humanities, natural and social sciences. I conducted a series of interviews with faculty and department chairs in Mathematics, Biology, International Relations/Studies and Philosophy. The interviews took place over a period lasting from August 2003 through February 2005.

To discover how language is used by departments to communicate with undergraduates, I asked faculty and department chairs a set of open-ended questions about their general departmental goals regarding students' thinking and writing, and about wider contexts like the role of the given discipline in society. Where relevant, documents such as course catalogs and departmental summaries, and observations of some classes and public lectures, supplement the interview data presented below. A set of more in-depth and extensive interviews took place at Cornell University, where a wider sample of faculty, staff, administrators and students was interviewed as part of an ongoing, separate research project.

A focus on language suggests, for the purposes of this study, at least three important levels of analysis. Language is, first and foremost, a locus for the ontological expression of the individual subject, identity or consciousness, as developed in works by Rene Descartes, Immanuel Kant, Martin Heidegger, Jacques Lacan, and Hélène

Cixous, to name a handful. Calvin Schrag writes that it is through language that we formulate the 'fragile presence' of the self which is both 'the who of discourse and the who of action', always embodied and active as a moral agent. Through narrative, we achieve the self against varying backgrounds of time and space, a self which is always 'an accomplishment, a performance' (1997: 33).

On a second level, we know that knowledge and authority/power become linked through language or discourse in many ways. This topic has invited rich analysis, ranging from structural-functionalist, linguistic models to semiotic, literary-psychoanalytical, critical discourse and social theory, and philosophical approaches (Austin, 1962; Burke, 1966; Saussure, 1966; Barthes, 1968; 1972; Foucault, 1970; 1972; Gramsci, 1971; Hymes, 1974; Eco, 1976; Fowler *et al.*, 1979; Fish, 1980; Ricouer, 1984; Bruner, 1986; Thompson, 1990; Bourdieu, 1992; Ochs, 1997; Rorty, 1998; Graesser *et al.*, 2003). Thirdly, in the specific contexts of knowledge production at the university, it is obvious but important to state that language, as in vocabulary, grammar and rhetoric, shapes the process by which ideas are transmitted. Humility, awe, wonder, control, fear – all are possible attitudes toward the unruly aspect of 'reality', which becomes disciplined and transformed through language into something manageable and clear, or at least partially knowable. At the same time, power relationships, expressed in part through ideological pronouncements and through the discourse of 'common sense', which Gramsci especially noted, work within and across disciplines and university contexts in a bewildering set of overlapping relationships which defy efforts to model them.

In one effort to pierce this complexity, Steve Fuller draws attention to the ways in which practitioners of the social sciences have controlled 'the circumstances under which they displayed their expertise'; elements of this control include 'a discourse that cannot be engaged without considerable prior technical training' and 'agreement on the generally progressive trajectory of the science's history' (1993: 146). John Hall uses the term 'the problem of values' to discuss sociohistorical inquiry and 'how contending discourses on ultimate purposes, goals, and routes to their realization frame the significance of an inquiry and its object' (1999: 33). This critical attention to technical discourse, narratives of disciplinary history, and value in scholarly inquiry is also applicable beyond the social sciences, as evidenced by the many studies of discourse, power, and practice in the natural sciences (Hesse, 1974; Zabusky, 1985; Latour, 1987; Bazerman, 1988; Traweek, 1988; Woolgar, 1988; Myers, 1990; Pickering, 1992; Halliday and Martin, 1993; Atkinson, 1999; Dear, 2001; Sapp, 2003).

While language is a means to invoke the 'spontaneous consent' of the subordinated, and to legitimize hegemonic or dominant power, for example through folklore and ideologies of what is 'natural' (Gramsci, 1971), it is also always a means for the imagination of 'emancipatory narratives', that is, alternative and counter-hegemonic, collective visions of society and the 'good life' (Lara, 1998). Understanding how the university is situated within this space of potentialities demands a multi-layered examination of what Schrag refers to as 'the narrating self ... [that] constitutes and understands itself as emplotted within interstices of stories already told and stories yet to be inscribed' (1997: 70-71). Individual narratives can reveal how institutional and disciplinary discourses either critique or reproduce dominant power.

Case Backgrounds

A brief review of the institutional histories of these three university cases will establish the institutional contexts for this study.

Cornell University: Located in Ithaca, New York, Cornell University had an enrollment of over 13,000 undergraduates and 19,620 graduate students in 2004. It was incorporated in 1865 by New York State as one of the 'land-grant' colleges and opened for business in 1868. While it has elite status as a member of the Ivy League, its distinctively public, foundational mission is still retained. The private, Research I university 'side'and the agricultural, veterinarian and other state school 'side' constitute a commonly assumed and referenced distinction at this geographically sprawling university.

Early documents reflect this enduring distinction. One sentence in the mission statement assumes a certain nobility in the learning process itself: 'There will be no petty daily marking system, a pedantic device, which has eaten out from so many colleges all capacity among students to seek knowledge for knowledge's sake' (*Catalogue of the Officers and Students of the Cornell University for the Academic Year 1868-1869, With an Announcement of the Terms, Courses, of Study, etc.* (1868): 68). *Cornell University: The Register 1900–1901* suggests the other side of the campus in stating that the leading object of Cornell is 'without excluding other scientific and classical studies, and including military tactics, to teach such branches of learning as are related to agriculture and the mechanic arts… in order to promote the liberal and practical education of the industrial classes in the several pursuits and professions of life'.

LeMoyne College: Le Moyne College in Syracuse, New York had 2,200 undergraduate students and 700 graduate students in 2004. The College was founded in 1946, after five years of planning and fund-raising. In a letter to the members of his diocese (who raised more than $1,600,000 for the school), Bishop Walter A. Foery wrote: 'Gigantic problems press in on us from all sides. Their solution rests fundamentally upon the knowledge of God's law and its application to these problems. To this effort Le Moyne is dedicated and consecrated' (*Preliminary Bulletin of Le Moyne College* 1946–1947: 5). Like SUNY Binghamton, an early emphasis on adult education was a distinctive part of LeMoyne's mission.

LeMoyne also has a long history of intertwining social justice issues into the curriculum. A major in Industrial Relations and a Bachelor's diploma in Business Administration were offered from the start. Both of these pursuits were described in terms of their relationship to Christian principles. For example, the Industrial Relations major is offered to help students understand 'problems confronting the three spheres of Industry, Labor, Management and Government' and 'the principles of justice and charity, upon which our industrial system must rest if it is to survive in our democracy' (*ibid.*: 15). The Bachelor's also includes 'ideals of justice and charity will be taught both on an intellectual and moral bases as criteria of the true Christian way of life' (*ibid.*: 16). The 1947–48 description of the School of Industrial Relations states that 'the philosophy underlying its courses is based on God's plan and law as applied to business and industry, labor and management, to the state and to citizens as individuals. The school is a laboratory of human values' (*Bulletin 1947–1948*: 41). Moreover, 'It offers a challenging answer to those who would destroy what is best in our Christian American way of life.'

State University of New York, Binghamton: In 1932, Syracuse University opened an Extension Division program in the Triple Cities area of Endicott, New York. A growing demand for courses led to the opening in 1946 of a branch of Syracuse University; its goals were to educate Second World War veterans in the area, to 'serve the people of the southern tier', and to offer 'complete sophomore sequences in Liberal Arts and in Business Administration' and 'preliminary courses in Applied Science and in Journalism' for first-year students, with work for Juniors and Seniors to be added 'as the College expands' (*Triple Cities College Bulletin 1947-1948*: 1). Another goal was to provide education so that those in the area could study 'while living at home'. The university was renamed Harpur University, moved to the Binghamton area, and then incorporated into the New York State university system in the early 1950s. The goals of this state system were described in the similarly humble terms: to provide 'a "comprehensive and adequate" program of higher education for the youth of this State', since its 33 separate post-high school units are intended to 'supplement, not supplant' the many existing schools in the state: 'what is perhaps the finest group of privately endowed colleges and universities of any State in the country' (*State University of New York: Annual Catalog, Triple Cities College, 1950-1951*: 7). SUNY Binghamton had 13,860 undergraduates and 2,826 graduate students in 2004.

The Value of a Major: Relevance and Philosophy

Across all three university sites which I studied, chairs of the Departments in Philosophy independently described their departmental goals in quite specific and similar ways. They referred to students as 'shopping' for a major, and to themselves as 'marketing' the major to students by making it 'relevant'. There was variation in the different qualities that were associated with relevance, a variation which seems to relate to differing institutional contexts and missions, which I will explain below. But, in general, while Cornell's Philosophy department has an emphasis on the analytical rather than the continental tradition, as opposed to the combination of both at SUNY Binghamton and LeMoyne, all three interviews shared the theme of relevance.

Obviously, no department representative would summarize her or his discipline in an interview as 'irrelevant'. Moreover, classroom experiences and curricular design yield very complex experiences for undergraduates beyond the wording of department chairs in an interview situation. But in the play of meanings surrounding the word 'relevance', there are notable dynamics across fields. These dynamics have implications for the planning of higher education in an era of university reform along 'rational' accounting principles.

The vocabulary of relevance may merely reflect the fact that campuses are becoming increasingly corporatized (although the alleged values of corporations are widely misapplied in university contexts (see Greenwood, Chapter 6, this volume); a stress on relevance may even be fairly unsurprising, given the tighter job markets which impact departments at all universities. Indeed, within the fields of Biology, International Relations and Mathematics there was also a focus on pragmatics and a discussion of preparation for future work. However, some faculty members in these latter disciplines also expressed the aesthetics of their respective fields freely, invoking for example the notion of 'a calling'. I will describe this sense of aesthetics further below, after a review of some key meanings of relevance.

The colloquial concept of 'selling' the Philosophy department or major to students was used in all three university contexts, as noted above. Ways of selling the major varied. The Philosophy department chair at SUNY Binghamton described the department's website and flexible curricula as among the efforts to make Philosophy (with over 100 majors) both appealing to students and relevant as an integral part of pre-professional training. This outreach has led to the department's openness to being part of double and triple majors, as well as its involvement in interdisciplinary programs like PPL (Philosophy, Politics and Law). PPL is a large liberal arts program that 'sells itself because people are convinced that it is pre-law and they take cognates from all over the university: economics, arts and sciences, and so on', as the chair stated. The department's hoped-for 'Learning Outcomes' for their majors include the ability to 'read with sensitivity to concepts, language, meaning context' and 'to develop arguments and communicate effectively', as well as to have 'knowledge of some major thinkers, periods, and fields of philosophy' ('Assessing the Philosophy Major', internal departmental document). These open-ended terms certainly lend themselves to the needs of the department, for they allow application by students to a variety of possible careers, including law. At the same time, scholars in the department were involved in and committed to the critical application of philosophy to contemporary political problems, as reflected in the comments of the chair and in research and publications displayed on bulletin boards in the hallway. This suggests a sense of relevance as related to current events.

This department chair also stated that members of the department 'assume that students and parents are interested in results beyond just a liberal arts education, so we repackage the field as useful, in other words, not just about the soul'. This juxtaposition of 'results' and utility in opposition to 'just the soul' is noteworthy. As May argues, relevance is an 'old and frequent visitor' to universities (Chapter 7, this volume: 123); in this case, its connection to 'utility' may suggest a relatively unexamined, cross-disciplinary usage that is simply a sign that people are being 'realistic'. But, are scholars of philosophy, in one sense, reducing the complexity and richness of meaning that has always been the province of their discipline? What is being lost in this shift? Since the first philosophers of ancient Greece, philosophy has been the realm of reflections upon the paradox, complexity and profundity of the human condition – the celebrations of life and the awe of confrontations with horror, with unknowability, with difference. Philosophy has been the branch of study where students confront the very issues of epistemology and certainty that underlie knowledge production: *how* is it that we know what we know. It is the process of introducing this kind of question that opens all authority claims to interrogation, allowing for the intellectual critique of the sciences, government and other powerful realms. While these aspects of study surely remain a part of the discipline of Philosophy, they are not explicitly a part of the message of relevance.

The pragmatics of disciplinary mission at SUNY Binghamton parallel those of the Cornell Philosophy Department's 2003–2004 course catalog entry: 'The study of philosophy provides students with an opportunity to become familiar with some of the ideas and texts in the history of thought while developing analytical skills that are valuable in practical as well as academic affairs.' This somewhat odd sentence humbly admits that such study is just one opportunity among many, while also invoking a more timeless, sweeping and grand reference: 'in the history of thought.' The stress on 'valuable' and 'practical' skills is notable. Even at a large, well-funded private research university like Cornell, with a heavy emphasis on pre-professional training, the Philosophy department (with about 90 majors) grapples with issues of relevance and seeks to make students competitive in a wider economy through an emphasis on 'rational' and 'objective' writing and thinking, for use in all fields and endeavors. The chair stated that the department aims to encourage students to engage in 'dispassionate, clear thinking and to be independent-minded, objective, rational thinkers', which she paraphrased as 'to not be swayed by the media'. They value 'thinking and reasoning with clarity, not just knowing facts, but learning to evaluate arguments and to engage in analytical thought, which is relevant in life, for example, in law'.

At LeMoyne College, the Philosophy department chair's mention of relevance was more explicitly grounded in the Jesuit and Catholic social justice tradition that is manifest in the college history. For example, he stated that the department is a bit 'weird' and 'off the radar' in relation to 'mainstream philosophy', in part due to the influence of the Catholic social justice tradition. His usage of relevance had a connotation that was less to do with practical job skills and careers, and more to do with an effort to be 'real' rather than esoteric. The areas covered in the department are 'diffuse, which is a worry; in general, we seek a balance between a historical emphasis (asking critical questions about figures and ideas) versus speaking to students in ways that are relevant to them right now. There is a big emphasis on political philosophy and ethics… an important analytical tool'. The department also aims at 'encouraging students to be critical of science and technology in an era that is so shaped by them, and to see language as a source of meaning and truth, with limits, as socially constituted, with potential'. Moreover, they seek to suggest: 'that living in the modern world should be seen by students as, in itself, a problem.'

Making social justice central to business and industrial relations, as described in early documents, thus remains an important aspect of LeMoyne's educational mission in the even wider contexts of the liberal arts degrees as well. Students are invited to study the subject of Philosophy on the grounds that they will develop analytical tools, but also that they will learn something which they can care about, which will be helpful in formulating critical assessments of social injustice. The possibility of combining practical and radical ideas seems unique and even exemplary in the cases of LeMoyne and SUNY Binghamton, campuses where inclusion of the less elite strata of student population is an explicit part of the institutional history. While Cornell too has its less elitist, 'vocational' or 'state school' side, a much deeper institutional history would be required in order to trace the threads of its social justice pedagogy.

The Relevance of International Relations and Mathematics

The notion of relevance was evident in the other narratives which I gathered, but with a different connotation. Besides the previously noted meanings – utility for students facing a tight job market, resonance with student realities, and a critical tool for those interested in problems of social justice – another sense of relevance emerged. In the discipline of global studies or international relations, relevance was related to characteristics such as timeliness, accuracy, depth of context, connection to history, ability to make a strong argument, and focus on current events in a complex world. A Cornell faculty member who teaches International Relations (which is not a major but rather a concentration offered through the Government Department) stated that undergraduate students should 'be able to articulate a relevant research question clearly, establish the criteria of evaluation, march through the relevant issues, and write a conclusion that explains what [the student] has learned'. His example of a relevant research question was 'the militarized crisis between India and Pakistan'. Another Cornell faculty member hoped that undergraduates: 'would develop a *non* US and *non* Eurocentric viewpoint … basically some knowledge of history and context.'

At LeMoyne College, the equivalent major is in the newly created Peace and Global Studies department, which evolved out of International Studies. While sharing with Cornell an emphasis on promoting non-Eurocentric perspectives, the sense of developing relevant skills was more explicitly phrased in moral terms by the chair of this department. For example, the documentation for the major reads: 'Like most Americans, LeMoyne College students need help understanding world affairs and other cultures. Their world will be one in which goods and services and capital move with breathtaking speed, one in which misunderstanding other cultures is not only unfortunate but dangerous, and one where ignorance and prejudice can result in horrible violence.' The chair of the department stated that the new major was 'part of the Jesuit approach that, especially with [the new President] coming from Central America, is consistent with the mission of the College, and that's a good thing'. He stated explicitly that the mission of the department was to prepare students to be better citizens in a complex world, and he hoped to also use its resources to promote a more global vision among the faculty as well.

In Mathematics, a dual emphasis on *both* relevance and aesthetics was evident, reflecting this discipline's unique position straddling both the more technical, applied fields and the humanities, through philosophy and logic. The Cornell mathematics department chair stated in an interview that 'Mathematicians almost universally see some kind of beauty in the work, almost an aesthetic sense in the way things fit together and different functions connect... .' With 150 majors and a flexible curriculum, this department graduates students who enter a variety of fields, pursuing PhDs in Math, Physics or Computer Science, or going into business or investment banking. The chair stated that while Wall Street employers might not see math itself as necessarily 'useful', the graduates are 'seen as capable of learning what needs to be learned, they can think clearly and logically'. Some students go into law school; again, in his view, they are valued because they 'have learned to think analytically'. Capturing both the relevance/utility and the more aesthetic aspect of the discipline, the course catalog text for this major notes: 'Mathematics is the language of modern science; basic training in the discipline is essential for those who want to understand, as well as for those who want to take part in, the important scientific developments of our time. Acquaintance with mathematics is also extremely useful for students in the social sciences and valuable for anyone interested in the full range of human culture and the ways of knowing the universe in which we live' (*Cornell University Course Catalog 2003–2004*).

After describing the relatively dismal job prospects in mathematics, a mathematics professor at SUNY Binghamton stated that he was 'not sure *why* students are coming into the major really, math is something that is in you, it's like a calling'. He himself had planned to be an electrical engineer, but then started taking math, and 'it just takes hold of you... mathematics is either in you or it's not'. Indeed, these uses of language suggested a certain comfort with the aesthetic and emotional side of knowledge, which is borne out in the Binghamton course catalog for 2003–04: 'Mathematics belongs both to the liberal arts and to the sciences. It is the language of the physical sciences (and, to some extent, of the biological and social sciences), and it is also studied for its own challenge and beauty. Current mathematical research spans a vast array of fields, from immediately applicable areas such as cryptography and optimization to beautiful problems in geometry and logic whose applications may not appear for many years.'

Biology: Beyond Relevance

Interviews with faculty in Biology did not contain explicit references to relevance. In fact, one could argue that the self-evidence of Biology's relevance to Cornell students is clear in a document distributed to the hundreds of students who take the intimidating Biology 101 course at Cornell: 'No matter what you have heard, this course is not used to "weed out" students from a pre-med track' (course handout). Rather than a discussion of relevance, the emphasis in interviews was on teaching undergraduate students one key parameter: what is science, and what is *not* science. This was stated with great firmness, although it turns out to be a fairly elusive concept.

Interviewees stressed that science has to do with a method, a process, a perspective on reality. The chair of LeMoyne's Biology department hoped that undergraduates would gain: 'an understanding of what science is, and more importantly, what it *is not* – that it is not an "end-all", but simply one way of asking and answering questions; there are only certain kinds of questions that science can answer: quantifiable, repeatable, measurable... an ability to read scientific literature and to assess what is valuable and to understand content; this is really important because it's all changing... You need to be able to read: to know enough and have basic information: to even know what to begin to ask about a subject... to know what you know. It's impossible to be an expert.' The Biology Department at LeMoyne has about 230 biology majors, and graduates 40–45 seniors each year. Of the latter, a few proceed to graduate (PhD) programs in some area of Biology, some enter health-related fields, and others obtain beginning-level research or technician jobs. The chair of this department hoped that undergraduates would be able: 'to express ideas clearly, concisely, and objectively... also, to analyze data and draw appropriate conclusions – a skill that takes longer to learn than undergraduates have.' The sense of trying to teach students within the context an overwhelming amount of constantly changing information was also evident in an interview with the chair of the Biology Department at SUNY Binghamton.

There are 1400 undergraduate students who major in Biology at Cornell; the program has a placement rate of 82 per cent into medical schools. As at the other university sites, the Director of the Office of Undergraduate Biology at Cornell stressed the need to communicate the enormous amount of factual content of biological sciences to undergraduates. He noted the many core requirements that students must take in a specific sequence, and the faculty's struggle to provide students with opportunities in what is being called 'The Century of Biology'. The Introduction to Biology course is an important introduction to 'the culture of Biology at Cornell' as well as a way to give them a 'factual preparation for the next tier'. The importance of students' experience of growing up at college was also an important issue, for, as he explained: 'we are responsible to give them what they think they need to get them out of here, and we need to be respectful of what they want to be.' He emphasized the need 'to educate them to be good citizens and functioning adults.' However, he acknowledged that with the 'credit-demanding' programs of study in biological sciences, there was little room for adding any more coursework on writing, ethics or diversity, issues which those on the curriculum committee realize should be emphasized. In this sense of regret, he echoed comments made by the Biology chair at SUNY Binghamton regarding writing issues and other tangential aspects of study.

The distinction between science and 'not science' deserves some elaboration, because it holds a key to a larger point about the aesthetics of knowledge and investigation. Humor and humility in the face of an awesome task was expressed by one Biology department chair in this sentence: 'You have to remember that you don't know the answer, or … you say "well, that may be the right answer, but it may be the wrong question".' This statement paralleled many other expressions that I heard. For example, a graduate student giving a presentation in mathematics at Cornell University on 'The Elliptic Curve Method of Factorization' stated during his talk: 'And the answer is, probably.'

This kind of sentence construction distills patterns that I observed at the graduate student and practitioner levels in biology and applied mathematics: notably, a high degree of informality and comfort within circumstances of intense paradox, complexity and uncertainty. Practitioners in these fields used metaphors of aesthetics, fun and pleasure in dealing with the huge amount of uncertainty within their fields of study, a usage directly at odds with the mainstream or popular image of science as a serious, objective, hardheaded, rational and even cold investigation into incontestable data and facts. The complexity of this point – paradox within rigidity – actually emerged most clearly in an interview with an undergraduate chemistry student at Cornell, who noted: 'They say in chemistry, you could try to memorize everything, but what you really need to do is "learn the chemistry" … That's what they say, it's not just rote: just think about what's happening in an experiment.' Later, explaining another point, he observed: 'The orbit view of electrons spinning is kind of wrong but kind of true, it's almost philosophical… Energy can only exist at certain levels; energy seems continuous to us, but it's not. Without certainty, it's just theory, not science… not a law.'

Interestingly, disciplinary histories include this sense of fun and express the random and creative nature of scientific discovery. 'Nothing in science can be proved', Graeme K. Hunter baldly states in a history of molecular biology (2000: xix). The physicist Erwin Chargaff once said 'molecular biology is essentially the practice of biochemistry without a license' (quoted in Hunter, 2000: 312). Data from interviews and lectures suggest that a sense of pleasure in profound unknowability permeates the world of both graduate students and practicing members of scientific disciplines.

This sense of fun in the face of mystery was, as noted, not so evident in the instruction of undergraduates. Professors in the natural sciences put far more emphasis on establishing, through language, exactly what is and is not 'science', always presuming that this dichotomy is discoverable and has nothing to do with values, with the observer, the context or 'the contingent'. This was evident for example in the corrections made to a first-year Cornell student's laboratory report for an introductory Biology class. The paper included the phrase: 'the eyes of hungry predators' as part of a lab report about a worm. The TA crossed out 'eyes of hungry' in red ink and wrote 'too dramatic' on the paper. A Biology professor at another university, upon hearing this anecdote, said 'Of course.' He went on to explain that a phrase like 'hungry predator' must be cut, 'because, how do you know they're hungry? Chances are they are, yes, it is poetic and probably accurate, but: *determining which data is inarguable is the key*' (emphasis added).

Such corrections on student writing are one means by which the apprehension of reality and the production of eventual knowledge are shaped. Fields like mathematics or biology, where the physical or embodied aspects of knowledge tend to be downplayed in epistemological, theoretical and methodological terms, not to mention in the kind of writing that is rewarded and expected, communicate a clear message that the fact of embodiment is irrelevant. This maintains what Karen Jacobs terms the 'long Western tradition of the disembodied observer... defined by their transcendence of the body – a body which, however, it remains their chief object to discover beyond themselves in another' (2001: 1).

Undergraduates experience this sense of rigidity and a de-emphasis on the embodied aspects of knowledge in their scientific education. Life is carefully distinguished into what is and what is not science, embodiment and emotion are irrelevant. The efforts to divide and distinguish between what can properly be called science and all else, or as Nancy Jay writes regarding sacrifice as both communal and expiatory, between 'A and not-A' (1992), occur at the undergraduate level. Yet at the same time, science seems to have also successfully claimed a position for itself at the graduate and practitioner level as the realm of inquiry into the unknown, into the boundless horizons of the as-yet-unimagined, into the nonlinear, the odd, the philosophical, the profoundly mysterious.

The language and style of academics as scientific *practitioners* reveals this in striking ways. For example, Cornell University lectures and presentations were marked by: (1) a disjuncture between the complex and even arcane abstraction of ideas expressed in signs, symbols and concepts (many of which are related to very grave topics such as illness and disease), and the informality, simple grammatical structure and playfulness in speech acts *about* these ideas; (2) a frequent attitude of humility and even self-deprecation on the part of presenters, in both informal and formal lectures; (3) in the informal talks, a taken for granted series of interruptions and good-natured but occasionally hostile remarks which were not necessarily disruptive of the process of proof, but which were actually cumulative, collaborative and productive of thinking, learning, and testing new knowledge; (4) few if any efforts to link the reported findings to wider contexts or implications; relevance was taken for granted.

One example of collaborative learning took place in the presentation on elliptic curves. The speaker began by defining **m** as 'a composite number', **p** 'as a prime dividing **m**', and so on. He then moved through a series of equations, which were written on the blackboard to support his overall argument. The small crowd of listeners gathered in the classroom grew increasingly restive. They interrupted the flow of his presentation several times, questioning and directly challenging his choices and assumptions. At one point, the audience was bickering among themselves over random numbers, nearly ignoring the speaker, and by the end of the presentation, he was met with silence and a few yawns, as someone admitted they were 'having trouble seeing how this is useful'.

Lectures that were delivered to larger groups differed from this general format, because spectator participation was limited to questions and comments, which took place only after a specific presentation by the speaker, but the sense of informality in speech was similar. In general, all of the scientific presentations were marked by very straightforward, basic sentence constructions, colloquial and informal nouns, verbs and adjectives. These simple forms of speech were used to explain individual components and systemic interactions that were impenetrable to outsiders. For example: 'As long as I have a GCD that's not **m**, I'm basically happy. The problem is, we might get **m**' and 'Basically you go forward with the thought that everything's nice, until it explodes.' Edited to remove the more technical aspects of the argument, the lecture on elliptic curves was structured in the following manner:

> So if we start off at a point whose GCD …
> and we add … a bunch of times…
> there exists a point such that this occurs…

In an example of comfort with nonlinearity, one lecturer on the topic of prediction and regulation of neuroplasticity in mammals focused on developing 'neuronal models with realistic dynamics, including a continuous remodeling character, using intra-cellular level aspects in system-wide contexts'. He admits that these cells are too small and inaccessible to actually do experimental data on, so they use in vitro data to extrapolate in vivo, 'with all the necessary caution'. Mathematics then becomes a key support in this extrapolation, because they can 'use a coherence matrix to characterize it even better … just put one in and see what it can do'. His findings were that 'at low frequencies, the I=O relation is *less nonlinear*', resorting to a lovely but vague concept: 'these are the harmonics of that… here they are higher harmonics.' Another lecturer stated that 'cardiac ganglia are involved in non-trivial integration of signals at the principal neuron level and the principal neurons are not just slaves of the brain, but able to take part in some local controls itself [sic]'. Another lecturer speculated about molecular processes thus: 'We think that the rate at which cargo is moving is driven by a mass action reflex. The number of molecules of VSVG being transported per minute is constantly changing, but is always a fixed percentage. This tells us it's *sensing* cargo in a very specific way; not just acting as an escalator. The rate is cargo-dependent … the cargo is in effect determining the rate. We're very interested in this.'

While phenomena which exhibit paradox, self-regulatory complexity and non-linearity are an assumed and accepted aspect of life in the natural sciences, the challenge becomes trying to, nevertheless, conduct something that all agree is 'science' within such intellectual uncertainty. This explains the humility of some individuals who speak frankly about scientific practices and ideas, but it also suggests that the traditional boundaries between disciplinary connotations may be shifting in important ways.

Aristotle categorized knowledge into the theoretical, practical, and productive or poetic. Edward Corbett writes that these distinctions are equivalent to knowing, doing and making (1984: vi). According to Corbett, the theoretical or scientific realm (*epistemē*) was, for Aristotle, different from art or *technē* in the same way that the necessary or inevitable differs from the contingent or probable. If, in fact, there is an ongoing exchange or shifting of metaphors and paradigms across disciplines, perhaps it can be understood as a recasting of these traditional, Western categorizations of knowledge, categorizations which were reproduced within both the modern and postmodern university but which are now being dissolved.

Perhaps the realm of the hard sciences is now able to combine all previously separate aspects of knowledge and claim them as its exclusive province: theory, practice and production, the latter in Aristotle's sense of poetics. Assured of their market niche and ample budgets, they are freer to signify themselves in the more 'emotional' or at least more descriptive terms, evoking humor, beauty, and humility, or phrasing ideas about careers around a notion of a 'calling'. Meanwhile the discipline of Philosophy, once signifying abstract and profound, timeless themes such as being, knowing and the pursuit of the good life, is being recast, at least to undergraduates, in more reductive, job-oriented terms. Faculty clearly perceive an imperative to present this discipline to students as one which is valuable primarily for its market relevance and its fostering of critical analytical skills. Imagining the reverse makes the point: for a Philosophy Department to try and attract students by invoking the 'calling' of studying the depths and complexity of being or the soul would probably be read as quaint, unrealistic, or outdated, not to mention irrational and overly subjective.

On one level, the simplest interpretation may be that language is emulating economic realities in this case. With changes in the job market and the wider economy, perhaps disciplines in the Humanities are redefining themselves using classic liberal arts terms that will sound attractive to undergraduates and their parents. But is that all that is going on? A slightly deeper analysis suggests that current hierarchies have established a privileged position for the harder sciences that enables them to co-opt the more glamorous adjectives and meanings associated with the pursuit of knowledge and higher education and thus to take advantage of students' idealism and enthusiasm. Students can be channeled into specific majors which are cast as having a 'higher' and deeper meaning, but which may lead to fairly rigid career paths, set increasingly by relatively unreflexive corporate- and government-driven research agendas. It is the subsuming of complexity and of moral and private meanings and the foreclosure of critique and reflexivity that may ultimately be most troubling, if the result is a decrease in the possibilities for non-scientists to engage freely in critical and alternative kinds of thinking and writing. One forum on ethical issues in nano-biotechnology held at Cornell featured a panel of 4 white males ranging from the age of 28–50, just one example of the aspects of privilege and power that I am suggesting here.

Conclusions

Linguistic framings of disciplinary relevance vary according to personal idiosyncrasies and institutional contexts. However, the dominant values of the consumerist society appeared in the many references to marketing a given discipline to undergraduates, or to students as shopping for courses and majors. While these terms may simply indicate the increasingly corporate aspects of university governance and social life, or a pragmatic awareness of the imperative to maintain numbers and thus departmental longevity and/or status, they also reproduce a rational attitude toward knowledge that is ultimately reductive of the rich and critical breadth in particular of the discipline of Philosophy. This suggests that many possible other meanings are being eclipsed, subordinated and lost. However, the discussion of responsibility to educate students as citizens who will have a role in promoting social justice, and who will critique dominant concepts, suggests that the imperative to redefine a departmental mission in terms of relevance does not necessarily imply a wholesale acceptance of corporate or consumer values.

My research also suggests the importance of mutually constitutive antagonisms between the humanities, sciences and social sciences. While hints of healthy agon may be more to do with personal and collective speech habits, the implications of these self-definitional struggles for those who manage university systems are worth considering. Can this sense of play and antagonism be effectively communicated to 'outside' stakeholders: taxpayers, parents, officials, policymakers? Or, perhaps the more important question is: can this sense of constitutive antagonism help in reconceptualizing the presumed 'town–gown' dichotomy to more usefully capture the multiple levels of interaction within knowledge production? Do we find this distinction to be reproduced *within* the university, in the form of adversarial relations between faculty on the one side, and staff/administrators on the other? If so, is this mutually constitutive antagonism productive of value in the workplace, or is it debilitating to participants? These and other questions can only be addressed with time.[2]

---

2   The research reported here was funded by the John S. Knight Institute's Writing in the Disciplines Program at Cornell University, which supplied me with a post-doctoral Research Associate position for the year 2003–2004. The Knight Institute's Jonathan Monroe was particularly supportive of my work. During the research and writing periods, Davydd Greenwood provided consistent support, and Bert Cramer was an invaluable source of research information, free exchange of ideas, and unique perspectives.

Chapter 9

Academics in the 'Knowledge Economy': From Expert to Intellectual?

Todd Bridgman and Hugh Willmott

Introduction

Universities are widely viewed as pivotal to the development of 'knowledge economies' in which 'brain power' is identified as key to maintaining established levels of material well-being and political stability. Simultaneously, established sources of funding – in most cases drawn from public taxation and supplemented by endowments – are insufficient to sustain a level of activity to compete effectively nationally and internationally. As a consequence, universities are under increasing pressure to work more closely, and in numerous ways, with other suppliers of funding – notably, the private sector.

The shifting landscape of higher education is not without significance for the positioning and role of academics within society. To meet the funding crisis, academics are encouraged and incentivized to emerge, in some cases kicking and screaming, from the closet, or ivory towers, of the university to engage with the wider world. Critics of the changing character of the academic's work and contribution – sometimes associated with so-called Mode 2 knowledge production (Gibbons *et al.*, 1994) – have cautioned that closer collaboration with the private sector indirectly fetters and compromises the distinctiveness and contribution of their role as economically independent producers of knowledge (Grey, 2001). There is a related fear that academics will hesitate to pursue their research or speak out (e.g. on social and environmental issues) whenever the exercise of 'academic freedom' could discredit their standing as experts and/or damage their chances of receiving Mode 2-type research programmes, especially when these provide an increasingly vital source of revenues.

In this chapter, we reflect upon the public role of academics, which, compared to the roles of teaching and research, has been neglected in the burgeoning literature on the contested character of higher education in contemporary Western societies (see, for example, Campion and Renner, 1995; Slaughter and Leslie, 1997; Doring, 2002; Graham, 2002; Willmott, 2003). Specifically, our focus is upon the contribution academics make as *intellectuals*[1] who, for us, are distinguished by a

---

1 We recognize that the meaning of, and the contribution ascribed to, 'intellectual' is contested. For some, its meaning is readily exchangeable with that of 'academic', on the grounds that academics are invariably highly educated, and therefore necessarily form part of

capacity to articulate and support views that transgress conventional understandings. Against the grain of current debate and analysis, we argue that the central position ascribed to universities in 'knowledge economies', and especially the incentives and opportunities to 'work in partnership' with new funding providers, can, in principle, serve to celebrate and extend this 'public role'.[2] Without denying that academics, who previously have been production-focused and transmitted their knowledge in rather esoteric and haphazard ways to potential 'users', are being urged to become more 'customer-facing', as a condition of receiving funding for teaching as well as research, we point to the contradictory process in which the commodification of knowledge production simultaneously creates spaces in which a positive value is placed upon academics as public intellectuals.

The privilege of 'academic freedom', combined with academics' social standing as 'authorities' and their experience in mass communicating through lectures makes it feasible, we argue, for academics to become 'public intellectuals'. There are increasing opportunities to play such a role as (late) modern societies become more dependent upon (risky) forms of scientific and technological knowledge to sustain and repair fragile social and ecological environments, and universities actively train and groom academics to engage with the media. While our discussion draws upon knowledge of higher education in the UK, we believe that our analysis has relevance for most advanced capitalist economies.

To orient our contribution, we compare and contrast two perspectives on the understanding of academics as public intellectuals: those of Weber and of Laclau and Mouffe. In Weber's thinking, academics are conceived as value-free experts working within specialized fields whose authority flows from their commitment to the ideals of science. This view, we suggest, has become the received wisdom. Laclau and Mouffe, in contrast, locate academics on a political terrain. Their thinking offers a fresh perspective on the academic's public role. The Weberian identification of separate spheres of fact and value is re-examined as a *performance discourse* that contributes to the constitution of the scientist as a value-free expert dedicated to scientific progress. That is to say, that Laclau and Mouffe do not regard the notion of the scientist as a value-free expert as a more or less accurate reflection of the role played by the scientist within a distinctive sphere of activity, but rather as an active participant in the constitution of a powerful myth. Applying Laclau and Mouffe's discourse theory, we argue that contemporary dislocations of social relations within higher education demonstrate the contingency of the identity of the

---

the 'intelligentsia', broadly defined. For others, it is important to differentiate these categories. Some academics may be 'well educated' and highly qualified, yet lack (or have had educated out of them) a questioning, 'intellectual' outlook on the world.

2   By public role, we mean communication between academics and audiences that extends beyond fellow academics, researchers and students. Amongst such audiences may be included policy-makers, business people, journalists, lobby groups as well as interested citizens. Interactions between academics and these diverse audiences often involve the articulation of expertise grounded in research activity, but cannot be reduced to this as academics may also comment upon matters that lie beyond their specialist sphere.

value-free scientist. Relatedly, we contend that the post-positivist critique of the notion of scientific progress, in combination with an increasing commodification of knowledge, is productive of antagonisms that destabilize established identities, including that of the value-free academic. Whereas Weber thinks of the academic as an impartial expert in a world of science, Laclau and Mouffe conceive of a multiplicity of identities forged and assumed in hegemonic struggles and through competing political projects. The academic as value-free scientist, as value-based critic, as entrepreneur and as activist (amongst others) – all such identities are articulated through discursive struggles and through processes of identification, and academics embrace and/or subvert elements of such discourses.

In reflecting upon the public role of academics, we enter a debate that explores the question of whether academics can/do/should adopt a value-free position as 'impartial experts' within a limited provenance of knowledge; or, alternatively, whether a value-based position should be favoured that allows comment and passing of judgements on matters within, but also outside, an academic's immediate specialization.

We begin by expanding upon our conception of the academic as a public intellectual in the context of 'knowledge economies'. We then examine the basis of the 'technical expert' position, its resonance with Weber's conception of science as 'value-free', and the implications of post-positivist attacks on these claims. Contrasting the Weberian standpoint with the thinking of Laclau and Mouffe, we reflect upon the implications of contemporary debates on science and the contemporary relevance of universities, and we argue that these debates are not unequivocally damaging for the role of academics as 'public intellectuals'. Laclau and Mouffe's thinking, we contend, can provide new insights into how hegemonic projects – such as the reconstruction of higher education as an arm of economic policy – produce (rather than encounter) their own limits as a consequence of the impossibility of fully suturing social space. We conclude by suggesting that there are conditions of possibility for academics to assume a more public role as 'critic and conscience' of society.

The 'Knowledge Economy' and the Public Role of Academics

Starkey and Madan (2001) have argued that a new articulation of the academic's role in society is critical to the future viability of the university within increasingly competitive markets for knowledge production. Universities, they contend, are the last bastions of Mode 1 knowledge (discipline-based and theoretical) in a world that increasingly demands and rewards Mode 2 knowledge (transdisciplinary and practical). Unless the role of the academic shifts to providing Mode 2 knowledge for external stakeholders, universities will find it increasingly difficult to demonstrate their relevance within the 'knowledge economy'. The counter-argument is that the 'competitive advantage' or USP of the academic universities over corporate universities is their independence. From this it follows that any move to negotiate the agenda of science with other, 'practical' parties risks compromising the very distinctiveness of universities and thereby endangers their *raison d'être* (Grey, 2001).

These conflicting assessments share a degree of recognition of how knowledge is produced within relations of power that differentiate and legitimize its claims. What counts as 'knowledge' is increasingly understood to be an outcome, as well as a medium, of power relations. An acknowledgement of this connection is symptomatic of the 'post-modern condition' (Lyotard, 1984: 7) where it is more readily accepted that 'the exercise, production and accumulation of knowledge cannot be dissociated from the mechanisms of power; complex relations exist which must be analysed' (Foucault, 1991: 165); in which case, the division made between Mode 1 and Mode 2, for example, is not an innocent one.

The identification of Mode 2 as having greater contemporary relevance is not without its own power/knowledge effects in shaping policy and legitimizing particular kinds of practices and identities. It aspires to supplant the dominant discourse of knowledge-for-its-own sake by a discourse where knowledge is a commodity – something that has an 'exchange value' (Willmott, 1995). In the knowledge-for-its-own-sake discourse, value freedom requires academics to be answerable to science alone – that is, to themselves. In the knowledge-as-a-commodity discourse, in contrast, the value of scientific practice is contingent upon its contribution to generating knowledge that has market value – either directly to a research sponsor or indirectly to a performance measure that operates as a quasi-market mechanism for resource allocation. Weber's value-free academic was, in principle, answerable to the community occupying the sphere of science, and not to commercial imperatives. In contrast, for the contemporary academic, the reverse is increasingly the case.

When reflecting upon the question of academics' public role, Furedi (2001) suggests that the key question 'is whether academics assume a public role as a technical expert or as an intellectual'. His answer is that, in relation to the public role of UK academics at least, the tendency is to be positioned as technical expert rather than intellectual. 'British university authorities encourage their staff to go public – not as intellectuals or members of an intelligentsia, but as "experts"' (Furedi, 2001: 5). *Experts* restrict their comments to their area of specialized knowledge, providing an ostensibly authoritative voice that rests upon an ascribed impartiality underpinned by a commitment to scientific objectivity. In contrast, the interventions of *intellectuals* encompass, but also extend beyond the confines of the expertise derived from specialist training and research. To be an intellectual is to 'rise above the preoccupation of one's own profession' (Bauman, 1987: 2).

Our analysis intersects with Foucault's (1980) thinking on 'power-knowledge', but we place greater emphasis on the increasingly commodified field of social relations, exemplified by the notion of the 'knowledge economy'. In the following section, we consider Weber's discussion of 'science as a vocation' whose celebrated focus upon value freedom remains central to established wisdom about the status of academics and the nature of their public role.

A Weberian Perspective on Value Freedom

For Weber (1919a: 9), specialization is the way of making a 'definitive and worthwhile' contribution to scientific knowledge; it is also the only legitimate means of contributing to the public sphere. Scientists contribute in two related ways. First, Weber argues, they provide factual, value-free knowledge that presents an alternative to prejudice and preconception; and, second, they recognize and respect the limits of scientific knowledge with regard to its impotence on matters of moral choice or value commitment. Intellectual integrity involves establishing facts and determining logical relations, which includes acknowledging 'inconvenient facts' (Weber, 1919a: 22); but it does not, for example, set out to provide politically uncomfortable evidence. Weber's identification of the limits of the scientist's sphere of competence is founded upon his appreciation of the irreconcilability of conflicts between different value spheres. The sphere of science is limited to answering 'if' questions, rather than 'whether' questions. Authorities in medical science, for example, can answer the (technical) question of how to prolong life, but they have no place in answering the politico-ethical question of whether life should be prolonged, just as technical experts in nuclear science can answer the question of how to make or destroy weapons of mass destruction but are not qualified to adjudicate on whether or when such weapons should be made, used or disarmed. Freedom from value judgments defines not just the limits of science as a vocation but also restricts its cultural reach and claims (Scott, 1997).

Qua scientists, academics are urged by Weber and his followers to avoid engagement in politics. Political engagement is seen to risk confusing and compromising the confidence of the public in scientists' producing and disseminating unbiased, factual, value-free knowledge. This position is illustrated by Tsoukas and Cummings (1997: 668) who first note how 'in organization studies, the opposition between facts and values has historically won wide-ranging acceptance' before observing how Simon (1976), for example, argues that 'unless we keep facts uncontaminated by values we risk not being scientific' and that 'ultimate goals such as particular notions of profit, efficiency, or human conduct, cannot be debated within scientific discourse' (Tsoukas and Cummings, 1997: 668). On this view, scientists must be free from political commitments and dependencies if their analysis is to produce the value-free knowledge that, for Weber, is pivotal for making informed value judgments (see Schluchter, 1979: 108; see also Alvesson and Willmott, 1996, Chapter 2). Unless this division is respected, knowledge claims made in the name of science become suspect or unreliable, as findings are understood to be susceptible to corruption by extra-scientific pressures. Any temptation to meddle in public life by blurring the boundary between the provision of factual information and the expression of opinionated views must therefore be resisted. The vocational challenge for scientists is to do everything in their power to expel values and politics from the sphere of science. It is for this reason that value freedom is the 'duty' of the scientist, as well as the distinctive quality of the sphere of scientific activity.

Shumway (2000) recently affirmed this view when he berated the humanities for departing from the Weberian ideal by encouraging relativism and/or endorsing political correctness. This departure, he believes, has undermined academics' authority by conveying the impression of deviating from the ideals of objectivity and disinterest upon which professional expertise and credibility is properly founded. Shumway urges academics to proclaim objectivity publicly as a goal even though 'our abstract knowledge holds that disinterest is impossible' (2000: 167). The condition of possibility, and perhaps also the justification of this seemingly hypocritical stance, which chimes with Weber's 'ethic' of responsibility (Weber, 1919b), is 'that the public continues to value disinterest and to believe that there is knowledge above politics' (Shumway, 2000: 167). It is by appealing to, and affirming, this popular belief that scientists can best secure credibility and authority for their knowledge claims.

Neo-Weberians acknowledge the force of the post-positivist critiques of Weber's intention to place 'facts' and 'values' in watertight compartments (e.g. Gouldner, 1973: 63). They argue, nonetheless, that this fiction can, and must, be maintained (with the collusion of a public that is willing, or has learned, to accept it) if modernity, founded upon the demystifying effects of scientific knowledge, is not to slide into irrationalism and nihilism. Academics are urged to reassert the established discourse within which they are inscribed as specialized experts who are distinguished, *qua* scientists, by an unequivocal commitment and capacity to distinguish facts from values, and politics from science. While recognizing that a stance of value freedom is unlikely to render academics politically dominant, the neo-Weberian claim is that it will at least make them politically relevant (Schluchter, 1979). In short, the commonsense idea and expectation of the academic as 'technical expert', which is legitimized by Weber's argument, is understood to empower, rather than impede, the contribution of the academic to the public sphere by limiting their role to advancing specialist fields of expertise.

A Laclau and Mouffe Perspective on Value Freedom

In this section we present a discourse-based account of academic identity, drawing primarily on the discourse theory developed by Laclau and Mouffe in *Hegemony and Socialist Strategy*. We interpret Weber's position, as set out in *Science as a Vocation,* not principally as a stance that distinguishes the realms of science and politics and demonstrates the value of this (essential) separation but, rather, as a discourse that operates to identify the academic as a value-free expert. Instead of conceiving of the 'value-free expert' as a successful detection of the distinguishing feature of the realm of science and the identity of its inhabitants, value freedom is understood as constitutive of science and scientists as essentially neutral and impartial. We argue that the critique of positivism has contributed to a weakening of its credibility and constitutive effects. Coincident with this disruption, we contend, is the dislocatory effect of commodification within higher education.

It is important to appreciate that Laclau and Mouffe's thinking marks a radical break with other uses of the concept of discourse in the social sciences. Rather than restricting its scope to linguistic phenomena, they include all social practices and relations, arguing that 'every object is constituted as an object of discourse' (Laclau and Mouffe, 1985: 108). While acknowledging that objects have an existence external to their discursive articulation, they contend that they have no meaning until articulated within particular discursive practices. Analysis, as Burgin (1982: 9) has argued, 'does not find its object sitting waiting for it in the world'. To take the example of water, it is 'not the same theoretical object in chemistry as it is in hydraulics – an observation which in no way denies that chemists and engineers alike drink, and shower in, the same substance' (*ibid.*). Discourses are social and political constructions that establish a system of relations between objects and practices, while providing positions such as 'scientist' or 'intellectual' with which social actors can identify or dis-identify.

One of the fundamentals of Laclau and Mouffe's approach is the '*openness of the social*' (Laclau and Mouffe, 1985: 113, emphasis in original) and the 'undecidability' (Laclau, 1990: 21) of what, in social analysis, is widely represented as the realms of 'agency' and 'structure'. For Laclau and Mouffe, identities are contingent and negotiable as there are no universal laws of history and no political agents motivated by preconstituted interests. Social conflict occurs as agents encounter antagonism in their efforts to establish and reproduce identities. They necessarily produce 'an Other' as the boundaries of identity are drawn: the other is produced by the very process of identification. Likewise, social structures are undecidable in that they presuppose a discursive exterior that both constitutes and threatens them. *Dislocation* is the process by which the contingency of identity becomes evident. The congenital 'failure' of the structure to confer identity on social actors 'compels' the subject to act in order to restore or affirm a sense of identity. Subjects are 'thrown' into history and are forced to take decisions. They are recurrently forced to identify with projects that are inescapably political (small 'p') in formulation and the discourses they articulate (Laclau, 1990).

Drawing on this framework, we can deconstruct Weber's writing to focus on how 'the academic' is discursively constituted through the organizing practices of particular discourses. Weber states that those who embrace science as a vocation are *engaged in science for science's sake* and not merely in order that others may achieve commercial or technical success or be able to feed, clothe, light or govern themselves better (1919a: 13, emphases added). Weber stresses that attributing value to the disinterested pursuit of knowledge cannot be justified by scientific means. 'It can only be interpreted with reference to its ultimate meaning, which one must accept or reject according to one's ultimate attitudes towards life' (1919a: 18). But he has no doubt that the value sphere of science is distinguished by its disinterested development of knowledge. In Weber's thinking, the academic is constituted within a discourse of progress that provides science with an identity distinct from other cultural activities. 'Scientific work is harnessed to the course of progress. In art, however, there is no progress in this sense. Each of us scientists knows that what one has worked through will be out of date in ten, twenty or fifty years. That is the fate of science; indeed, it is the true meaning of scientific work, to which it is subjected and devoted in a sense specifically different from all the other elements of culture, where the same thing is generally true' (1919a: 12). If science means knowledge for its own sake, then scientists are positioned as people who have no interest *qua scientists* in dealing with questions of value or in exploiting the technical or commercial potential of their work. In this discourse, the academic-as-scientist is constituted as a value-free expert pursuing a project of progressive knowledge production within a specialized field of inquiry.

Attention to Laclau and Mouffe's discourse theory highlights the contingency of identification with the value-free 'technical expert'. From this perspective, attempts by academics to identify with its position produces 'an Other' that cannot be represented within that discursive field. A discursive field is characterized by a 'surplus of meaning' that can never be exhausted by any particular discourse. While particular discourses attempt a universal fixation of meaning, they are disrupted by a radical contingency that prevents this from occurring. Discourses and identities are both relational: they depend on their differentiation from other discourses and identities. They are therefore inescapably and recurrently vulnerable to meanings that are excluded in a discursive articulation (Laclau and Mouffe, 1985).

Returning to Weber's writing, his attempt to fix the meaning of scientific work around the identity of the value-free expert produces 'an Other': namely the value-based academic, who cannot be represented within the discourse of the pursuit of knowledge for its own sake. The discursive outside is, in this case, represented by 'anti' or 'post'-positivism. Whereas positivism articulates an aspiration to attain higher forms of consciousness that anticipate a limitless future, post-positivism incorporates an awareness of limits; of reason and of ideals (Laclau, 1990). The antagonism between positivist and post-positivist discourse has a dislocatory effect, not least within the social sciences where the positioning of the social scientist as 'value-free' expert is destabilized as it is subjected to critical scrutiny.

Our argument is that the positivism/post-positivism antagonism is a key moment in a postmodern crisis of identity for academics within the contemporary university that has coincided with an intensifying process of commercialization and commodification. Talk of commodities immediately takes us back to Marx, for whom market capitalism is inherently expansionary and 'all production becomes commodity production' (Marx 1978: 220). One route for this expansion is through the extension of market relations into previously non-market sectors, including higher education. Laclau and Mouffe acknowledge the central importance of capitalist production and its commodification of the world. But they reject what they detect as residues of economic reductionism and determinism in Marx's theorizing. From their standpoint, commodification is analysed discursively. Following their thinking, it is within a discourse that represents economic life as a 'knowledge economy' that knowledge becomes a commodity. In other words, a vital precondition of capitalist development is the discursive identification of artefacts as commodities. This has also created spaces for critique from a variety of different discursive standpoints

– spaces that have been further expanded by growing public wariness of science and its effects in the aftermath of experimentations with science-based forms of energy generation, housing development, land cultivation, soil propagation, oil transportation, animal husbandry, etc. In this context, the contemporary university is a key institution in, and object of, a discursive struggle concerning the status and value of knowledge, and the capacity of scientific knowledge to provide fixes for social and ecological as well as economic problems.

The role of universities in addressing such problems is articulated through New Right discourse – comprising elements of neo-liberalism, public choice, neo-conservatism and libertarianism (Harris, 1998) where students are viewed as investors, as well as consumers, in the educational market place. Relatedly, New Right discourse mistrusts the collegial governance of universities preferring instead a private sector model in which vice-chancellors operate more like CEOs and full-time managers replace rotating heads of departments, deans, etc. Only a version of a private sector model, it is believed, will successfully implement the changes – in teaching as well as research – required to harness universities directly to the demands of product and labour markets. In this discourse 'students' are constituted as 'consumers' who undertake a university education to acquire 'skills' and 'knowledge' that have value in the new 'knowledge economy'. Academics are 'service providers' who strive to meet the needs of these individual consumers (Prichard, 2000). As researchers, academics are incentivized to undertake work that has a commercial or technical application or which, at least, can be turned into publishable outputs that have 'exchange value' in attracting funding. For university management, the discourse of commodification is articulated in packaging and selling the university on the basis of the exchange value that is attributed to its value-adding activities.

What, then, of the significance of these changes for the public role of academics? Academics have long been respected and rewarded for presenting themselves as value-free experts. New Right discourse endorses and reinforces this identity: academics and their institutions risk denigration as 'politically motivated' or 'biased' when their actions are construed to depart from the expectations of such discourse. In the contemporary university, academics are strongly encouraged to foster links with industry. The 'sale' of publicly subsidized and seemingly impartial expertise to private contractors offers an attractive, or at least expedient, way to supplement the income of universities, their departments and their staff who are increasingly 'incentivized' to participate therein. The development, harnessing and promotion of expertise then become part of a departmental or corporate competitive strategy to attract funding from sponsors. In addition to the appeal of comparatively low-priced contracts subsidized by public funds, the positioning of academics as independent technical experts provides a competitive advantage relative to other suppliers. This market-positioned commitment to value freedom is most probably not what Weber had in mind when he talked of a vocational and moral commitment to value-free science founded upon the pursuit of knowledge for its own sake. But the discourse of value freedom does lend itself to such (ab)use. The value of Laclau and Mouffe's thinking is that it leads us to understand value freedom as a discourse that is readily aligned to the technical application and exploitation of knowledge. It is a commitment based on an instrumental concern with the maintenance of scientific authority, a concern that directly coincides with the neo-Weberian 'management of appearances' (Shumway, 2000).

Discussion: Implications for the Academic as Public Intellectual

Much of the literature on the commodification of higher education is pessimistic about the preservation of the identity of critic, especially those works which employ Marxist conceptions of society to suggest that economic logics determine political and discursive processes (e.g. Slaughter, 1988; Winter, 1995; Soley, 1996; Taylor *et al.*, 1998). Laclau and Mouffe forcefully reject this determinism. For Laclau and Mouffe, social relations are becoming increasingly dislocated through commodification, but 'this does not mean that the only prospect thrown up by such dislocations is the growing passive conformity of all aspects of life to the laws of the market' (Laclau, 1990: 51). New Right discourse attempts to fix the identity of academics' as experts. Yet, this discourse is located within a discursive field that is suffused by a surplus of meaning and therefore can never be exhausted by any specific discourse. No matter how dominant the project of the New Right becomes, it can never completely articulate all elements in the discursive field as it is defined by what it opposes. Just as the discourse of positivism created the conditions of possibility of post-positivism by what it denied and suppressed, so too, according to this logic, will the discourse of the New Right act to construct the identity of that to which it is opposed.

Departing from both structuralist and humanist conceptions of Marxian or leftist formulations of social change, Laclau and Mouffe do not advocate a straightforward resistance to commodification. Instead of waging a defensive struggle against an inexorable structure by constructing a project that opposes it, they argue that struggles should acknowledge the reality of commodification: 'Commodification... should not necessarily be resisted. Rather, one should work within these processes so as to develop the prospects they create for a non-capitalist alternative' (Laclau, 1990: 56). These new historical possibilities are political constructions formed by hegemonization of the social space, and are not determined by the internal logic of capitalism.

Consider, then, the prospects for the value-based academic or 'public intellectual' who ventures outside of a disciplinary specialization to contribute to public debates. We have already acknowledged that identification with the hegemony achieved by the knowledge-as-a-commodity discourse is impeded by the low exchange value credited to the critic's role. Yet, there are academics who embrace the role of critic. The standard explanation of their actions offered in non-deterministic accounts of such defiance is that some academics are not completely captured by dominant discourses. Some agents develop and embrace alternative subterranean discourses and through their resistance transform structures that are constituted by those discourses. Laclau and Mouffe's post-Marxist thinking, in contrast, conceives of how the public intellectual is accommodated and represented *within* the discourse of knowledge as a commodity. Encouraging a faculty member to embrace the role of a public intellectual is not necessarily inconsistent with a competitive strategy intended to attract more students and funding. In a fiercely competitive context, building a distinctive profile becomes a strategic goal for departments and institutions; faculty being in the public gaze is consonant with this strategy. If their contribution is controversial, it is more likely to attract media attention. Even though the views might not reflect the views of senior university management, it is generally the case that 'any publicity is good publicity' so long as it does not bring the institution into disrepute.

Notably, Noam Chomsky, Professor of Linguistics at MIT, is a valuable asset for MIT not just because of his work in linguistics, but because of the publicity he has attracted from his staunch criticism of American foreign policy and other developments in society, including commodification. As a recognized public intellectual, Chomsky implicitly demonstrates the *independence* of his university which, unlike private corporations, think-tanks or other policy-forming institutions, is ready and willing to retain staff who, in some quarters, are castigated as enemies of the state. In the UK, the most prominent media pundit in the field of management, Cary Cooper, was recently hired by Lancaster University in a move to raise the wider public profile of its academically excellent Management School. While Cooper is not a radical critic of industry policy, he has repeatedly raised uncomfortable questions about the quality of working life, the attitudes of managers towards employees and issues of work–life balance. His value for Lancaster, however, resides primarily in the 'name check' they receive on every occasion that he appears on radio or television and each time he provides a 'sound bite' for the press.

According to Furedi (2001), universities in the United States are, on the face of it surprisingly, more active than their UK counterparts in encouraging such work. 'It appears that their support of the public intellectual is motivated by the conviction that achieving a high media profile is essential to safeguard the viability of the institution.' The University of Chicago, for example, prides itself on its stable of public intellectuals, including John Dewey, Susan Sontag and Allan Bloom. It is part of the university's brand that differentiates it from 'lesser' institutions that cannot afford – symbolically rather than materially – to accommodate such independent voices, as they would risk the loss of the endowments and grants from industry upon which they have become increasingly dependent. We foresee that a similar trend will emerge in the UK as universities seek to attract, train and actively support staff who are capable of fulfilling the profile-raising role of stimulating or developing public debate. The voicing of concerns about public issues can, of course, be interpreted as a form of resistance against commodification, but it is work that is legitimated by that discourse and, thus, operates productively yet subversively within it. The academic as value-free expert is not the only identity possible within the commodified context of the contemporary university.

Conclusion

A recognition of the political character of academic interventions in public life as contended by Laclau and Mouffe's discourse theory will doubtless disturb those who believe the future of the university depends on academics respecting and defending the ethos of the value-free expert. This includes followers of Weber who are persuaded by the idea of value-free science: a science that can provide impartial facts with which to inform political decisions; and also neo-Weberians, who advocate that academics should maintain a façade of objectivity in order to remain politically relevant. In our view, it is necessary to surrender the myth of value freedom as an ideal, and as an instrument of professional legitimacy. It is also necessary to challenge the assumption that abandoning this myth renders academics defenceless against the pressures of commercialization. Jettisoning the role of the academic as impartial expert opens up space for an appreciation of the interdependence of politics and knowledge; and, accompanying this development, there is the prospect of forging a more legitimate role for the academic as a public intellectual who acts as 'critic and conscience' of society.

The public intellectual can accommodate many of the demands of Mode 2 knowledge without compromising the 'independence' that lies at the heart of the university's traditional *raison d'être*. Since 'independence' contributes to the added-value or 'unique selling point' of universities in the market for knowledge, it can be maintained in a commercialized and competitive context. In an environment where universities are anxious to raise their profile, the role of the academic as public intellectual may be actively encouraged, even, and perhaps especially, when he or she speaks out against the status quo – so long as this challenge to orthodoxy is regarded by the public as an indicator of the institution's independence and its determination to stand firm in the face of political pressures to silence such critics.

§2: Organising Engagement: Practices and Impacts

Building Bridges over Troubled Water – A Tale of the Difficult Cooperation between University and Region

Stephan Laske, Maximilian Egger and Claudia Meister-Scheytt

Introduction

Do you know Mr Tur-Tur? He is a character from the children's story 'Jim Button and Luke the Engine Driver' by Michael Ende (1963). The strange thing about Mr Tur-Tur is the fact that – contrary to our usual everyday experiences – he reaches ever bigger, more threatening and more terrible dimensions the further away you are. This is why he belongs to the species of 'fake giants'. Looking at the relationship of universities to their surrounding regions, one often gets the impression that they also see each other as 'fake giants' – better to avoid them and keep contact to a minimum. It certainly is difficult to gauge in detail whether the often found mutual ignorance stems from a lack of common interests, the arrogance of academia (or praxis!), a lack of common language, pronounced mutual prejudices, a shrinking away from the effort needed for discourse, or an inability or unwillingness on the part of each to fulfil the expectations ascribed to them by the other. It is clearly a whole bundle of possible reasons that complicates the relationship. Still, there are numerous arguments in favour of a closer connection between university and region, and examples of functioning co-operation. What we want to show in our example is that successful cooperation is not just a matter of goodwill, but depends on a number of preconditions, coincidences and the ability of all involved to resolve inevitable ambiguities again and again.

University and Region – Casual Affair, Marriage of Convenience or Love Match?

Universities are impressive – sometimes oppressive – organizations. Their existence is usually seen (in the abstract) as a bonus to the locality (Czarniawska and Wolff, 1998). On the other hand, it is often hard for people outside the university to come to terms with the particular culture that is specific to the university as an organization and to the people socialized into it. After all, the image of the ivory tower, shut off from its surroundings and society at large, is no empty phrase.

It expresses emotional and probably also cognitive distance even where there is geographical proximity.

But are universities not organizations that do not care where in the world they happen to have been founded and where they are currently located?[1] Have they not always been orientated towards international scientific communities, which are suspicious of strong references to local conditions and regard them as provincialism (Pellert, 1999)? Does an emphasis on the regional role of a university not mean that you are failing to see the bigger picture in academic and academic-policy terms? Does it not make you an anachronism, given globalization and the creation of ever larger political, cultural and/or economic entities? And, lastly, does this not also mean that the development potential of those working in the university, and of its future users, is gravely restricted, if its (mental) horizon ends at its regional boundaries (Laske, 1988)? Such questions suggest that the relationship between region and university is by no means unproblematic. Let us consider this in a bit more detail.

If one looks more closely at the challenges facing universities in the twenty-first century, it becomes clear that in many places the state is withdrawing more and more from education policy decisions and leaving the universities to their own devices under the appealing slogan of 'accountable autonomy'. In countries where the state traditionally takes on a weak role in matters of education, it abandons the universities to the 'forces of the market'. Linked to this retreat from (education) policy is usually also a financial withdrawal, at least de facto a more or less deep cut in state budgets. Economizing is now the order of the day, with all the inherent risks to university identity. Autonomy therefore is often more a 'child of the crisis' than an outcome of improved understanding (cf. Clark, 2004). Hence universities must reorientate and reposition themselves. State universities, at least those in Austria, are changing from being a state-dependent 'service units' to being more or less 'autonomous organizations', where, increasingly, processes must be initiated and implemented to formulate strategy and vision, create new management and control structures, and to establish new reporting systems for evaluating how resources are being used (Pechar and Pellert, 1998; Pechar, 2003; Meister-Scheytt and Scheytt, 2005; Burtscher, Pasqualoni and Scott, forthcoming). The universities must ask themselves how they can and will fulfil their public service responsibilities as convincingly as possible – and answer to others on the same point too. Then, if not before, and to the extent that the state releases them from its (financial) care[2] and they gain distance from it, the universities will also

---

1   Given the influence of new information and communication technologies, universities can no longer be clearly localized in any one region. Just think of those universities that are pursuing regional diversification strategies (like, for instance, the Australian universities in Asia-Pacific).

2   In fact this is, say, a sort of financial abandonment dressed up with ideology and phrases. All the same, the management instruments associated with the intended framework control, e.g. management by objectives, evaluation, knowledge reporting, strategic controlling and not least the governance structure are meant to ensure permanent if a bit more subtle state influence on the university. This form of governance without government seems to be inherent

realize that it is precisely a grounding in the region which can become a central political and strategic element in their future development (Davies, 1997). The re-rationalization of the universities might become a building block in a 'marriage of convenience' at precisely that moment when 'politics' is emphasizing the privatization of the public domain (Atkins *et al.*, 2000; cf. Marquand, 2004).

From the point of view of the region, two broad arguments can be identified in support of such a trend. On the one hand there is an *economic rationale* (Parellada, 1999): universities create jobs for academic and non-academic staff; the universities, their personnel and students act as customers for products and services within the region; university spin-offs provide stimuli to the economy; research foci are established in order to develop regionally relevant expertise in cooperation with local firms, etc. Altogether successful cooperation brings a climate of openness, readiness for innovation and future orientation into the region. Companies and public institutions have a need for qualified staff and expert advice that academics can supply, while the university can hope for financial support from the region if it is able to offer services that are relevant to the development of the region. In short: in economic terms, university and region is a potentially fruitful pairing.[3]

There is an additional dimension, which remains largely invisible but has its effect nonetheless. It involves mainly the actors who build up a more or less emotional relationship with *their* university. Starting points are personal experiences as a student, the wish to belong, knowing someone at the university or an alumnus, the simple pull of 'the place where you are from', the fact that one's children study there or might even work there later. Systematic efforts to keep the relationship of the alumni to their university alive would be another element in looking after indispensable 'social capital'.[4]

There are a number of structural aspects that form obstacles to a closer cooperation between university and region (we are referring here to the model of state universities that predominates in Austria). There is the constitutional responsibility of the Federal State for university matters, that is to say that *de jure* the regions are not required to support the universities in any respect and therefore find it relatively easy to deflect their requests. In addition there is the loose coupling within the universities (Weick, 1976; Orton and Weick, 1990) – to date the university governing body has only very limited powers to demand specific cooperation from the relatively autonomous

---

in the new public management praxis and is often not obvious straight away (Moldaschl and Fischer, 2004; Loacker *et al.*, 2005).

3   This idea is not new, by the way: as far back as the thirteenth century, the city of Bologna got into trouble when the frustrated students left and the city realized its considerable economic loss.

4   Austrian universities have a considerable potential for building goodwill and relationships around the public graduation ceremonies, which draw thousands of visitors (usually from the region) each year. However, the actors do not seem to be aware of this. Meanwhile the celebrations themselves have developed into a considerable economic factor.

sub-units. The legal status of university teachers as civil servants strengthens this independence further.[5]

Good intentions for cooperation in themselves are clearly not enough – in order to become effective they need particular preconditions. In one respect university and region should have a sure head start for developing mutual relationships and understanding: universities are *eo ipso* a collecting point of pluralist concepts of the world, values, logic and rationality systems, in which the paradox and the contradictory are constitutive elements. In our opinion, the same is true for regions. Any regional development that restricts itself to knowledge transfer into the region, spin-offs from universities and so on, reduces the region to an economic complex and ignores the fact that cultural, public, social and ecological concepts of the world, values, logic and rationalities are at work here too and need to be balanced. Just think of HGV transit on the north-south routes crossing the Alps, a phenomenon experienced and suffered by the region every day. In this case, economic considerations and interests are in diametrical opposition to ecological, health and social policy demands.

Whatever the details, the task of making university and region future-proof, the fact that they are mutually dependent and the opportunity of making use of the other for one's own goals, make the expansion and intensification of a cooperation a reasonable proposition for both sides. The strategic advantage of a close cooperation lies in the fact that, on the basis of equality in the sense of a cooperation of equals (Goddard, 1997), the difference between the partners – in the sense of differing competences and potentials – can be leveraged (see also Greenwood, chapter 6 this volume). This presupposes that both sides know these potentials, a matter with which we shall deal later. Next, we shall present the concrete situation that provided the basis for our case study.

The Case Study

Starting Point: Who was Sleeping Beauty?

Any situational analysis, any narrative includes an intrinsic arbitrariness: where does the story start?; what criteria are being included?; what is being left out?; when and how should you end?; how should you interpret acts, situations, effects and side-effects? Such subjectivity in the selection applies all the more if one is or has been involved in the processes, as is the case here. We shall at least try to reduce the risk of blind spots, of viewing things through rose-tinted glasses or creating heroes, of post hoc justifications – in short, the risk of establishing a mere façade of rationality (Meyer and Rowan, 1991) – at least to a degree, by employing the different extent of our involvement in the case in question in a collegial triangulation, that is, in the form of a constructively critical reading and checking of the various interpretations.

---

5   This does not stop them, however, from entertaining private (and sometimes quite lucrative) relationships with companies and institutions in the region.

The case itself concerns the University of Innsbruck, a medium-sized state university in Western Austria. The time span for our example extends from 1984 to 2005.

Until recently the university consisted of seven faculties (the faculty of medicine was hived off in the course of the most recent organizational reform of 2003 and turned into a separate university). The regional catchment area is comparatively large. The university is a so-called *Landesuniversität* (regional university) for the provinces of the Tyrol, Vorarlberg and the Alto Adige; currently there are roughly 23,000 students who come mainly from the surrounding regions. For a very long time there was no comparable institution of tertiary education within a 150 km (nearly 100 mile) radius.[6] Within the last few years, however, several *Fachhochschulen* (praxis-oriented university-level institutions) have successfully established themselves within the catchment area, not least due to continuous political support at federal and provincial level.

Our case concerns the situation in the Faculty of Social and Economic Science (*SoWi-Fakultät*).[7] It only became an independent faculty after separating from the *Fakultät für Rechts- und Staatswissenschaft* (a combination of law, jurisprudence, economics and social and political science) in 1976, and for years afterwards suffered under a legacy of quality defects. In terms of student numbers, *SoWi* is one of the largest faculties in the university (containing, on average, roughly 25 per cent of all registered students); in terms of staff, however, it is considerably worse off.

The faculty contains three subject areas: economics (traditionally overrepresented, given its student numbers), the – internally somewhat fragmented – social sciences, and management studies, which carries the main burden of education but has not managed to present a coherent stance to the outside world due to its internal heterogeneity. Cross-disciplinary cooperation used to be the exception and relied mainly on personal contacts. In the mid-1980s the lack of identity and common purpose manifested itself tellingly in the fact that the institutes that made up the faculty were distributed over nine different sites across the town.[8] Initially, there was little external pressure for change. The university budget rose continuously, enough to quieten latent inner distribution conflicts. There were de facto no systematic contacts between faculty and region, even if academics from individual institutes carried out regionally relevant studies (for instance, on the economic effect of the university or the regional hospital, or on community finance).

The economic structure of the region is dominated by SMEs, with relatively few internationally active big companies. The service sector accounts for a very large part of regional economic performance, not least because of the strong position

---

6   In 1997 the Free University of Bolzano was founded. To date it has four faculties and is on target to establish itself in the region.

7   Our arguments in the following sections are made essentially from the point of view of this faculty.

8   A former dean summed up the situation like this: 'Running this faculty is comparable to the role of a flea circus director – but without a sack to put the fleas into ...!'

of tourism (roughly a third of the regional share of the domestic product depends directly or indirectly on this sector of the economy). Therefore work opportunities for graduates are limited. For better or worse, they have to hold their own in national and international job markets. Only over the last few years has the provincial government been pursuing an active regional economic policy targeted at creating economic clusters. Nor has there been much discernible interest in cooperation with the faculty on the part of the economy or social institutions in the region, except in a few individual cases. And in those cases where a visible cooperation might have been possible, controls were introduced to ensure that the university teachers involved had not in the past cooperated with the 'wrong' (political) partners.[9]

Sleeping Beauty was practically everywhere. Regardless on which side you want to localize her, she was fast asleep most of the time and did not even dream of the kiss of a fairy-tale prince…

Where Did Impulses for a Change Come From?

As the description of the initial situation should have demonstrated, the faculty received no lasting external impulses for development in the 1980s, nor was there much cause for change within. The major trigger eventually came from rising student numbers, which necessitated a substantial expansion and an influx of younger staff, particularly in the area of management studies. In this context, the lines of decision-making in appointing new chairs took on an important role. At the time the University Organization Act 1975 (UOG'75) was in force, which envisaged appointments being carried out by autonomous commissions. Once the shortlist had been drawn up by these commissions, there was no higher body within the university that could officially challenge it, rather it was sent directly to the ministry. This central authority was responsible for negotiating with the shortlisted candidates and implementing the appointment. In the composition of the appointment commission, which was regulated by law – professors made up only 50 per cent of the members, the other 50 per cent were made up of non-professorial faculty [*Mittelbau*] and of students. Therefore new appointments were sometimes made against the preferences of the majority of professors.[10]

In our concrete example, in addition to this important structural condition, there were several major factors that added an impetus to the proceedings.

---

9   Even though Austrian industrial relations are characterized by pronounced fraternizing tendencies (social partnership), at the same time there were – and still are – clear 'demarcation lines' between left and right and a concomitant thinking in camps.

10 One can easily imagine the wealth of informal attempts on the part of the universities to intervene in the wake of such decisions. They aimed either at underscoring the short list or at 'flipping' it. In the mid-1980s the responsible Ministry for Science and Culture did not automatically view it as discrimination if a shortlist had support mainly from the non-professorial faculty or the students, therefore interventions on the part of the professors were not always successful.

A growing number of students were frustrated with the quality of education on offer. With a few exceptions, it hovered at a rather low academic level; teaching was strangely 'anaemic' and abstract, with little reference to practice and little intellectual challenge; international cooperation was rare. Nor were these deficits always balanced by a corresponding strength in research. The substantive interest shown by students and the formally generous possibilities for their becoming involved in decision-making made up an important potential resource for the ensuing process.

Substantive demands for innovation in teaching methods were made by several newly appointed, younger colleagues, who brought with them professional experience and expectations from other university sites and other – sometimes international – university cultures and identified a need for concrete action. Here, the existing image problems of the faculty constituted an important push factor. The bad reputation of a place also damages individual reputations and with it future working opportunities, career chances and professional mobility. The initiative also happened to fall into a phase, during which innovation in teaching methods was being proposed in higher education policy but was in most cases only implemented half-heartedly.

Moreover, behind the measures described below stood the interest of the initiators in demonstrating that internal and external cooperation was possible and beneficial to all involved. At the same time this was an attempt to enhance intra-faculty coalitions between individual institutes and the students, in other words, the activities also had a clear micro-political perspective.

While these things were going on inside the university, there was increasing public suspicion that the universities were not taking on their public service responsibilities in a sufficiently active manner and so were not contributing enough to an ongoing knowledge transfer between academia and society. Talk of the 'demystification' of science (cf. Habermas, 1971) could be seen as the synonym for a growing legitimation crisis of the universities.

Preparations for the First Date ...

The first public 'performance', that is, the presentation of the offer of cooperation by the initiators to the region, was based on the following considerations:

- The search was on for a 'product' that would promise students, potential partners in the region and the university teachers involved a clear benefit, that could be provided without great financial input and was consistent with academic values.
- The 'product' was to have the potential for a brand, should, if possible, have a direct regional reference and should be on offer over an extended period.
- Access to this 'product' had to have a low threshold; it had to show a positive cost-benefit-ratio for all involved and still break even in the medium term.

These more abstract criteria were matched by idealism on the part of the protagonists and by a very concrete and almost limitless 'resource' that is rarely activated in university education processes in a systematic manner and to a sufficient extent: hundreds of students, having started their courses with great enthusiasm, were ready to be intellectually challenged, to be infected with the enthusiasm of their teachers, and to prove their own capacity in practice.[11] As they get nearer to finishing their studies, soon-to-be graduates are quite keen to explore their future employment possibilities and to gather experience that will enhance their chances of getting a job.

Meanwhile numerous organizations in the region potentially had a considerable need for consultative services, which often remains latent, whether for financial reasons, out of insecurity vis-à-vis professional consultants or out of a concern that consulting external advisors might be understood as weakness. In SMEs in particular, management often comes across issues that would benefit from an enquiry but cannot be processed in the course of everyday activity due to lack of time or the means to let a third party professional deal with it. If one could assess this demand, so the thinking went, and link it with the knowledge and the commitment of the students as well as the substantive competence of the academics at the faculty, it would add up to a proposal that would meet the conditions listed above. However, one would have to take into consideration that SMEs take a fairly sceptical view of university institutions and often doubt that 'otherworldly theoreticians' could be of use to them.

The Size and Shape of the Dowry

To avoid the bureaucratic restrictions associated with state universities, the initiators established a private charity, invited colleagues from neighbouring institutes to join[12] and negotiated a start-up grant from the ministry of about € 35.000 with the assurance that the project with the brand name *Patenschaftsmodell Innsbruck* (P-INN) would be self-funding after two years if not earlier.[13]

For the public institutions, associations and companies as (main) regional partners and the students of the faculty there was a differentiated bundle of services on offer:

---

11 At the beginning of the project there were around 3800 students registered at the faculty. It would, of course, be naive to assume that all students corresponded to this 'ideal type' and that there were not also some 'marginalists' among them trying to 'go for the easy option'. Experience over many years, however, shows that students are ready in principle to get enthusiastic if they have found a task that makes sense and represents a challenge to them (see also Kappler, 2004). Another important aspect was the fact that most students came from the region and were fairly level-headed.

12 The invitation was only accepted by the younger professors and their assistants. It is hard to gauge what the motives behind the rejection by the others might have been: stand-offishness vis-à-vis the world of praxis, a fundamentally different concept of the university, a more distant attitude towards the students, an a priori individualistic stance – there are many possibilities (and most likely multiple causes).

13 This promise was kept. For 17 years now the model manages to reach an average annual turnover of between 80,000 and 100,000 Euros.

it was made up, for instance, of joint training events for students and practitioners in the area of project management and social skills, systematic organization analyses by students within the scope of seminars,[14] regular involvement of entrepreneurs as teachers, presentations of companies as future employers etc. The core element of the cooperation, however, was a project dealing with a practical issue in an organization, which had to be worked on by two students within a limited time-frame. The project was coordinated by one member of staff from the client and one academic from the faculty who supervised it in terms of content as well as method. The client had to pay the direct cost of carrying out the project, a contribution to the overhead costs of the association (the amount of which has risen from an initial € 350 to € 2000 at the time of writing) and a freely negotiable performance bonus to the student project workers.

Two concrete examples may serve to illustrate the course of such a project. A manufacturer of cable cars with a site in Western Austria turned to P-INN to find students who would produce a feasibility study on the profitability of a materials transport cable car along the mountaineering route up Mt Everest. The company paid for two students to go to Nepal and explore the situation. In their final report the two also mentioned the potential ecological and social implications of such a project, so that in the end it was not realized. The other example is that of a small retailer in Innsbruck selling fair-trade products. In view of the difficult market situation, the shop manager was invited to develop a marketing concept for his shop in order to contribute to its survival.[15]

For the students there were three main incentives for committing themselves to a P-INN project: first, it satisfied their desire to apply their recently gained knowledge; second, the project usually provided the basic content for their diploma thesis; third, cooperation in the project often represented a way into permanent employment.[16]

Acceptance in the Region

The media presentation of the concept triggered an instant and unexpected reaction: professional management consultants feared the emergence of new competition behind a university 'front'. At that time, access to the consulting

---

14 A report on the implementation of this type of event with several companies from the region by one of the authors and his team was awarded the *Österreichische Staatspreis für besondere Leistungen in der Hochschuldidaktik* [Austrian state prize for outstanding performance in teaching in higher education].

15 In this case, of course, all costs were covered by the association. As a token of public responsibility, every year 2–4 projects are carried out free, for instance, for social service institutions.

16 This effect is not to be underestimated: SMEs are traditionally very reluctant to employ business administration graduates. In direct cooperation with the university they were now able to observe at close quarters that the students were efficient and committed and that the lack of suitability ascribed to university graduates was based mainly on their own prejudices.

profession was controlled by the consultants themselves and carefully guarded against intruders. The argument that this was a training model and that competent consultants could not possibly have anything to fear from a competition with students, while formally unassailable, did nothing to lessen bad feelings.

The real intended recipients, however – public and private companies in the region as well as students – reacted very positively. The benefit for the people involved had been successfully and clearly communicated, which prevented the emergence of any significant reservations vis-à-vis this new form of cooperation. On the contrary, the participating companies as well as the P-INN students emerged as excellent carriers of the message and references for the acquisition processes that followed. Here is a selection of indicators for the positive regional impact:

- Altogether, over the past eighteen years, around 560 projects involving public institutions and companies have been successfully concluded, 420 of them in the geographical vicinity of the University of Innsbruck.
- A number of partners brought several projects into the cooperation. Innsbruck City Council, for instance, negotiated a bundle of twelve simultaneous projects, which were realized over roughly eighteen months.
- The cooperation partners are really diverse: as expected, small and medium-sized enterprises dominate. On top of that there are public institutions, for example, old people's homes or the manpower services, as well as large companies with international business. Very occasionally even the university itself has taken advantage of its own resources.
- Approximately 25 per cent of the students have found jobs in the initial partner organization. By now this has led to 'second-generation projects' being offered quite regularly.

A Critical Reflection: On Balancing Ambiguities

Even if the cooperation model can be described as successful in principle, it would be incorrect and at the same time naïve to present it as just a success story. It would mean losing most of the inherent potential lessons, were one to skip over the obstacles that had and still have to be overcome by all involved in the precarious balance between cooperative partnership and market-like expectations. We therefore want to reflect critically on those almost inevitable tensions emerging from the impact of region, students and university on each other, which has to be shaped and dealt with time and again. Triangular relationships have a reputation for being difficult social set-ups and this applies to our example too. Expressed in a more abstract fashion: as a general problem for the cooperation between university and region in our case we identify the fact that the parties involved each orientate themselves according to the logic of action of their own system of reference, that is, the logic of market, money, scarcity and development interest on the one hand, and the logic of science, learning, limited abundance and interest in truth on the other.[17] These logics are often in conflict with each other, as we shall demonstrate below.

The first area of potential conflict is the individual *concepts of time* of the partners. The problem starts with the fact that project definitions often stem from a pressing practical problem and therefore quality solutions are needed as quickly as possible. The students, however, are participating on a voluntary basis, so the management of P-INN must present the projects and partner organizations in such an attractive light that competent interested students and staff supervisors come forward as quickly as possible and start working on it. Especially in non-teaching periods – 'black holes' in the schedule of the university – this cannot always be achieved, so that some cooperations have stalled at this early stage. Time pressures in the world of companies and regional institutions are difficult to synchronize with the idiosyncratic temporal rhythm of the university system.

Moreover the relative *standards of success* of university education and practical work seemed to contradict each other in several cases. For the praxis side, functionality has priority and not a theoretical 'correctness', as in the saying, 'practice is what works but is not correct – theory is what is correct but does not work'. Here the students often got into a fix between pragmatism and reflection. This became particularly apparent in the assessment of diploma theses. While the regional cooperation partners were usually very satisfied with the work of the students, the supervisors often criticized a lack of theoretical reflection.

In this context *quality assurance* must also be mentioned as a potential area of conflict. Although on acquisition it was made clear in principle that the project work by the students could not be equated with that of a professional consultant, the university actors found themselves under pressure to succeed. After all, each successfully completed project was a step towards building up the reputational capital essential for the continuation of the concept as a whole. This not only meant carefully assessing the potential of the students when assigning them to projects; in the odd crisis, the supervising university teachers felt obliged to take on more responsibility within the project than had been envisaged initially, even if all participants would have learned more from a 'failure'.

Just as informative and instructive for students, academic supervisors and the management of the partner companies alike was an area of conflict that we shall call *the impossibility of non-interference*. An example: in the course of a company analysis, about 35 students in working groups studied ten different issues in a medium-sized enterprise in the region over three days. The questions initially envisaged by the supervising professor covered factual and staff-related issues in an even spread, for instance about stock keeping, distribution, the competitor situation, the leadership quality of the management, support for junior staff, etc. The management only agreed to the study after all topics that they considered risky had been struck off the list and replaced by functional questions. When the staff was

---

17 On the ensuing problems for the development processes of the universities see for instance Meister-Scheytt and Scheytt, 2005.

interviewed, however, the eliminated issues – particularly those concerning HRM – de facto re-emerged. When the results were presented by the students, the CEO, despite his previous announcement to the contrary, stayed for four hours instead of one and took an active part in the discussions.

A highly sensitive problematic area we identified concerning *differences of status*: Critical external feedback is accepted in the companies and organizations, if the person giving the feedback is considered sufficiently competent and experienced. If the criticism comes from students, however, it has to be justified in a lot more detail. The owner of a fast-growing software company, for instance, ordered a study into the recognition of the product he distributed. In the final discussion he freely admitted to getting more and more irritated while reading the report, because the results were clearly more negative than he had anticipated. Initially he assumed that the two people working on the project must have got their methods wrong. In the course of his reading, however, he realized that the problem did not lie with the methods applied but with his own over-optimistic assessment.

Lastly we identified a particularly difficult problem, which transcends our case study really. It is the *system of incentives in academia*. Time and again, it makes it very hard to apply the principles of volunteer spirit and solidarity, but these are precisely the principles on which the cooperation model rests. Those university teachers who agree to supervise projects are not getting any financial or other extrinsic incentives for their extra commitment. This is not a problem, 1) as long as the time invested is recognized as work by the university system and it does not conflict with other input demands made on them, and, 2) as long as there is internal solidarity throughout the institutes involved.[18] With a rather narrowly defined idea of efficiency gaining in importance and the number of publications becoming a central criterion for careers, investing time in activities that are probably good for shaping the relationship with the region but are irrelevant for an individual career seems an increasingly irrational move for the staff. Here you hit the limits of the chosen form of organization: private associations must be seen as a thorn in the flesh of control-orientated, centralist systems like the Austrian universities after UG2002.

Summary

Looking at the common experience of region and university over the past two decades (as represented by our model), one can distinguish constant and changing aspects. Among the constant aspects are eager and committed students looking for challenges and tasks within their courses that stretch them. Constant, too, are the practical questions and issues, the answers to which may change over the decades but the questions remain. Constant, lastly, is the fact that the companies, regardless of size, industry or site, are looking for cost-effective and innovative answers and

---

18 This call for solidarity must be understood in two senses: on the one hand to achieve a relative balance of commitments and on the other to avoid free-riding, i.e. relationships built up within the framework of the model must not be exploited for the benefit of individual institutes.

solutions to their problems and are convinced that university and students can help them find these. So what has changed?

Let us remind ourselves of the initial metaphor of Sleeping Beauty. In the course of the last two decades, Sleeping Beauty has greatly changed her looks. Several operations involving the instrument of 'university reform'[19] were supposed to make Sleeping Beauty more beautiful, radiant and attractive than ever (that was the hope of the initiators, the state and higher education policy). A new name was found as well: Sleeping Beauty was now to be known as www.weltklasse-uni.at. However, the operation did not proceed without complications and unintended side-effects: complex systems often defy a trivializing make-over.[20]

An increasing orientation towards quantifiable performance indicators, combined with the persistent upholding of values from traditional academia, are leading to a potential devaluation of cooperations with the region. In universities that focus on individualized and individually apportionable academic performance like the ones that, in line with international developments, have come to dominate the Austrian higher education scene, research, i.e. publications in internationally renowned journals, is taking on an *overriding* importance. This shift of emphasis alone systematically reduces the weighting of all other activities, and among them cooperation with the region.

At the same time, the loose coupling typical – if not the raison d'être (Weick, 1976; Laske, 1997) – of educational organizations, is being replaced more and more by a tight coupling. The loose internal coupling of the organization that is the university made – and as yet still makes – it possible to retain precisely those open ends at the boundaries of an organization which are essential for making quick and unbureaucratic contact with what lies beyond – the region, 'the practical realm', the companies. Increasing hierarchization and efficiency-driven control of the university necessitates the deployment of resources in line with strategy and in a homogenizing manner, thus coupling the universities more tightly (Leitner, 1998). This in turn endangers the continued existence of those loose ends for ties with the region. One can observe tendencies to make P-INN fit into the 'programmed' system of performance constitution. In areas where the proven model balks at the process of 'making it fit', it runs the risk of being excluded – the system brooks no opposition.

Another systematic problem that is becoming relevant in this leverage-orientated age of audit at the universities, is how to present the positive effects of the cooperation model for the university and the region. It is obvious that around 420 completed projects with comparatively little expense and a lot of voluntary commitment must have positive effects on the knowledge and problem-solving capacity of the students, on the reputation of university and faculty and on the professionalization

---

19 From the University Organization Act 1975 on to the University Organization Act 1993 and then on to the University Act 2002 plus several curriculum reforms.

20 We can see this kind of trivialization, for instance, in the unconsidered application of business control instruments that were designed for companies to universities, without taking into account the latter's organizational particularities.

of the management in the region. These effects, however, are not individually *measurable and calculable*. This makes it hard to include them in the usual key figures systems that dominate the university context and serve as focal points for goal-setting and contract management. P-INN must therefore legitimize itself by qualitative-argumentative means beyond key figures. In the current indicator climate this means a systematic disadvantage in legitimization vis-à-vis other, more easily quantifiable performance areas (for example, exams held, talks given at conferences, publications in academic journals).

Another, somewhat critical, conclusion concerns the manner of the cooperations developed. If one looks at how the structure of the cooperations between university and region has evolved over the past two decades, then individual actors from the region addressed individual questions to the university or to P-INN, which were then dealt with as described above by individual students and their supervisors. The people involved have developed extensive competence in generating practicable individual solutions. Essential for the future, however, given the much-hyped knowledge society, is for the university in its entirety to be understood by the region as a knowledge pool and as a societal and cultural factor that can be productive for the region in a variety of ways. This has several implications. One, other parts of the university must also open themselves more to the outside world and must no longer see this as the sole privilege and duty of the management studies section. Two, university and region must consider much more systematically what they need the other for and what they can and will learn from each other beyond the solution packages offered by P-INN. Three, from the point of view of the university it would be desirable for the region to reflect more critically and constructively on the development of the university than it has done up to now. It is not very helpful to accuse the university constantly of lacking in management quality, efficiency and benefits for the region and practical life. If the university is to learn from the practical realm, as is often demanded publicly, then this cannot mean copying over concepts into the university that have long proved to be dysfunctional in practical life. Rather, it means finding appropriate forms of cooperation that facilitate learning from each other repeatedly, and making proper use of them. An attitude of 'I know better' would not contribute much for either side.

One often neglected output that is just as important for the university and its sub-units at faculty level, is the evolution of a particularly committed network of alumni. The vast majority of the so-called P-INN graduates are much closer to their faculty and their former supervisors than other students. From this network stem not only the second-generation P-INN projects described above, but also a readiness to commit more thoroughly (sometimes also financially) to the development of the faculty. Caring for this potential, nurturing it and expanding it with new projects, is not just a duty, but can be a beneficial activity for the key figures in faculty and university. After all, the status of alumnus of a university stays with you all your life and therefore remains as a permanent aspect of the activity in P-INN – at the least as a nostalgic reminder, at the most as the prospect for an ongoing productive form of gaining experience and orientation for your actions.

Chapter 11

Community Engagement in Developing a New Campus: The Griffith University, Logan Campus Experience

Christine Smith and William Lovegrove

1. Introduction

This chapter documents the establishment of a new campus of Griffith University in a socioeconomically disadvantaged area close to a major metropolitan city. Original planning for the campus involved considerable community consultation and involvement to ensure the development of career-relevant and innovative degrees, delivery modes and learning-support mechanisms that both matched regional needs and interests and took advantage of modern communications technology. Engagement with the local region has been continued and enhanced over time with a strong focus on facilitation of socioeconomic change and development through the establishment of strategic alliances with community organizations and increased interaction with local and state economic development agencies as well as industry and business leaders.

Recent years have seen a significant growth in interest in the role of universities in regional and community development in many developed countries (see, for example, National Committee of Inquiry into Higher Education, 1997, Robson et al., 1997 and OECD, 1999a in the European context; Garlick, 1998, 2000, and 2002, and Nelson, 2002a and 2002b in the Australian context; and Kellogg Commission, 1999 and W.K. Kellogg Foundation, 2002 in the North American context). Changes in national higher education policy in Australia as well as high levels of economic and demographic growth in the South-East Queensland region have seen Griffith University change from a single-campus-based institution of around 5000 students in 1986 to become a large multi-campus-based institution with more than 26,000 students spread across a corridor of 70 kilometres from Brisbane to the New South Wales border by 2002 (Griffith University, 2002b). Most of the new Griffith campuses emerged between 1989 and1992 as a result of amalgamations with small former non-university-sector higher educational institutions – for example the Mt Gravatt and Gold Coast campuses were former colleges of advanced education, while the South Bank campuses were formerly the Queensland Conservatorium of Music and the Queensland College of Art. These amalgamations took place in response to federal government policy arguing that economies of scale could be achieved in higher education and that a reduced number of larger institutions should result in improved corporate governance for the sector as a whole (Dawkins, 1987; 1988; Smart, 1997). No other Australian university entered into as many amalgamations or experienced such rapid growth in student numbers over this same period (Griffith University, 2002b). By contrast, Griffith's Logan campus was established in the late 1990s on a 'green-field' site to the south of Brisbane and commenced teaching in 1998 with federally funded student load places transferred from elsewhere in the institution – primarily its original Nathan and Mt Gravatt campuses. The original impetus for the Logan campus originated in the Logan community and considerable care and attention has been given to linkage with this community in its short history. This chapter documents this relationship while at the same time attempting to place it in the context of global and national trends in both higher education and economic development more generally.

In section 2 we discuss recent changes in the nature of the global economy and, in particular, the growth in importance of the so-called 'knowledge economy'. Implications of these changes for regional development processes and policies are also highlighted. In section 3 we shift the focus onto how universities are increasingly being seen as having an important role to play in enhancing the ability of their regions to adapt to this changing economic environment. In sections 4 and 5 we provide an overview of key regional engagement strategies put in place by Griffith University at its Logan campus. It is too early to evaluate in detail the impact of a number of these strategies, however an attempt is made in section 6 to identify areas for improvement based on a comparison with strategies adopted by other institutions and from the results of evaluations conducted to date.

2. Knowledge Economy and Its Implications for Regional Development

Since the mid-1970s enormous transformations have been observed in the nature of the world economy. In particular the capitalist system is generally agreed to have changed as OECD observes:

> from a system based on mass production, Keynesianism, macro-economic management and the welfare state to one characterized by widespread economic and political deregulation and the emergence of more decentralized forms of economic organization. (OECD, 1999a: 18)

This has resulted in what some (for example, Goddard and Chatterton, 1999a) term a 'new geography' of capitalist activity resulting from an increase in internationalization of production and enhanced mobility of capital on the one hand and a decrease in the capacity of nation-states to regulate and control economic behaviour within their territorial boundaries.

These factors have combined to create a renewed interest in the role of regions in the economic development process, with Kanter (1995) in a book entitled *World Class: Thriving Locally in the Global Economy* arguing that the regional (or local) environment has become as relevant as the national macroeconomic situation in determining the ability of enterprises to compete in the national, supra-national and global economies. In this context then the role of state and regional authorities has shifted from being an arm of a national welfare state to a catalyst for local cooperation and linkage of local firms and organizations to national and global networks (Storper, 1997; OECD, 1999a).

Within this environment Florida (1995; 2002) argues that knowledge creation and transfer, learning and creativity become the major determinants of regional economic growth and sustainability. Successful regions within this new age of capitalism must in effect become 'learning regions'. The latter concept derives from studies on national systems of innovation, for example Lundvall (1992), Lundvall and Johnson (1994) and Morgan (1997) wherein a learning economy is defined according to Chatterton and Goddard as:

> an economy where the success of individuals, firms and regions reflects the capability to learn (and forget old practices); where change is rapid and old skills become obsolete and new skills are in demand; where learning includes the building of competencies, not just increased access to information; where learning is going on in all parts of society, not just high-tech sectors; and where net job creation is in knowledge intensive sectors (high R&D, high proportion with a university degree, and a job situation worsens for the unskilled). (Chatterton and Goddard 2000: 479)

In the Australian context the 'Knowledge Nation' and 'Smart State' strategies of the Federal Opposition and the Queensland Government can be seen as local responses to these emerging global economic trends (see Chifley Research Centre, 2001 and Queensland Government, 1999, respectively).

Storper (1997), among others, questions the importance of nationally initiated regional and urban regional policy initiatives in this environment and warns that knowledge embeddedness in a learning region needs to be 'built simultaneously and synergistically from the bottom up' or else a new type of regional periphery will emerge based on the access to such knowledge. Along a similar vein Garlick (1998; 2000) notes that there has been a shift in regional development policy in Australia away from a top-down compensatory approach to bottom-up facilitation in which regional development authorities need to come up with solutions to their own economic viability issues and service needs and map out initiatives to generate sustainable futures. In a later paper he goes further to speculate that:

> Vulnerable regions in a knowledge world are not only those that make themselves unattractive to new knowledge accumulation, but are also those places that do not make the effort to mobilize the knowledge and learning resources they already have. While all regional communities have creative, 'ideas people', of one kind or another, resilient regions increasingly will be those that are able to extract the full extent of this knowledge and promote learning around it to meet their regional priorities. Without this focus, the growing divide between wealth creating and welfare creating regions will only continue to widen. (Garlick, 2002: 4)

This view is also articulated by Feldman (2001).

3. Emergence of a Policy Interest in the Role of Universities in this New Regional Development Climate

Where do universities fit in with this? Historically, universities have played a key role in nation building and have been, for the most part, preoccupied with promoting interaction with national and international research and academic communities. For example, Goddard and Chatterton argue:

> In the past, higher education in most countries has been primarily funded by national governments to meet national labour-market needs for skilled manpower and to provide a capacity to meet national research and technological development needs. (Goddard and Chatterton 1999a: 686)

As national economies have become more regionalized in response to the changes outlined in section 2, universities are increasingly being expected to play a more significant role in regional networking and capacity building. This expectation is highlighted in recent UK policy reports, case studies and evaluations (Centre for Urban and Regional Development Studies, 1997; Court, 1997; Davies, 1997; National Committee of Inquiry into Higher Education, 1997; Robson *et al.*, 1997; Binks and Otter, 1998; and Atkins *et al.*, 1999), in the OECD (1999a) Report, in European case studies and evaluations (Holtta and Pullianen, 1996; de Gaudemar, 1997; Simonyi, 1999; Butera, 2000; and Holtta, 2000), and in North American reports, case studies and evaluations (Kellogg Commission, 1999; Holland, 2001; and W.W. Kellogg Foundation, 2002). Within the Australian context too, a number of recently commissioned reports (Garlick, 1998; 2000; Stevenson *et al.*, 1999; 2000; Shoemaker *et al.*, 2000), policy documents (Kemp, 1999; Nelson, 2002a; 2002b) and research forums (for example, Department of Transport and Regional Services, 2001) have been launched, pushing for an enhanced regional role for universities especially those located in non-metropolitan areas. As Garlick notes, the high expectations placed on universities in many of the latter type of regions relate to the fact that these institutions 'represent the only institution with the critical mass, longevity of presence, independence, and networks to make a significant difference to their futures' (Garlick 2002: 2). A similar observation was made in the Canadian context by Weller (1998).

Not only has global economic change generated pull factors causing regional authorities to be interested in interacting with universities, but a number of the above-mentioned studies also highlight the presence of push factors causing universities to be more interested in partnerships with their regions. Funding cutbacks by central governments and a focus on state and regional institutions as alternative sources of revenue have been cited as one such push factor by a number of authors, especially in the European context (see, for example, Holtta and Pulliainen, 1996; Davies, 1997; Goddard and Chatterton, 1999a; Simonyi, 1999; and Garlick, 2002). Another push factor frequently cited is the shift in many countries from an elitist higher educational system to a mass higher educational system and the need for equitable access and participation possibilities (see, for example, Hollta and Pulliainen, 1996;

Davies, 1997; de Gaudemar, 1997; Goddard and Chatterton, 1999a; and Garlick, 2000). Other factors of significance are the potential for modern information and communication technologies to open universities up to increased competition from other educational providers even for local students (see, for example, Court, 1997; Wilson. 1997; and Chatterton and Goddard, 2000), the increasing shift of the cost of education onto a full-time student's present or future family resulting in increasing proportions of such students choosing to attend a university close to their home in order to minimize such costs (see, for example, Court, 1997; Atkins *et al.*, 1999; and Chatterton and Goddard, 2000), the lifelong learning needs generated by changing patterns of skills requirements in the labour market producing demand for higher education retraining by less geographically mobile mature aged students (see, for example, Court, 1997; Goddard, 1997; and Atkins *et al.*, 1999) and a perceived thrust by government funded research bodies to give priority to research proposals that demonstrate direct and/or immediate industry relevance (OECD, 1999a).

The net result of these push and pull factors is that universities worldwide are in the process of formulating and implementing strategies for enhancing engagement with their regions. However, the latter may need to be defined differently for different aspects of a university's operations – for, as Chatterton and Goddard (2000) note, universities have allegiances to multiple territories rather than being tied exclusively to a specific territory for all purposes. In addition, the term 'region' itself does not have a single definition – it can refer to the immediate hinterland, to the area within a reasonable commuting distance, to the state in a federated system or even to entities that combine several nation states. Indeed, in recent policy debates and media circles in the Australian context the term has somewhat perversely become synonymous with rural and/or remote communities (see, for example, Nelson, 2002a; 2002b).

Early studies on the regional economic impact of universities were limited in focus to the multiplier effects of expenditure by the university on a fairly narrowly defined geographic region – using much the same type of impact analysis as conventionally employed for any other large organization (see, for example, Bleaney *et al.*, 1992; Brown and Heaney, 1997). These studies point to direct expenditure by the university in the local area as well as expenditure by its students and employees while resident in or visiting the local area on a regular basis during the academic year. As Garlick (1998) and Goddard and Chatterton (1999a) note, these are primarily passive impacts of universities on their host regions and do not indicate active and systematic engagement with this region.

More recent studies of higher education institutions (HEIs) have incorporated a considerably larger range of factors under the regional economic impact umbrella (see, for example, Hudson, 1974; Armstrong, 1997; Brown and Heaney, 1997; Court, 1997; Davies, 1997; de Gaudema, 1997; Weller, 1998; OECD, 1999a; Keane and Allison, 1999; and Thanki, 1999). In particular, emphasis is increasingly being placed on the impact on human capital endowment of regions (through the teaching role of HEIs), the impact on competitiveness of local businesses and/or the attraction of new business investment to the region (through the research role and training programmes of HEIs), and the impact on social and cultural development of region (through the community service role of HEIs). Examples of such more extensive impacts are listed by OECD as:

> technology transfer to industry; recruiting students from out of the region and placing them with local companies; the flow of students and staff into the regional labour market; programmes of continuing and professional development to enhance the skills of local managers; raising skills and educational levels in the region; locally embedding global businesses by targeted training programmes and research links; ... providing a gateway to the global knowledge base of SMEs ...providing media expertise and commentary, access to public lectures and facilities, providing leaders for civic society, offering impartial knowledge to regional organizations and promoting the region. (OECD 1999a: 40)

However, conducting these more all-embracing impact studies is fraught with difficulty since it requires, among other things, data on the proportion of graduates employed locally, net income received by locally employed graduates in excess of what they might have earned without a university education, and so on. Indeed, it is clear that some of these impacts (for example, the impact of access to university facilities on the cultural development of the region) could never be quantified accurately in economic terms.

Having a regional university or a regional campus of a well-regarded metropolitan-based university has become a matter of considerable civic and regional pride in many countries, with regions who cannot claim to have one viewing this as a blight on their self esteem (see, for example, Davies, 1997; Weller, 1998). However, the fact is that the mere presence of a university in a region does not guarantee regional development (Garlick, 2002). Similarly, the establishment of a university in a region will not necessarily act to increase participation rates by local population (Stevenson *et al.*, 1999; 2000). Universities need to adopt proactive strategies on both of these fronts if they are not just enclaves within a largely unaffected region. Nevertheless, many universities are reluctant to invest significant resources in achieving a high level of engagement with their 'region(s)' – especially as doing so is seen as shifting resources away from the achievement of a higher national and/or international profile for its teaching and research activities. Others have argued, however, that this need not necessarily be the case since performing the regional role well will contribute positively towards excellence in teaching and research (see, for example, OECD, 1999a; Garlick, 2002; Holland, 2002; and W.K. Kellogg Foundation, 2002). The proactive regional engagement strategies implemented by Griffith University at its Logan campus are outlined and evaluated in the following sections.

4. Griffith University's Logan Campus and Its Region(s) of Concern

Griffith University was founded in 1971 and commenced teaching on a single campus to the south of the Brisbane CBD in 1975. Along with other Australian universities established around this time, the aim was to offer a consciously different set of educational programs from those associated with more traditional universities.

In particular, these initial programs were interdisciplinary in focus, centred around a problem-solving approach, delivered via team teaching, and emphasized a strong commitment to principles of equity and social justice (Griffith University, 2002b). While many of its contemporaries in the Australian educational system have remained small and specialized around their original set of programs, the profile of Griffith University has become more comprehensive as it has grown dramatically in size over its 30-year history.

This change was most dramatic during the 1989–92 period when the University was involved in amalgamations with the Mt Gravatt campus of the Brisbane College of Advanced Education, the Gold Coast College of Advanced Education, the Queensland Conservatorium of Music and the Queensland College of Art to become a multi-campus institution serving a 70-kilometre corridor stretching from Brisbane to the Gold Coast. This expansion meant that Griffith could no longer be just an alternative to longer established tertiary institutions in the Brisbane city area, since for communities in the corridor south of Brisbane it was the sole provider of tertiary education with the expectation that it would adopt a more comprehensive research and teaching profile (Griffith University, 2002b).

Expansion continued through the 1990s with the addition of a new campus established within this corridor at Logan City to commence teaching in 1998. It took place partly in response to national higher education policy and funding encouraging institutional amalgamations during the late 1980s and early 1990s – however, the corridor serviced by the University is the fastest growing region within Australia and this growth is projected to continue over the next 10 years.

During the period 1986–2002 Griffith's student population grew from 5000 to over 20,000, yet this is projected to need to expand to around 35,000 by 2012 if the estimated resident population in the corridor were to have access to tertiary education places in their region at the current national average (Griffith University, 2002b). Table 12.1 and Figure 12.1 show the growth of Griffith University over the period 1997-2002, with the Gold Coast and Logan campus absorbing the vast majority of this growth. Indeed the original Nathan campus has absorbed a decline in student load in order to enable the establishment and/or growth of these southern campuses. In the case of the Logan campus this was necessary since although the state and local governments were instrumental in the establishment of this campus, the federal government allocated no additional funded places to Griffith University to support this initiative.

The creation of the Logan campus arose out of the enthusiasm and aspirations of the Logan community to bring about social and economic change in what has been widely acknowledged as a disadvantaged region (Taylor and Blaik, 2002). The Queensland premier, as the local state member of parliament, and the leaders of the surrounding local governments (Logan City, Redlands Shire, Beaudesert Shire and Gold Coast City) were extremely supportive at the time of initial planning for the campus (1995) – with this strong local support continuing to date.

Some indication of the socioeconomic indicators of the region are insightful as background to understanding the nature of the engagement strategies described and

Table 11.1   Griffith University student load (EFTSU) by campus

Campus	1997	1998	1999	2000	2001	2002
Nathan	8687	7630	7634	7440	7419	8369
Mt Gravatt	2585	3094	3126	3274	3303	3437
Gold Coast	4623	5183	5573	6181	6391	7525
College of Art	899	862	742	765	901	979
Conservatorium	569	607	590	556	555	533
Logan	0	474	1139	1519	1649	1973
TOTAL	17363	17850	18804	19735	20218	22816

Source: Griffith University Statistical Collections

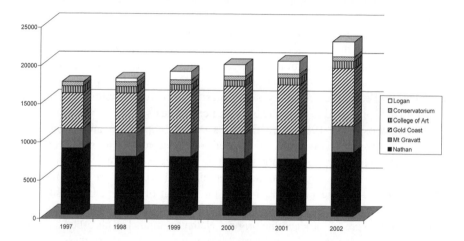

Figure 11.1   Griffith University student load (EFTSU) by campus
Source: Griffith University Statistical Collections

evaluated in the remaining sections of this chapter. Logan City is the third largest
city in the state of Queensland and it is located in the southeast corner of the state
approximately midway between two larger cities – Brisbane to the north and Gold
Coast to the south. Logan City and the surrounding region (including Redlands and
Beaudesert Shires and the northern part of the Gold Coast) contain approximately 10
per cent of the state's total resident population and is projected to have an average
annual population growth rate of around 1.7 per cent per annum between 2001 and
2021 compared with the state average of 1.6 per cent (Australian Bureau of Statistics,
2002). Approximately 25 per cent of the region's population is aged under 15 and the
unemployment rate is significantly higher than the state average especially for young

people (with some areas in the region recording over 30 per cent of their youth unemployed in 1999) (Taylor and Blaik, 2002). Individual average annual taxable income was AUS$32,035 in 1999–2000. This was 5 per cent below the corresponding state average, yet seventeen per cent below income in the neighbouring Brisbane City. Welfare dependency is also higher than the state average as are crime rates, especially juvenile crime rates. (Office of Economic and Statistical Research, 2002a; 2002b; Australian Bureau of Statistics, 2002). Only 5.3 per cent of the region's resident population have completed a university degree compared with the national average of 10.6 per cent; while the comparable statistics for vocational qualifications are 11.9 per cent for the region and 8.2 per cent for the nation as a whole (Cumpston *et al.*, 2001). A significantly lower proportion of the region's resident population are employed in managerial and professional occupations than the corresponding state and national averages, while a significantly higher proportion of the region's resident population are employed as tradespersons, labourers and clerical, sales and service workers. A large proportion of the resident population commute to the neighbouring cities of Brisbane and Gold Coast for employment, with the result that much of the local service sector employment is of the population servicing rather than business servicing variety (Office of Economic and Statistical Research, 2002a; 2002b; Australian Bureau of Statistics, 2002). Finally, high school completion rates and higher-education participation rates were significantly lower than the state and national average for urban areas during the 1980s and 1990s (Australian Bureau of Statistics, 2002).

5. Examples of Regional Engagement Strategies at the Logan Campus

A task force (including representatives of state and local governments and chaired by the Vice Chancellor) was established in August 1995 to plan the Logan campus. The work of the task force involved considerable community consultation and involvement to ensure the development of career-relevant and innovative degrees, delivery modes and learning support mechanisms that both matched regional needs and interests and took advantage of modern communication and information technology. Engagement with the local region has been continued and enhanced over time with a strong focus on facilitation of socioeconomic change and development through the establishment of strategic alliances with community organizations and increased interaction with local and state economic development agencies as well as industry and business leaders. Discussion of the various regional engagement activities is grouped under the headings of teaching, research and community service (although deciding under which category to classify a particular activity is sometimes problematic).

Teaching Activities

The initial selection of areas of teaching programs to be delivered at the Logan campus was based around identified and agreed local needs for the community's development, as well as targeting areas of anticipated job growth in state, national and international economies. The degree programs currently delivered focus on the areas of nursing, business management (accounting, financial planning, e-commerce, employment relations, business systems), photography, human services (aged care, disability services, welfare and child studies), education, arts, communication, information technology, science, food science and nutrition, and public and environmental health.

In recognition of the potentially prohibitive cost of mounting such a broad offering of programs in a campus with comparatively small initial enrolment levels, a number of strategies were employed in the attempt to minimize these costs. Examples include the formation of cross-campus schools, use of modern technology (videoconferencing facilities, the internet and computer technology more generally) in the delivery of course materials, the nesting of programs within a shared teaching and learning experience rather than proliferating stand-alone offerings, and the introduction of a systematic whole-of-campus teaching innovation labelled 'flexible learning'. (Flexible learning is a student-centred approach that seeks to provide choice and options for the learner, using campus and home or workplace based access to the internet and specially designed course resource packages in addition to on-campus student-staff and student-student interaction.)

Not all of these strategies have worked as well in hindsight as originally anticipated. The cross-campus school was envisaged as a means by which small groups of campus-based academic staff could interact with a critical mass of colleagues in similar disciplines for research and professional development purposes. At the same time, however, it was also used as a means to have lower levels of academic and/or administrative staff based on the Logan campus than otherwise would have been necessary, with staff members servicing Logan students travelling from their home campuses as and when required and being provided with access to shared office facilities at Logan. Students have often found it difficult to access academic staff when needed, a problem often exacerbated if those staff teach across multiple campuses and do not have a dedicated office at the Logan campus. The introduction of 'Common time' is one School's response to these problems. It involves scheduling a weekly block of time when all staff involved in teaching courses in a given semester are available on campus for consultation and during which optional skills development sessions that are course-specific are offered in adjoining computer laboratories, learning centres and/or workshop rooms.

Similarly, while flexible delivery using modern technology can work very well, teething problems in relation to the accessibility, reliability and capacity of the Griffith University network proved difficult to resolve in the short term generating high levels of frustration and disillusionment on the part of both staff and students. Videoconferencing, originally envisaged as a means of enabling students on different campuses to participate in lectures given by world-class scholars on other campuses, is in general loathed by students and staff alike. Unreliability of the link and the tendency for the resulting 'lectures' to become one-way communications with limited opportunity for real interaction on remote campuses are cited as the main reasons behind these negative sentiments.

Finally, while flexible learning has been found to have many benefits for students and staff it too has suffered from ambiguities relating to its meaning and unrealistic expectations being placed on it, with a recent evaluation leading to a series of recommendations for reform. In particular, the adoption of flexible learning has not resulted in the 'independent' form of resource-based learning that was expected by its initial proponents. The majority of staff and students have, as a result, adjusted to using the flexible learning resources (including on-line resources) to augment more traditional face-to-face class-based interactions. The result has been a critical shortage of conventional teaching spaces, especially for large classes. Additionally, while the initial roll-out of flexible learning materials was well funded, concern has been expressed about a lack of adequate recognition of the time and resources required to change and update these materials in the light of experience with their use by staff and students (Taylor and Blaik, 2002).

Nevertheless, the campus has experienced significant growth in student demand for its programs and in the quality of the students applying for entry, especially when compared with campuses of similar age and size in the Australian context (Taylor and Blaik, 2002).

In response to the low higher-education participation rates traditionally associated with the expected primary catchment area for school leavers, a series of initiatives has been implemented to encourage a greater number of young people in this region to develop career aspirations that include completion of a university degree and to ease the transition to university education for those who choose to act on these newly developed aspirations. Examples include the Griffith Early Start to Tertiary Studies (GUESTS) program, a Student Ambassador program, an Early Admission program, the Logan Orientation program and associated Orientation Guide, as well as Transition to University programs (including Uni-key and Uni-reach). See Appendix A for details of each of these initiatives, which have worked extremely well for both Griffith University and its students. For example, the campus has strong regional representation in its student population with around 70 per cent of its enrolments coming from the Greater Logan area in 2002. Additionally, retention and progression rates for students at the Logan campus are comparable with those on other Griffith campuses (Taylor and Blaik, 2002). Finally, Griffith University's Logan campus is highlighted as an example of national best practice in facilitation of local student access in a recent report to the federal government (Garlick and Pryor, 2002).

In recognition of the high youth unemployment rate and the cumulative effects of past low higher-education participation rates among the resident population, community consultation suggested that strategies aimed at encouraging and supporting mature age entry had the potential to reap significant rewards for the local community. As a result a series of initiatives have been implemented with this goal in mind, the most significant of which is the Logan Tertiary Access Course described in detail in Appendix A. Other initiatives involve inclusion of mature age students in promotion campaigns for the various 'transition to university' programs discussed above. This has also been an area of considerable success for the Logan campus, although some concern has been expressed that the quality of students being recruited under these schemes has begun to decline. To some extent this should have been expected, however, and it should be interpreted as a sign of success rather than failure if the local pool of highly motivated yet previously under-achieving mature-aged applicants dries up. There has also been concern raised within the Logan campus community, however, that students given access under special equity programs make disproportionate ongoing use of support services such as the Learning Assistance Unit are placing strain on limited resources (Taylor and Blaik, 2002).

Collaborations with other regional institutions in the areas of designing and implementing teaching programs have extended beyond the direct student recruitment area. Examples include the Logan 4x4 Learning Link, the Logan Education Alliance and partnership arrangements with the Logan hospital. The Logan 4x4 Learning Link is a regional partnership involving four institutions (Griffith University, the Logan Institute of TAFE, the Logan Hospital and Loganlea State High School) and focusing on the four areas of facilitating learning pathways, supporting academic and practical enrichment of staff and students, fostering joint research initiatives and sharing physical and other resources. The Logan Educational Alliance was formed in 1999 and involves Griffith University, the Logan Institute of TAFE, three local state high schools, and their nine feeder primary schools. The Alliance is involved in the development of strategies to improve literacy standards in the Logan community. The partnership with the Logan hospital embraces clinical placements for students, cooperative conduct of graduate programs in Infection Control and Sexual Health Nursing, and access to hospital facilities by academic staff where necessary to facilitate research endeavours.

Concern to ensure that Logan graduates have good employment prospects was a guiding principle in initial course and program design. As a result, all academic programs include practical experience components. Partnerships with local industry, business and government service providers have been important to the implementation of these program components. Thus, wherever possible, nursing students (as mentioned above) obtain practical experience at the Logan hospital, education students undertake practice teaching blocks in local schools, management students spend time working on problems confronting local businesses and human services students are required to undertake work experience with local community-based welfare agencies. Unfortunately, however, as the student intake levels at Logan have increased, local placements offering sufficient scope for the development of the requisite specialist skills have been exhausted in a number of fields (especially business management). This has necessitated expanding such university–community partnerships beyond the local region and into the Brisbane and Gold Coast communities.

It is too early for any detailed analysis of the proportions of graduates finding employment in the local region – since only one cohort of students has passed through the system. However, since many businesses currently located in the Greater Logan region are of a type that would be highly unlikely to employ university graduates, most students set their sights on graduate employment opportunities in the Brisbane and/or Gold Coast labour markets. Others have moved interstate or even overseas with the aim of obtaining access to superior career progression possibilities. Leaders in the Logan community regard these 'exports' as a sign of the success of the campus in providing opportunities for local youth, rather than as a sign of failure of regional engagement strategies as has been suggested by some national and international commentators in this field. This is consistent with the findings of Atkins *et al.* (1999) and Weller (1998).

Research Activities

Some examples of research collaboration involving local educational institutions were mentioned in the previous section. The partnership with the Logan hospital highlighted above also involves developing research collaborations in the fields of nursing, public health and health promotion, and human services. These examples of regional engagement in the research arena are essentially spin-offs from arrangements originally put in place to facilitate core teaching activities.

Examples of other non-teaching-related research collaborations have been more slow in emerging. Part of the explanation for this lies in the fact that, in the early stages of operation of the campus, comparatively few staff were based full-time at Logan, and those that were found that their workload became disproportionately skewed towards curriculum development and bedding down new teaching programs leaving little, if any time, for research activities – especially those which involved devotion of time to establishing meaningful contacts with relevant local businesses, government agencies and community organizations (Taylor and Blaik, 2002).

This is beginning to turn around now with the following examples indicative of the range of projects currently underway:

- Staff from the School of Human Services are engaged in substantial research collaboration with Logan employment and welfare agencies and government offices, primarily in the areas of return to work following injury, stress in the workplace and the development of community playgroup activities for socioeconomically disadvantaged students.

- Staff from the School of Public Health are involved with the Logan City Council in developing and implementing plans for more efficient public and environmental health services and conditions within its jurisdiction. This research collaboration has its genesis in the WHO 'Healthy Cities' program.

- Staff from the Schools of Management and International Business are also involved with the Logan City Council, in this instance concerned with the development of improved image building and marketing strategies for the region.

- Research in Australia and overseas suggests that collaboration between firms within a common field of interest can act to enhance the economic development of a region, especially if this region is one like the Greater Logan region whose businesses are predominantly small or medium sized enterprises. (See, for example, Perry, 1995; Held, 1996; Staber *et al.*, 1996; Porter, 1998b; Bergman and Feser, 1999; Marceau, 1999; Enright and Roberts, 2001). With this in mind, staff from the School of Management have taken a leading role together with staff from the Logan Office of the Department of State Development and the Logan Office of Economic Development in identifying the potential benefits from and facilitating the establishment and ongoing work of a Food Industry Cluster comprising approximately 100 businesses from the Logan region. Numerous local firms such as Qantas Snap Fresh, Grove Fruit Juice, Carlton and United Breweries, Golden Cockerel and Bunny Bite Farms meet regularly on campus together with academic staff and regional government officials to share experiences, brainstorm solutions to common problems and hopefully harness opportunities previously unavailable as individual enterprises (Brunetto *et al.*, 2002).

These projects are for the most part in the embryonic stage so that direct benefits to the local region in terms of enhanced socioeconomic development are difficult to document. They do demonstrate, however, that there exists significant potential for further developing this aspect of regional engagement at the Logan campus. It should be acknowledged, however, that teaching activities at Griffith University's Logan campus are largely focused on providing undergraduate training across a broad range of areas and that the campus has not been given the necessary authority or funding levels by the federal government to initiate the range of professional schools (such as medicine, engineering and law) found elsewhere to generate maximum impact on regional economic development through research spin-offs related to technological innovation.

Community Service Activities

Logan campus facilities are widely used by local community groups. For example, students from local schools and the Logan TAFE are regular users of computer and scientific laboratories, photographic studios and darkrooms and library facilities. The regional office for Open Learning Australia is located on the campus, as is the Learning Network Queensland.

The Logan campus head, normally one of the University's Deputy or Pro-Vice Chancellors, serves as a Director of the Board of the Logan Office of Economic Development. Unfortunately, there has been considerable turnover of Logan Campus heads in its short history, which has been somewhat disruptive for the identification and implementation of long-term research and other collaborative ventures aimed at assisting the region in this area. Nevertheless, operating through this link, the University recently worked cooperatively with the Logan City Council, government departments, local developers and the above-mentioned food industry cluster group to submit a bid for the establishment of a $20 million 'Food for Life Centre of Excellence' on the Logan Campus as an important regional development initiative. The successful site has not yet been announced, but the bid was one of only a handful short-listed for detailed examination.

Griffith University has been an on-going sponsor of Business Achiever Awards in the Logan region, and funds awards and scholarships to reward academic excellence on an annual basis to local schools. Additionally work is being undertaken jointly with the Logan City Council to develop sister city relationships with a number of overseas locations.

To date the community service activities undertaken by academic staff associated with the Logan campus has been somewhat haphazard. Although excellent individual examples of successful and ongoing engagement with local community organizations exist, involvement in such activity is purely voluntary with a strong perception among staff that the rewards in terms of annual review of performance and/or promotion are negligible in proportion to the time and energy involved.

6. Evaluation of Current Engagement Strategies and Identification of Areas for Improvement

Recent literature has shifted from a focus on documenting examples of regional engagement strategies that either could be or are being employed by universities to a focus on developing procedures for evaluating the effectiveness of such engagement strategies (see, for example, Goddard, 1998; Keane and Allison, 1999; Symoni, 1999; Butera, 2000; Kellogg Commission, 2000; Garlick, 2000; 2002; and Holland, 2001).

Garlick (2002: 9–11) refers to an engagement spectrum ranging over:

- *a fully engaged university* characterized by: a committed leadership; a course structure that links with regional priorities; staff contracts that acknowledge regional engagement aspects of their research and teaching activities; faculty arrangements that facilitate interdisciplinary operations; consultative mechanisms with the regional community; mechanisms for evaluating the success or otherwise of regional engagement activities; dispute resolution procedures in place; and simple and accessible entry points and contact mechanisms for all members of the local community;
- *a partially engaged university* in which: some engagement activities are in place but they tend to be incidental to mainstream institutional operations; some key university staff members are involved in key positions on a variety of community bodies, some of which are significant in influencing outcomes for the region; the university regards their participation as part of its social obligations only and not as a significant partnership arrangement based around mutual learning and outcome achievements;

- *a non-engaged institution* where excuses will be given to explain why engagement activities are not appropriate or necessary – such excuses ranging from conflict with achieving international academic excellence, lack of identifiable or meaningful regional partners and lack of financial incentives provided under current funding arrangements.

Where does Griffith Logan campus fit in within this spectrum based on the analysis in sections 3 and 4 of this chapter? While it would be fair to acknowledge that it has many of the characteristics of a 'fully engaged institution', it would also be important to recognize that changes are necessary in other areas before it can claim to have achieved this status. Some suggestions for improvement are highlighted below.

A number of researchers have pointed to the need for higher education institutions to be more systematic in their approach to regional engagement, especially in the areas of research and community-service-oriented collaborations (see, for example, OECD, 1999a). It has been suggested by some that the more fully engaged institutions have been successful in part because they have established a dedicated section of university charged with responsibility for managing the regional engagement processes (see, for example, Goddard and Chatterton, 1999a). This has been recognized by Griffith's newly appointed Vice Chancellor, and an Office of Community Partnerships is to be established with its headquarters located on the Logan Campus. This office will headed up by a new Pro-Vice Chancellor with responsibility for equity and community partnerships for all of the Griffith campuses (Griffith University, 2002b).

A number of researchers have pointed to the fact that while regional policy initiatives may be agreed to in a formal board setting by chief executive officers (or their delegates) from higher educational institutions and regional development authorities, this is often not followed through appropriately at a grass roots level within either organization. (see, for example, Atkins *et al.*, 1999; Goddard and Chatterton, 1999a; and OECD, 1999a). Repeated instances of this lead to a build-up of disillusionment and mistrust, and the opportunity for meaningful engagement through this channel is lost. There needs to be recognition that top management can sanction the initiation of collaborative initiatives of various types, but rarely do they have time to nurture and develop these collaborations to the extent required for them to achieve their maximum potential. The latter work requires a different set of skills and commitments than is required to carry out the core duties as a CEO. As a result, each CEO needs to identify staff within their organization who are willing and able to undertake this work, and to provide them with the resources needed to carry it through to completion. This is an area where Griffith can improve on past performance, and hopefully the new Pro-Vice Chancellor (Equity and Community Partnerships) will introduce the required mechanisms to make his/her position as a Director of the Board of the Logan Office of Economic Development a highly effective vehicle for enhancing the University's impact on regional economic development.

Research has also pointed to the need for revised performance criteria for staff that give greater emphasis to time allocated to regional engagement/community service role, if higher-education institutions are to make the transition from partial to fully engaged organizations (see, for example, OECD, 1999a; Goddard and Chatterton, 1999a; and Holland, 2002). This too has been recognized by Griffith's newly appointed Vice Chancellor and an undertaking given to review performance appraisal mechanisms and promotion criteria currently in place to allow for a greater range of career profiles (Griffith University, 2002b).

Finally, given that many external research funding agencies will only fund proposals judged to be at the cutting edge of national and/or international research in their field it can be argued that there may be a structural barrier in place discouraging regional engagement in research activities for many high-profile academic staff. Where this can be demonstrated to be the case, yet the regional community could benefit from a given research task being undertaken by a particular Griffith academic researcher, then a strong case could be made for internal research or community service grants to be allocated by the university. A similar case could by made for University-funded scholarships or bursaries to be earmarked for allocation to students selecting region-specific topics for their Honours, Masters and PhD theses.

APPENDIX

Details of Equity and Access Programs available to Students at Logan Campus of Griffith University

The Logan Tertiary Access Course

The Logan Tertiary Access Course is a collaborative program jointly funded by the Logan Institute of Technical and Further Education (TAFE), where it is delivered, and Griffith University. It was first introduced in 1989 and comprises a one-year full-time course designed to prepare students for successful tertiary study in a degree in science, information technology or social science (including education). It targets mature-age individuals who are socioeconomically disadvantaged, do not meet normal university entry requirements, and yet wish to undertake studies in the above-mentioned areas at Griffith. These individuals typically under-achieved at high school, may even have dropped out prior to completion due to a range of personal circumstances including teenage pregnancy. They must demonstrate adequate language and mathematical capacity prior to entry to their chosen strand within the course – with a range of opportunities to brush up on skills being offered to prospective students prior to sitting the entry tests. Upon successful completion of the Access Course, graduates have guaranteed non-competitive entry to designated Griffith University undergraduate degree programs. Periodic evaluations of the course have been undertaken (Bond, 1996 and Pendergast, 2000), and the course has evolved as a result. Approximately 50 per cent of enrolled students have successfully completed the Access Course in the period 1989–99 and 90 per cent of these students made the transition to Griffith University. Rates of subsequent successful completion of degree programs is not as high as for the general student population, but not inconsistent with completion rates for mature-age students in the Australian higher education system. The majority of the participants in the course were unemployed or working in unskilled jobs or in the home prior to commencing the course. Of those successfully completing both the access course and the subsequent degree course, the overwhelming majority have obtained professional/skilled employment or continued on with further studies at the postgraduate level. Perhaps more significant from a community or regional development perspective is the 'ripple effect' reported by Bond (1996):

> the study found evidence of positive change in perceptions of higher education amongst the participants and their children. Students reported that where previously there was little expectation of a university education, now their children were assuming that higher education would be part of their lives. Students' partners and friends were following their example and participating in the Access Program. This effect was seen to be a significant factor in the 'breakdown' of the cycle of socio-economic and educational disadvantage. (Bond 1996: 6)

The Griffith University Early Start to Tertiary Studies (GUESTS) Program

This program offers high-achieving Year 12 (final year) students from the local area the opportunity to undertake a first-semester Logan-campus-based university course while still at high school. The students must have the support of their school to undertake these additional studies and receive full credit for the course completed upon subsequent enrolment in a degree program at Griffith. The aim is to stretch the academic horizons of the region's high-achieving students and enable them to sample university life prior to making the decision as to whether and/or where to enrol in tertiary studies the following year. It is anticipated that positive experiences by GUEST program participants will spread by word-of-mouth to fellow classmates when they begin weighing up their future options towards the end of Year 12. GUEST program participants pay no fees to study at Griffith, but must be able to afford to purchase textbooks, stationery, photocopying, etc as well as meet any local transport costs (from school to university campus, for example).

The Griffith Student Ambassador Program

Research shows that interest in studying at university increases when prospective students have an opportunity to discuss their study options directly with academic staff and current students. To this end, our Student Ambassador Program involves visits being made to secondary school students (usually Years 10 to 12) at their place of learning. During these visits student ambassadors discuss on a one-to-one or small group basis their experiences in choosing where and what to study and whether what they are interested in now has changed from their original plans. Wherever possible student ambassadors visiting Logan schools were themselves recent graduates from the region.

The Logan Early AdmissionProgram

This program was initiated in 1997 and provides an interview-based means for local students to apply for acceptance into campus programs on the basis of their commitment and motivation rather than relying exclusively on high school performance as measured by the OP score. An analysis of academic achievement by students admitted under this program is comparable to other Logan students.

The Logan Campus Specific Transition to University Program

This is a program, conducted over three evening sessions, made available to all students offered early admission prior to their first semester of enrolment. Issues addressed include expectations of university life, time management, support programs available, flexible learning and the use of computer facilities.

The Griffith Uni-Reach Program

This program is available to Year 12 (final year) students from six state high schools in the Logan campus catchment area. These schools were selected because of the widely acknowledged financial disadvantage of many of their students. The program aims to encourage and assist students who feel motivated to undertake higher education by providing participants with a mentor who visits the school offering assistance with current studies, advice on university life and courses as well as moral support at final examination times. These mentors are specially trained Griffith students who are in turn supported by the Student Equity Programs Officer. High school students taking part in Uni-Reach are eligible to participate in a number of special admission schemes at Griffith – for example, the Logan Early Admission Program. It is currently planned to extend this program to students in Years 10-12 (Griffith University, 2002a).

The Griffith Uni-Key Program

This semester-long program provides a structured transition to university for commencing students from socioeconomically disadvantaged backgrounds. It features customized orientation to university sessions, academic and general skills development workshops and additional peer mentoring/tutorial assistance. Students from socioeconomically disadvantaged backgrounds are widely acknowledged to be at greater risk of not completing their studies or struggling through the system passing their subjects but never achieving their full potential. This program aims to increase completion rates and GPAs for these students (Griffith University, 2002a).

Chapter 12

Managing a University Merger in a Post-Industrial Context (the Ruhrgebiet)

An Interview with Lothar Zechlin, Founding Rector
of the University of Duisburg-Essen

The University of Duisburg-Essen, with around 30,000 students and 3400 academic and non-academic employees, was founded on 1 January 2003 through the merger of the University of Duisburg and the University of Essen (http://www.uni-duisburg-essen.de). Both universities had been founded in 1972 with a distinct regional mission. Primarily out of financial considerations, the state government of North Rhine-Westphalia had decided to merge the two universities and passed the relevant law. This decision concerning higher education policy led to considerable turbulence, not only in the two affected universities, but also within the region.

Lothar Zechlin (**LZ**), Professor of Public Law, ex-President of the Hochschule für Wirtschaft und Politik (Hamburg) – a 'reform university'[1] – and one-time Rector of the University of Graz (Austria), became the Founding Rector of the University of Duisburg-Essen on 1 October 2003. In the following interview with Stephan Laske and Alan Scott (**SL/AS**), conducted at the Essen Campus on 12 May 2005, he sketches the history, the context, the process and the consequences to date of this 'financial rehabilitation measure', which is – as yet – highly unusual in continental European higher-education policy. The regional context is one of the readjustment of the Ruhrgebiet to processes of deindustrialization. In line with similar – and well-documented – cases elsewhere, cultural as well as economic policies play a key role in urban-regional regeneration. The place of universities and science within such a post-industrial scene is thus a central theme.

Background and Process

SL/AS: Can you describe the context and the history of the merger in some detail? What were the driving forces behind it?

---

1 The Hochschule für Wirtschaft und Politik, founded in 1970, counted as a *Reformuniversität* because it, in contrast to the state universities, was open to those with work experience rather than with the *Abitur*. Beyond this, the curriculum was explicitly designed for modern adult education.

LZ: In the mid-1960s, the *Land* North Rhine-Westphalia started to declare education a notable feature and cornerstone of its policies. There were already the traditional and respected universities of Bonn, Cologne, Münster, and Aachen. That is, in the south of the Rhineland and in the north there were already old venerable universities. But within the entire vast area in between – in the Ruhrgebiet – there was absolutely nothing. Already in the 1960s, with the foundation of the University of Bochum under the CDU, but above all under the SPD from 1966, the government of the *Land* sought to bring universities to the children of workers in order to tap these unexplored talents and to increase the participation rates among working-class families who were to go to the universities within the region. The following decades were to be the golden age of education.

SL/AS: So that was the vision of the government of the *Land* at that time?

LZ: Yes, they really did have a vision. The whole process was, by the way, closely associated with Johannes Rau, who was first Minister of Higher Education and Science, then Prime Minister of the *Land*. Under his rule, in the 1970s North Rhine-Westphalia founded five new *Gesamthochschulen* [comprehensive universities] in Duisburg, Essen, Paderborn, Siegen and Wuppertal, which were to integrate features of the *Fachhochschulen* [universities of applied science] and the universities.[2] All was going well until the second half of the 1990s when two factors came into play. The first was the financial situation of the *Land*: it could no longer pay for everything it had created. It was no longer possible to finance so many universities. Politicians had to look for ways through this bottleneck. With that, a whole debate broke out everywhere under the catchphrase 'creating profile'. Do we need physics and chemistry everywhere? Can't one prune out some multiply offered degree programmes and have a discussion about where what should be located? In this context, the radical idea surfaced as to whether one shouldn't merge two institutions of higher education in order to save money. The second development was the discussion about quality. In 1999 the Science and Higher Education Minister [of the *Land*] set up a committee of experts which was to examine these issues. Thus, it soon became apparent that in many respects the *Gesamthochschulen* could not keep up with the real universities in terms of research and theoretical developments, and, more seriously still, that they could not always compete with the *Fachhochschulen* with respect to teaching performance. The latter are more efficient when one looks exclusively at teaching. They have lower dropout rates, shorter degree programmes,

---

2   Germany has a two-tier system (similar to the old polytechnic–university divide in the UK). Both the universities and *Fachhochschulen* are financed by, and are the political responsibility of, the *Länder*. The traditional universities tend to cover the full range of disciplines. The *Gesamthochschulen* offered, under one roof, both the six-semester *Fachhochschulstudiengang*, and the traditional (university) eight-semester *Diplomstudiengang* (roughly a MA/MSc). This developed into a problem, as did the divisions between academic staff with varying levels of qualification, and distinct working conditions and status. In the meantime, the *Gesamthochschulen* have been formally rechristened 'universities'.

and their graduates do well in the labour market. Taken together, this produced a specific pressure within the higher education landscape.

And then things started to move due to an initiative originating from within the universities of Duisburg and Essen. The two rectors asked themselves whether they could not increase the level of cooperation; after all, they were only about 20km apart. It was in the context of this cooperation that the discussion of a merger came about. The experts noticed this and said: 'yes, this idea has our support'; while politicians thought to themselves: 'yes, this is a really good idea, it looks good, it also sounds modern; merger, yes, go for it.'

As soon as word got round within the universities that there was a discussion concerning a merger, things really started to heat up. With every merger, there are always those who say: 'we are much better, they are weaker; we can't be expected to join them.' That was the case here too. If you don't plan a merger exactly you'll get a quite destructive group dynamic.

Then the politicians took a quite forceful step and simply passed a law, which was brought before the State Parliament (*Landtag*) in the autumn of 2002 and passed, in order to realize the merger. This pushed the two universities into a position of fundamental opposition. For example, in the summer of 2002 the Rector in Essen was voted out of office with a two-thirds majority – just imagine that! This could only happen if the Senate had already agreed with the same majority on a new candidate. She had been one of the very few women rectors. This was an enormous debacle!

As a response to this, the politicians dissolved the two universities by law, and on the 1 January 2003, there was a completely new university: the University of Duisburg-Essen. This move was challenged in the courts, which slowed down the process such that the *Land* was unable to appoint a founding rector on 1 January. On 31 December, however, the law had already come into effect, the law that said that the two universities no longer existed as legal entities. There was a complete vacuum such that the *Land* had to put in a kind of state commissioner – a ministerial civil servant who somehow had to deal with the situation. On top of this, came the many suspicions within the two (old) universities. In Essen they thought that the Duisburgers had got the politicians on their side otherwise they could not have been rescued at all. The Duisburgers claimed that the people from Essen had somehow started the whole process. The whole situation was a disaster. Eventually, the politicians and the University agreed to form a search committee that was to unanimously agree on a candidate. This was the oil that calmed the troubled waters.

SL/AS: How active were the politicians? Did they consciously put pressure on the universities? Was there a coherent strategy behind these moves or were they merely reacting to developments?

LZ: No, by passing the law the politicians quite consciously created pressure. Regarding strategy: there are three logical steps as to how mergers should be shaped: pre-merger, the merger itself, post-merger in which integration should actually occur. The pre-merger phase lasted until 31 December 2002, at which point the University of Duisburg-Essen was legally formed: the two universities fused. The end of the merger phase was also fixed by law for 31 December 2006. And, as one can read in the literature, in the pre-merger phase the vision must be identified, the whole sense of the merger must be communicated. None of this actually happened. They talked a bit, the politicians said 'give it a go', and universities said 'we won't do it'. There was a very active role for politics, but it was not thought through, not planned. In the meantime, because the conflict had got so out of hand, the politicians withdrew their direct influence. This was a good thing. They now made a real effort to give us advantageous conditions in order to secure the merger: the universities would benefit from the synergy effects that the merger would bring. In this way, they did not really produce savings [for the *Land*], but they did create the conditions for increased efficiency within the University. That had a real motivating effect: where there had been duplication of effort, we could merge and relocate on a single campus – thus requiring fewer professors – while at the same time being able to create new middle-level posts in order to make workable structures.

So, in the first phase, the politicians thumped the table, and in the second, they largely withdrew.

Internal Process

SL/AS: So, you inherited a pretty hot potato. How did you deal with this situation? Did you manage, and if so how, to build trust among faculty from the two old universities?

LZ: What was important in this situation was intensive communication between all those affected. Although it may sound strange, I must say that we, the Rectorate, had a good starting point because, in light of what had happened in the previous year or so, the whole process had become completely blocked, and both sides had noticed that they couldn't win. They were exhausted and thought the main thing was that something sensible should happen. I could already sense this when, after my election, I presented myself to the Senate. I noticed that I had considerable support: at last, someone who didn't come from the Ministry, someone completely neutral. That made my job much easier. In this respect, the potato was no longer quite so hot by the time I had to pick it up.

In any case, I had to meet people. I knew no one here. When you come from the outside, the pressure to go and meet people is all the greater. When you've already been in the system for ten years, you think you know everyone. And in this way something surprising happens: after a relatively short time, I thought to myself that I still knew no one, but when I went into groups I noticed that they knew each other even less well. So, I approached the hot potato in the first place by talking. Naturally, I told them what I had in mind. But that was initially a very crude notion. Thus, I told them that the Bologna process was important to me, and, as an ex-*Gesamthochschule*, we had to strengthen research. And then I pointed to two areas in which there were no systems in place: there was nothing like systematic quality development, nor was there anything for personnel development, whether for academic or for non-academic staff. So, I had a couple of keywords: this and that are important to me, but are they also important to you? That worked very well at the beginning. And so, after half a year I looked up and thought 'where's the problem?' Everything appeared to me to be ideal. Everyone was very nice. And then, after about nine months, things really started to happen. Then I really did notice where the problems lay. But the beginning was actually quite straightforward.

SL/AS: So, where did the problems lie?

LZ: My plan was that by reducing the level of replication between Duisburg and Essen we could create campus profiles that were as complementary as possible – i.e. with as little overlap as possible. By the summer of 2004, we had largely managed to achieve this for the natural and social sciences, and for the humanities. There was a bit of grumbling, but in the end, everyone thought 'okay, it might have been decided differently, but that may not have been better'. We left the economic sciences[3] at both locations because they each had around 4000 students, and were thus each working to full capacity.

Then we noticed that we not only had these structural issues to deal with, but also a precarious financial situation, even a crisis. The Rectorate had not been full aware of this – financial – aspect of the merger process. So, we had once again to revisit decisions, and then things boiled over. Our suggestion was to merge the economic sciences and locate them in Duisburg, and in return give Essen the entire educational studies. But what really made the emotional temperature rise was the idea of taking the economic sciences away from Essen. This is related to the distinct local function of these two universities within their respective cities, and with the nature of those cities themselves. Duisburg is in the middle of a structural transformation from being a classical industrial centre on the Lower Rhine; it's still very much workers, steel, and docks. Essen sees itself as the Ruhrgebiet's 'writing desk': the boardrooms are located in Essen. Thus, they felt it an affront that it should be they who were to give up the economic sciences. One should know that the cities here are quite nervous and have to restructure themselves at a time in which their budgets are in the red. Essen itself is currently in the process of working its way up, and precisely because of this is highly sensitive about such matters. Of course, there was a big fuss in the newspapers and among local politicians. Therefore, the scene was highly politicized.

To make matters more complex still, the 'filleting' of a university is more analytically complex that one might imagine from the outside. For example, the simple idea that we didn't need business studies twice, and that they should go to Duisburg and work sensibly with engineering and industrial engineering, and with the social sciences, could not be implemented. As business studies in Essen is closely linked to economics and business informatics, should they go too? A new building

---

3   *Wirtschaftswissenschaften* (economic sciences) include economics (*Volkwirt-schaftschaftlehre* – VWL), business/management studies (*Betriebswirtschaftslehre* – BWL), and business informatics (*Wirtschaftsinformatik*).

had just been put up for business informatics at a cost of several million Euros, and, in addition, mathematics was closely linked to business informatics. And then there was the problem of teacher training in Essen – i.e. all the teacher-training students are here, and they require business studies courses for their programme. Should they have to constantly travel to Duisburg? (e.g., study English in Essen, business studies in Duisburg). There simply are these established interconnections that have developed within the University, and which one cannot so easily disentangle. To found a new university is quite a different task from going into already established structures and saying 'let's take this bit out and put this bit in'.

Therefore, we had both external and internal political pressure. After the emotional temperature had risen so high, in the end I believe we managed to get things under control very well because we managed to stick to our basic line. We had said that we wanted at least a serious discussion within the university. We don't have money, so we can't finance duplicate structures, and we can show you the figures. If we don't manage to solve the problem by savings in the economic sciences, then we must find alternative sources of income. Therefore, it really was a serious situation. However, we also always said that, in case of massive resistance by the University – i.e. when the Senate was against us with a large majority – the Rectorate still has the legal right to make decisions, but that we would in fact not do so. We thereby gave the Senate a degree of responsibility. This created a very constructive dialogue in which we were able to agree on small-step solutions: business studies will only be offered in Essen as a BA with no master programme, they will become service teachers for economics and business informatics. In this way, we saved money. In Duisburg, we are establishing a strong School of Management. These structural decisions represented the critical phase of the merger, and we're pleased to have them behind us. Above all, it was only in this process that we acquired a kind of master plan that was clear also to ourselves; only now had we a clear idea as to how the merger might be accomplished.

SL/AS: What shape did the 'masterplan' take?

LZ: We made it clear that there are three distinct steps in the process of the merger: 2004 was the year of structural decisions; that is to say, which disciplines should be located in Essen, which in Duisburg, and what the organizational structure should look like – i.e. which departments [*Fachbereiche*] or faculties should we have. These were the issues marked by a high level of group dynamics. We said that the decisions had to be made in 2004, telling people: 'you can be sure that after that these themes will not appear again, and you'll have your peace, but for now we have to impose these discussions upon you.' In 2005, we said that within these new structures we shall write development plans. These are our guidelines that have been agreed with the Senate; now make your own development plans, but in the process take note of our guidelines, we shall later balance things out with you. In summer, we want to have discussions with you about our respective concepts. The results of these discussions will be written into internal performance contracts [*Leistungsvereinbarungen*] in late summer or autumn. The result was that the University no longer bickered about the

Duisburg-Essen divide, but rather each newly formed department had to think about where it wanted to go.

And now we are in the middle of this process. We have the first round of these discussions about the development plan and developmental aims behind us. It took three full days from early on a Thursday until 6pm on the Saturday. We have also developed instruments in order to balance out these matters. And these were really productive discussions. It was no longer primarily relevant what our cornerstones were. They served more as a kind of thread for the discussions. In this process, quite new things came out. We shall have one of two further rounds of discussion before the summer break [2005] in which we shall agree internal performance contracts. In this way, we shall ensure that these discussions produce concrete and binding results. So, in this year energies were directed, so to speak, forwards.

The third step in 2006 is to be our last. This we named the year of 'quality and evaluation'. We are building up an internal evaluation agency and workable management accounting system. Beyond that, however, we want to re-examine the initial structural decisions; that is, let them be examined by external advisors. In the case of the structural decisions in 2004, we said we wanted to move quickly – i.e. within a half year we would have the basic outline and in this way, once again, there would be organizational quiet, and people would know with whom they have to work, and with whom they no longer have to argue. But we knew that these structural decisions would possibly be suboptimal. If you decide very quickly, this will be at the cost of quality; but, at the same time, we said clearly that we would re-examine the effects. Today we say to ourselves that we could have done some things better. In 2006 let's look at things in peace; people will know each other better, and we can decide then whether there should be any further adjustments, or whether we should leave things as they are. In the end, people require stable behaviour. In this way, we introduced a degree of peace into the system.

SL/AS: That means you worked with the principle: treat structures as hypotheses! Structures are merely temporary possibilities. By viewing them as such the sting is taken out of the decisions. If people think the current structural decisions will last for eternity they turn it into a kind of holy war. The next decisive stage is to plausibly communicate the reviseability of these structures; that is, that you are genuinely prepared to put in place these revisions, but recognize that they may then require fine tuning.

LZ: Yes, that's a useful way of putting it.

External Factors and Regional Actors

SL/AS: Earlier in your account of the process, you said that they put pressure on you. Who were 'they'?

LZ: 'They' were the players here within the University who had fixed interests of their own, and who concealed themselves behind local politicians, who likewise had their own interests. Also the respective local papers in Duisburg and Essen see only the things they don't like. That is what they really give column inches to. That they also won out in the process – well, if you're lucky that might get a mention, but as a rule not even that. Because we are located within two such different cities, it is difficult to develop a coherent university.

SL/AS: Has the Rector's Office sought to speak with external actors?

LZ: You have to realize this office had to overcome the same schism. There are two people from Duisburg and two from Essen, and they tended to see themselves as representing the different interests. It took time before our team emerged out of this, and mutual trust had been established. We have spoken to externals; with the politicians, with the Lord Mayors, and so on. But we only really spoke to local politicians and journalists when I noticed that things out there were really heating up. In the everyday workings of the cities, the University is not really a presence. It plays only a marginal role within the cities. Only when there is a danger of losing something, does the University become important. One cannot really say that the University is a formative influence here. It makes all the difference whether the merger of the universities is taking place in a city; in a major metropolitan centre – e.g. Munich, Berlin, Vienna or Manchester – or in two cities with different identities. In our case, there is even another city between Duisburg and Essen, namely Mülheim. The campuses cannot yet grow together, otherwise they would have been more willing to assist in the process.

SL/AS: Is there some kind of rivalry between the two cities?

LZ: No, I don't think there is such a rivalry between Duisburg and Essen. It's more a matter of the self-image of Essen as a city on the way up. This meant that they did not want to lose the economic sciences. There was also the argument that firms were dependent upon business studies students. That is ridiculous because Duisburg is 18 km away, and in any case they live in the general area, not always in Essen itself. No, I think it was about self-image and anxiety, and we are in a region that is in any case not very self-confident. For decades, they experienced decline. In the first half of the twentieth century, this was the industrial powerhouse of Germany. There is a lot of symbolism here.

SL/AS: If these cities are so obviously in need of support in respect of their own self-image, what is the university doing now to meet this need?

LZ: Probably too little. I do not take a very active part in the issue of the regional embeddedness of the university or its regional presence. Of course, I'm constantly invited to receptions, and naturally, I go, and there I talk to people. We have also created a board of trustees, but that is just starting to take up its activities. It is due to have its constitutive meeting in four weeks time. There are fifteen top-ranking people from within the region on it, for example both Lord Mayors, and the chief representatives of industry and commerce. We expect of them a stronger connection to the region, and also, of course, support, up to the point of bringing in money for us. But the regional interdependences are mainly decentralized: the banks cooperate with the economists, or the Research Institute for fuel cell technology in Duisburg runs joint projects with private companies, and so on. There is a lot going on, but less at the level of the University as a whole, and more at that of the respective departments.

SL/AS: Have the cities ever attempted to use the universities in order to raise their own profiles?

LZ: If that is the case, it hasn't been successful. Both Duisburg and Essen are cities with universities, but they are not university cities. A one-time Duisburg Lord Mayor made considerable efforts in the early 1970s to get a university in Duisburg. And they made available an absolutely first-rate piece of land, in the middle of the best part of town. At that time, they even had to fight the local elite because the latter lost some of its tennis courts and golf course. And yet the University is – well I wouldn't say a foreign body, more a nobody in both cities. It simply isn't present. The University doesn't bother anyone; it doesn't do them any good either.

For twenty years now the talk in the Ruhrgebiet has been about the fact that it is one of the largest conurbations in the world, something like Los Angeles; that it's really a metropolis with over five million inhabitants. The rhetoric is highly developed, but when there is really something at stake, parish pump politics takes over. That's incredible. Each of them tries to grab the last crumb off the plate. There is no sense of common interest. It is also true of the administrative structure here: there is a regional administrative district Rhineland, in which the western part of the Ruhrgebiet is included; and there is an administrative district Westfalen, in which the eastern Ruhrgebiet is included. Thus, they are split. The Ruhrgebiet is not a political entity; rather it emerged out of 100 years of economic development. The political structures did not keep up. So, in the last instance, it's up to us what we make of ourselves. If we manage to position the University reasonably well, if our ranking improves, if we can strengthen research, we will then make our mark on our surroundings. It is less a case of orientating ourselves to what the environment expects from us. That is important too, but the priority is what we make of things ourselves.

SL/AS: How do you deal with other regional players; that is with other institutions of higher education and other universities?

LZ: Shortly after I got here we made contact with Bochum and Dortmund. We are trying to create a type a of strategic alliance. We Ruhrgebiet universities have to secure and defend our position vis-à-vis the traditionally well-established universities. We want to see how far cooperation can go, but short of merger. For example, although the two construction engineering departments here in Essen and in Bochum are not going to fuse, they are trying to create a common centre for construction engineering science. Here, in the case of new professorships, we consider which chairs we should advertise and which they should advertise. The three universities also have a single office in New York, and we offer a common programme for younger women scientists. Here things are beginning to move. But this is something we must do in a relaxed fashion. There should be a working relationship going, not something that has been imposed from above.

Issues of Research, Teaching and the Positioning of the University

SL/AS: The age structure of the professoriate must create a relatively advantageous scope for action. The *Gesamthochschulen* were created in the 1970s and that's when most of the professors were appointed. That means that in the coming years a whole raft of colleagues will retire. In turn, that will probably create an opportunity for the university to reposition itself.

LZ: Yes, that's right. In physics, for example, we already have more young people, and you notice that a fresh wind is blowing. And in those areas in which professors of my generation are in the majority, in the next five to six years these too will be in a restructuring phase. I believe that is a good position to be in. With the merger, we have reorganized the structures, and if in the next six or seven years there is an exchange of personnel within these structures then they can do something new with them.

SL/AS: A central aspect of every university is now its research profile. In the course of the merger, this too must have been a key concern. How is the new University of Duisburg-Essen seeking to position itself?

LZ: In order to reposition a university one has to concern oneself with the research profile. Here we are working with a step-by-step model. The first step is that each faculty must decide for itself, but we make the assessments; that is to say, we shall examine how much external funding is coming in, how many doctorates have been completed, how many Humboldt grants, and how much DFG money.[4] Up to now there has been no proper managerial accounting, everyone worked as they saw fit. And then there is a second step, namely that concerning the university as a whole and research across faculties. We have identified four areas of future investment. The first is nanoscience. In Duisburg, we are strong in engineering and physics and a lot is going on in medicine, which is located here in Essen. This is quite astonishing

---

4   The Alexander von Humboldt Foundation (http://www.humboldt-foundation.de) is a prestigious non-profit foundation established by the Federal Republic of Germany for the promotion of international research cooperation. It enables highly qualified scholars not resident in Germany to spend extended periods of research there and promotes academic contacts. The foundation supports a worldwide network of scholars. The self-governing DFG (Deutsche Forschungsgemeinschaft/German Research Foundation – http://www.dfg.de/) is the main research funding body – for both the humanities and sciences – for universities and other publicly financed research institutions in Germany.

– in this area one no longer notices that there are two city sites. In the meantime, in my view, here we are competitive at an international level. The second area where we are strong, and could be stronger still, is in empirical educational research. There are number of groups working in this area, e.g. in cooperation with a Max Planck Institute in Berlin. For example, one group is examining empirically the didactics of natural-science education. There is a third cluster, the life sciences, which also involves the medical people, but now together with biology and chemistry. And then there is a forth area: logistics, traffic, and environment. In this region, there is an astonishing amount of traffic, on both the roads and the waterways: Duisburg is a port city, and is connected to the North Sea via Rotterdam. Here our business studies people in Duisburg work alongside our environmental scientists, chemists and geographers in Essen.

So, in addition to regional cooperation with other universities, we try to improve the quality of our research. One inherits particular material – with particular strengths and weakness – with which one has then to work. So, you have to examine what there is that you can build upon, and here you can't do much more than make some money available and talk to the people concerned.

SL/AS: You make an important point in suggesting that the central task of the Rector's Office is to create structural conditions that enable people to work across the boundaries of disciplines, faculties and departments. If you manage to facilitate work across the boundaries within the University, or create conditions in which these can be more easily overcome, then you've already achieved a great deal. You mentioned four research clusters. That is quite ambitious. What would count as success for you here?

LZ: Success for me would be acquiring more DFG-financed graduate programmes, more special research areas, and in particular widening the range of DFG funding. And if, beyond that, we manage to train more young scientists who manage to get Junior Professorships in other universities, then so much the better.[5] Whether that takes place in all four clusters, or only in three, or whether a fifth joins them; this isn't so important for me.

SL/AS: What is striking about the four clusters you have mentioned is that, with the exception of education, these are primarily in the natural sciences, and perhaps also

---

5   The Junior Professorship is a new position introduced in the course of higher education reform in Germany. It is an attempt to address the serious problem of the generation(s) 'lost' to the universities. The Federal Ministry of Education and Research (BMBF) has also sought to phase out the Habilitation, traditionally the cornerstone of the German academic career, but at the time of writing this move has been blocked by the Constitutional Court on the grounds that such competences lie with the states (*Länder*) not with the federal ministry. The combination of the new Junior Professorship and the abolition of the Habilitation would represent a paradigmatic shift from a national to an international – or, more specifically, US – model of the academic career, something that Max Weber, rather prematurely, predicted in 'Science as a Vocation' (1919).

primarily tending towards an applied orientation. What are the possible consequences of this for the humanities and for the social sciences, particularly where they have no immediate application?

LZ: We say to those areas that are not yet within a cluster that this is not a closed shop. Right now, we are getting into these four areas, and for that we are making resources available. But we are also creating incentives for other interdisciplinary research. If good proposals come from management scientists, sociologists, historians, or political scientists then each year we finance, on a competitive basis, between one and three interdisciplinary research groups, each for three years, in order for them to prepare research applications and undertake preliminary research. But after three years, they must be in a position to acquire external funding, to fund themselves. Will this actually happen? I don't think one can do much to direct this from the centre. And if the offer is not taken up then nothing will emerge. I do not believe that a university of this size can be good in all areas of research; rather there is normally an internal differentiation. There simply are areas that are more geared towards teaching and training. And as long as the university has enough islands of strong research then that is acceptable for me.

SL/AS: The inherent logic of the attempts to create university profiles is that not everyone can succeed. In the long run, there will be winners and losers. And usually it is clear fairly early on who they will be.

LZ: Yes, it will come to that. Yes.

SL/AS: What does that mean in the longer term for the 'losers'? What kind of incentives can one create in the future for people who work in areas that are outside the profile of the university's research? How can one recruit good people for such areas?

LZ: That is a difficult question. I have no patented solution. How is one really to value performance in teaching? Honestly, I'm unclear about this. Have you got a good tip!?

SL/AS: No! But we would be sceptical about decoupling teaching and research activities.

LZ: Yes, the complete division is also something I too find bad. However, the creation of research foci makes sense. And in those areas where teaching is predominant, I expect research not to disappear. They also need to have doctoral students and they should do research-based teaching, but they do not have to create a large postgraduate community. So, I believe that a complete division of teaching and research – that is to say a purely teaching unit – is not suitable in a university context.

SL/AS: There are also areas of poor staff–student ratios. It is difficult to look after large numbers of students and at the same time do top research. Here one has the make a distinction.

LZ: Yes, of course. But research is always more highly valued. I do indeed believe that a university is ultimately legitimized through its research. If one puts together under one roof, as was done in the UK, the polytechnics and universities, then naturally an internal differentiation will emerge between research and teaching universities.

SL/AS: We would like to thank you for the interview and for your time.

Bibliography

Abbott, A. (1988) *The System of Professions*. Chicago: University of Chicago Press.

Abbott, A. (2001) *Chaos of Disciplines*. Chicago: University of Chicago Press.

Ackoff, R. (1999) *Ackoff's Best: His Classic Writings on Management*. New York: John Wylie & Sons.

Albrow, M. (1996) *The Global Age: State and Society beyond Modernity.* Cambridge: Polity Press.

Allen, J. (2000) 'Power/Economic Knowledge. Symbolic and Spatial Formations'. In J. Bryson, P. Daniels, N. Henry and J. Pollard (eds) *Knowledge, Space, Economy*. London: Routledge.

Allen, T.J. (1977) *Managing the Flow of Technology*. Cambridge, MA: MIT Press.

Altbach, P.G. (2004) 'Globalization and the University: Myths and Realities in an Unequal World'. *Tertiary Education and Management* 10. 1: 3–25.

Alvesson, M. and H. Willmott (1996) *Making Sense of Management: A Critical Introduction*. London: Sage.

Amit, V. (2000) 'The University as Panopticon: Moral Claims and Attacks on Academic Freedom'. In M. Strathern (ed.) *Audit Cultures: Anthropological Studies in Accountability, Ethics and the Academy*. London: Routledge.

Anderson, A. and J. Valente (2002) *Disciplinarity at the Fin de Siècle*. Princeton: Princeton University Press.

Anderson, L. (2003) *Pursuing Truth, Exercising Power*. New York: Columbia University Press.

Appadurai, A. (1990) 'Disjuncture and Difference in the Global Cultural Economy'. *Theory, Culture and Society* 7. 2&3: 295–310.

Argyris, C. and D.A. Schön (1978) *Organizational Learning: A Theory of Action Perspective.* New York: Addison Wesley Publishing Company.

Argyris, C. and D.A. Schön (1996) *Organizational Learning II. Theory, Method, and Practice.* New York: Addison Wesley OD series.

Argyris, C., R. Putnam, and D. McClain Smith (1985) *Action Science: Concepts, Methods, and Skills for Research and Intervention*, San Francisco, Jossey-Bass. Also available at http://www.actiondesign.com/action_science/index.htm.

Armstrong, H.W. (1997) 'Maximising the Local Economic, Environmental and Social Benefits of a University: Lancaster University'. *GeoJournal*, 41. 4: 339–50.

Arthur D. Little Ltd. (2001) *Realising the Potential of the North East's Science Base*. Report to One NorthEast. Harrogate: ADL.

Asheim, B.T. (1996) 'Industrial Districts as "Learning regions". A condition for Prosperity'. *Journal of Planning Studies*, 4. 4: 379–422.

Asheim, B.T. and A. Isaksen (1997) 'Location, Agglomeration and Innovations: Towards Regional Innovation Systems in Norway?' *European Planning Studies*, 5.3: 299–332.

Atkins, M., J. Dersley and R. Tomlin (1999) 'The Engagement of Universities in Regional Economic Regeneration and Development: A Case Study of Perspectives'. *Higher Education Management*, 11. 1: 97–115.

Atkinson, D. (1999) *Scientific Discourse in Sociohistorical Context*. Mahwah, NJ: Lawrence Erlbaum Associates.

Austin, J.L. (1962) *How to Do Things with Words*. Cambridge, MA: Harvard University Press.

Australian Bureau of Statistics (2002) *Regional Statistics, Queensland*. Accessible at http: //www.abs.gov.au.

Baert, P. and A. Shipman (2005) 'University under Siege? Trust and Accountability in the Contemporary Academy'. *European Societies*, 78. 1: 157–85.

Baggen, P. (1998) *Vorming door Wetenschap: Universitair Onderwijs in Nederland 1815–1960* [Education through knowledge: university teaching in the Netherlands 1815–1960]. Delft: Eburon.

Bahrenberg, G. (1974) 'Zur Frage optimaler Standorte von Gesamthochschulen in Nordrhein-Westfalen. Eine Lösung mit Hilfe der linearen Programmierung' [On the question of optimal locations for *Gesamthochschulen* in North Rhine-Westphalia. A solution with the aid of linear programming]. *Erdkunde* 28: 101– 14.

Bargh, C., P. Scott and D. Smith (1996) *Governing Universities: Changing the Culture?* Bristol, PA: Taylor and Francis Inc.

Barnett, R. (1990) *The Idea of Higher Education*. Buckingham: Society for Research into Higher Education and Oxford University Press.

Barthes, R. (1968) *Elements of Semiology*. New York: Hill and Wang.

Barthes, R. (1972) *Mythologies*. New York: Hill and Wang.

Bates, A.W. (1997) 'Restructuring the University for Technological Change'. Paper presented at the Carnegie Foundation for the Advancement of Teaching. conference: *What Kind of University?*, London, 18–20 June, 1997, London.

Bauman, Z. (1987) *Legislators and Interpreters: On Modernity, Post-modernity and Intellectuals*. Cambridge: Polity Press.

Bauman, Z. (1997) *Postmodernity and its Discontents*. Cambridge: Polity Press.

Bazerman, C. (1988) *Shaping Written Knowledge*. Madison: University of Wisconsin Press.

Beck, U. and N. Sznaider (2006) 'Unpacking Cosmopolitanism for the Social Sciences: A Research Agenda'. *British Journal of Sociology* 57. 1: 2–23.

Bell, D. (1973) *The Coming of the Post-Industrial Society. A Venture in Social Forecasting*. New York: Basic Books.

Bell, D. (1980) 'The Social Framework of the Information Society'. In T. Forester (ed.) *The Microelectronics Revolution*. Blackwell; Oxford.

Benneworth, P.S. (1999) 'The future for relations between higher education and RDAs'. *Regions* 220: 15–22.

Berger, P.L. and T. Luckmann (1971 [1966]) *The Social Construction of Reality.* London: Allen Lane.

Bergman, E.M. and E.J. Feser (1999) *Industrial and Regional Clusters: Concepts and Comparative Application.* Regional Science Research Institute, West Virginia University. Accessible at http: //www.rri.wvu.edu/WebBook/Bergman-Feser/ contents.htm.

Bernard, N. (2002) *Multilevel Governance in the European Union.* Dordrecht: Kluwer European Monographs.

Bijker W.E., T.P. Hughes and T. Pinch (1987) *The Social Construction of Technological Systems.* Cambridge, MA: MIT Press.

Binks, M. and S. Otter (1998) 'Realising the Potential Contribution of Higher Educational Institutions to their Regions and Communities'. *Tertiary Education and Management* 4. 3: 209–21.

Bjarnason, S. and P. Coldstream (eds) (2003) *The Idea of Engagement. Universities in Society.* London: Association of Commonwealth Universities.

Bleaney, M.F., M.R. Binks, D. Greenaway, G.V. Reed and D.K. Whynes (1992) 'What Does a University Add to its Local Economy?' *Applied Economics*, 24: 305–11.

Boezerooy, P. and F. Kaiser (2001) 'Nieuwe Lijnen in het Hoger Onderwijs. Statistische Trends in Negen West-Europese Landen. Periode 1990–1998' [New lines in higher education. Statistical trends in nine West European countries during the period 1990–1998]. CHEPS – higher education monitor, trend report. Enschede: Center for Higher Education Policy Studies (CHEPS), Enschede.

Bok, D. (2003) *Universities in the Marketplace.* Princeton: Princeton University Press.

Bond, C. (1996) *Access to Griffith University: A Study of the Impact of the Logan Institute of TAFE Certificate in Tertiary Access to Griffith University*, Report to Griffith University. Available at http: //www.gu.edu.au/ua/aa/ss/equity/Tertiary. htm (accessed June 2005).

Bourdieu, P. (1986) *Distinction: A Social Critique of the Judgement of Taste* (translated by R. Nice) London: Routledge.

Bourdieu, P. (1992) *Language and Symbolic Power* (translated by G. Raymond and M. Adamson). Cambridge: Polity Press.

Bourdieu, P. (1993) *Sociology in Question* (translated by R. Nice). London: Sage.

Bourdieu, P. (1998) *Acts of Resistance: Against the New Myths of Our Time* (translated by R. Nice). Cambridge: Polity Press.

Bourdieu, P. (2000) *Pascalian Meditations* (translated by R. Nice) Cambridge: Polity Press.

Bowring, F. (2002) 'Post-Fordism and the End of Work'. *Futures,* 34: 159–72.

Boyte, H. and N. Kari (1996) *Building America: The Democratic Promise of Public Work.* Philadelphia: Temple University Press.

Braun, D. and F.-X. Merrien (eds) (1999) *Towards a New Model of Governance for Universities? A Comparative View*. London: Jessica Kingsley.

Brenner, N. (1998) 'Global Cities, Global States: Global City Formation and State Territorial Restructuring in Contemporary Europe'. *Review of International Political Economy* 5. 1: 1–37.

Brenner, N. (2004) *New State Spaces: Urban Governance and the Rescaling of Statehood*. Oxford: Oxford University Press.

Brint, S. (1994) *In an Age of Experts: The Changing Role of Professionals in Politics and Public Life*. Princeton, NJ: Princeton University Press.

Brint, S. (ed.) (2002) *The Future of The City of Intellect: The Changing American University*. Stanford: Stanford University Press.

Brown, J.S. and P. Duguid (1991) 'Organizational Learning and Communities-of-Practice: Towards a Unified View of Working, Learning, and Innovation'. *Organization Science* 2. 1: 40–57.

Brown, J.S. and P. Duguid (2000) *The Social Life of Information*. Boston: Harvard Business School Press.

Brown, K.H. and M.T. Heaney (1997) 'A Note on Measuring the Economic Impact of Institutions of Higher Education'. *Research in Higher Education*, 38. 2: 229–40.

Bruner, J. (1986) *Actual Minds, Possible Worlds*. Cambridge, MA and London: Harvard University Press.

Brunetto, Y., J.A. Campbell, R. Farr-Wharton and A. Greenhill (2002) 'Analysing the Potential for Collaborative Business Activities: A Case Study Examining the Contextual Capability of a Region to Foster Business Clustering'. Paper presented at the *Australia and New Zealand Regional Association International Conference*, Gold Coast, October.

Brusco, S. (1982) 'The Emilian Model: Productive Decentralization and Social Integration'. *Cambridge Journal of Economics* 6: 167–84.

Bryson, J., P. Daniels, N. Henry and J. Pollard (eds) (2000) *Knowledge, Space, Economy*. London: Routledge.

Buck, N., I. Gordon, A. Harding and I. Turok (eds) (2005) *Changing Cities: Rethinking Urban Competitiveness, Cohesion and Governance*. Basingstoke: Palgrave.

Burawoy, M. (2005) 'Provincializing the Social Sciences'. In G. Steinmetz (ed.) *The Politics of Method in the Human Sciences*. Durham and London: Duke University Press.

Burgin, V. (1982) *Thinking Photography*. London: Macmillan.

Burke, K. (1966) *Language as Symbolic Action: Essays on Life, Literature, and Method*. Berkeley and Los Angeles: University of California Press.

Burton-Jones, A. (1999) *Knowledge Capitalism. Business, Work and Learning in the New Economy*. Oxford: Oxford University Press.

Burtscher, C., P.-P. Pasqualoni and A. Scott (forthcoming) 'On the Way to Market: The Austrian University System in Transition'. *Social Epistemology*. Special issue on higher education, edited by T. May and B. Perry.

Butera, F. (2000) 'Adapting the Pattern of University Organisation to the Needs of the Knowledge Economy'. *European Journal of Education*, 35. 4: 403–19.

Buursink, J. and P. Vaessen (2003) *De Regionale Functie van de Katholieke Universiteit Nijmegen* [The regional function of the Catholic University of Nijmegen]. Nijmegen: Department of Human Geography, University of Nijmegen.

Cairncross, F. (1997) *The Death of Distance: How the Communications Revolution Will Change our Lives*. Boston: Harvard Business School Press.

Campion, M. and W. Renner (1995) 'Goal Setting, Domestication and Academia: The Beginnings of Analysis'. In J. Smyth (ed.) *Academic Work: The Changing Labour Process in Higher Education*. Buckingham: Society for Research in to Higher Education and Open University Press.

Cannell, W. (2001) 'Afterword'. In S. Dresner and N. Gilbert (eds) *The Dynamics of European Science and Technology Policies*. Aldershot: Ashgate.

Castells, M. (1996) *The Rise of the Network Society*. Oxford: Blackwell.

Castells, M. and P. Hall (1994) *Technopoles of the World*. London: Routledge.

Catalogue of the Officers and Students of the Cornell University for the Academic Year, 1868–1869, with an Announcement of the Terms, Courses of Study, etc. (1868) Ithaca: Cornell University Press.

Centre for Urban and Regional Development Studies (1997) *Universities and Regional Development*. Newcastle upon Tyne: University of Newcastle Upon Tyne.

Charles, D.R. (2001) 'Universities and Regions: An International Perspective'. Paper presented at the conference *Universities and Regional Development in the Knowledge Society*, Barcelona, 12–14 November.

Charles, D.R. and P. Benneworth (2001) 'Are we realizing our potential? Joining up science and technology policy in the English regions'. *Regional Studies* 35: 73–79.

Charles, D.R. and C. Conway (2001) *Higher Education Business Interaction Survey*. Bristol: HEFCE.

Charles, D.R. and J. Howells (1992) *Technology Transfer in Europe: Public and Private Networks*. London: Belhaven.

Chatterton, P. and J. Goddard (2000) 'The Response of Higher Education Institutions to Regional Needs'. *European Journal of Education* 35. 4: 475–96.

Cheshire, P. and I. Gordon (1998) 'Territorial Competition: Some Lessons for Policy'. *Annals of Regional Science* 33, 321–46.

Chifley Research Centre (2001) *An Agenda for the Knowledge Nation*. Canberra, July. Available at www.chifley.org.au/publications/kn_report_020701.pdf (accessed June 2005).

Clark, B. (1998) *Creating Entrepreneurial Universities: Organizational Pathways of Transformation*. New York and Oxford: Pergamon Press.

Clark, B. (2004) *Sustaining Change in Universities: Continuities in Case Studies and Concepts*. Maidenhead: Society for Research into Higher Education and Open University Press.

Coldstream, P. (2003) 'Engagement: An Unfolding Debate'. In S. Bjarnason and P. Coldstream (eds) *The Idea of Engagement. Universities in Society*. London: Association of Commonwealth Universities.

Collini, S. (2003) 'HiEdBiz'. *London Review of Books*, 25. (21): http://www.lrb.co.uk/v25/n21/coll01_.html (accessed August 2005).

Communiqué of the Conference of Ministers Responsible for Higher Education (2003) *Realizing the European Higher Education Area*. 19 September, Berlin.

Cooke, P., M. Gomez Uranga and G. Etxebarria (1997) 'Regional Innovation Systems: Institutional and Organizational Dimensions'. *Research Policy* 26: 475–91.

Corbett, E. J. (1984) 'Introduction'. In E.J. Corbett (ed.) *The Rhetoric and the Poetics of Aristotle*. New York: Random House.

Cornell University: The Register 1900–1901 (1900) Ithaca: Cornell University Press.

Court, S. (1997) 'The Development of a Regional Role for the UK Higher Education Institutions with Particular Reference to the South West Region of England'. *Higher Education Management*, 9. 3: 45–63.

Crouch, C. (2004) *Post-Democracy*. Cambridge: Polity Press.

Cumpston, A., R. Blakers, C. Evans, M. Maclachlan and T. Karmel (2001) *Atlas of Higher Education: A Community Focus*. Canberra: Department of Education, Training and Youth Affairs.

Czarniawska, B. and R. Wolff (1998) 'Constructing New Identities in Established Organization Fields'. *International Studies of Management and Organization* 28. 3: 32–56.

Davies, J.L. (1997) 'The Regional University: Issues in the Development of an Organizational Framework'. *Higher Education Management* 9. 3: 29–44.

Davies, J.L. (1997) 'The Development of a Regional Role for UK Higher Education Institutions with Particular Reference to the South West Region of England'. *Higher Education Management*, 9. 3: 45–66.

Davies, J.L. (2000) 'Reflections on the Outcomes of Discussions on "Beyond the Entrepreneurial University"'. Paper presented at the IMHE General Conference, Paris, September.

Davies, J.L. (2004) *Issues in the Development of Universities' Strategies for Internationalisation*. Anglia Polytechnic University, U.K. available from: www.ipv.pt/millenium/davies11.htm (accessed May 2004).

Davis, D. (1999) 'Cellulose Valley: Southern Cross University and Regional Development'. In Z. Klich (ed.) *Universities and Regional Engagement*. Lismore, NSW: Southern Cross University.

Dawkins, J. (1987) *Higher Education: A Policy Discussion Paper*. Canberra: AGPS.

Dawkins, J. (1988) *Higher Education: A Policy Statement*. Canberra: AGPS.

Dear, P. (2001) *Revolutionizing the Sciences*. Princeton: Princeton University Press.

de Gaudemar, J.-P. (1997) 'The Higher Education Institution as a Regional Actor'. *Higher Education Management*, 9. 2: 53–64.

Delanty, G. (2001) *Challenging Knowledge. The University in the Knowledge Society*. Buckingham: Society for Research into Higher Education and Oxford University Press.

den Hertog, P., E. Bergman and D.R. Charles (eds) (2001) *Innovative Clusters: Drivers of National Innovation Policy*. Paris: OECD.

Department of Trade and Industry (1998) *Our Competitive Future: Building the Knowledge-driven Economy* London: Her Majesty's Stationery Office.

Department of Trade and Industry (2000) *Excellence and Opportunity – A Science and Innovation Policy for the 21ˢᵗ Century*. White Paper (Cm 4814). London: The Stationery Office.

Department of Trade and Industry (no date) *Clusters: Higher Education and Business Collaboration for Success*. London: DTI.

Department of Trade and Industry/Department for Education and Employment (2001) *Opportunity for All in a World of Change: A White Paper on Enterprise, Skills and Innovation*. London: The Stationery Office.

Department of Transport and Regional Services (2001) *Universities and Regional Development Forum*. Accessible at http: //www.dotars.gov.au/regional/urdf/.

de Weert, E. (1999) 'Contours of the Emergent Knowledge Society: Theoretical Debate and Implications for Higher Education Research'. *Higher Education* 38: 49–69.

DiMaggio, P.J. and W.W. Powell (1991) 'The "Iron Cage" Revisited: Institutional Isomorphism and Collective Identity'. In W.W. Powell and P.J. DiMaggio (eds) *The New Institutionalism in Organizational Analysis*. Chicago: Chicago University Press.

Doring, A. (2002) 'Challenges to the Academic Role of Change Agent'. *Journal of Higher Education* 26. 2: 139–48.

Douglas, M. (1996) 'Introduction'. In *Natural Symbols* (new edition). London: Routledge.

Douglas, M. and B. Isherwood (1979) *The World of Goods*. London: Routledge.

Drennan, M. (2002) *The Information Economy and American Cities*. Baltimore and London: Johns Hopkins University Press.

Drucker, P. (1969) *The Age of Discontinuity*. New York: Harper and Row.

Drucker, P. (1998) 'From Capitalism to Knowledge Society'. In D. Neef (ed.) *The Knowledge Economy*. Boston: Butterworth-Heinemann.

Duderstadt, J.J. (2000) *A University for the 21st Century*. Ann Arbor: University of Michigan Press.

du Gay, P. (2000) *In Praise of Bureaucracy*. London: Sage.

Dunning, J. (1997) 'Technology and the Changing Boundaries of Firms and Government. Some Notes'. Paper presented at the OECD *International Seminar on the Changing Nature of the Firm*, Stockholm, February 19, 1997.

Dunning, J. (2000) 'Regions, Globalisation and the Knowledge Economy'. In J. Dunning (ed), *Regions, Globalisation and the Knowledge Economy*. Oxford: Oxford University Press.

Eco, Umberto (1976) *A Theory of Semiotics*. Bloomington: Indiana University Press.

Edquist, C. (1997) *Systems of Innovation*. London: Pinter.

Ehrlich, T. (ed.) (2000) *Civic Responsibility and Higher Education*. Phoenix: American Council on Education/Oryx Press.

Elvemo, J., J. Munkeby and P. Lynne Hansen (2001) 'National Strategies and Local Diversities: Adding Value through Broad Participation – Experiences from the Norwegian Enterprise Development 2000 Program'. In R. Markeby, P. Gollan, A. Hodgkinson, A. Chouraqui and U. Veersma (eds) *Models of Employee Participation in a Changing Glocal Environment. Diversity and Interaction.* Aldershot: Ashgate.

Ende, M. (1963) *Jim Button and Luke the Engine Driver*. London and Edinburgh: Harrap.

Enright, M. and B. Roberts (2001) 'Regional Clustering in Australia'. *Australian Journal of Management* 26: 66–85.

Etzkowitz, H. (2002) *MIT and the Rise of Entrepreneurial Science*. London: Routledge.

European Commission (1997) *Communication from the Commission: Towards a Europe of Knowledge*. COM (97)573 final. Luxembourg: Commission of the European Communities.

European Commission (2000) *Communication from the Commission: Towards a European Research Area*. COM (2000) 6. Luxembourg: Commission of the European Communities.

European Commission (2001) *Communication from the Commission: The Regional Dimension of the European Research Area*. COM (2001) 549 final. Luxembourg: Commission of the European Communities.

European Commission (2003) *Communication from the Commission on The Role of the Universities in the Europe of Knowledge*. COM (2003) 58 final. Luxembourg: Commission of the European Communities.

Evangelista, R., S. Iammarino, V. Mastrostefano and A. Silvani (2002) 'Looking for Regional Systems of Innovation: Evidence from the Italian Innovation Survey'. *Regional Studies* 36. 2: 173–186.

Feldman, J.M. (2001) 'Towards the Post-University: Centres of Higher Learning and Creative Spaces as Economic Development and Change Agents'. *Economic and Industrial Democracy*, 22: 99–142.

Filmer, P. (1997) 'Disinterestedness and the Modern University'. In A. Smith and F. Webster (eds) *The Postmodern University: Contested Visions of Higher Education in Society*. Buckingham: Open University Press.

Fish, S. (1980) *Is There a Text in this Class?* Cambridge, MA: Harvard University Press.

Florida, R. (1995) 'Towards the Learning Region' *Futures*, 27: 527–36.

Florida, R. (2002) *The Rise of the Creative Class and How It's Transforming Work, Leisure, Community and Everyday Life*. New York: Basic Books.

Flyvbjerg, B. (2001) *Making Social Science Matter: Why Social Inquiry Fails and How It Can Succeed Again.* Cambridge: Cambridge University Press.

Foucault, M. (1970) *The Order of Things*. New York: Random House.

Foucault, M. (1972) *The Archaeology of Knowledge*. New York: Pantheon Books.

Foucault, M. (1980) *Power/Knowledge: Selected Interviews and Other Writings 1972–77*. New York: Pantheon.

Foucault, M. (1984) *The Foucault Reader*. Harmondsworth: Penguin.

Foucault, M. (1991) *Remarks on Marx: Conversations with Duccio Trombadori*. New York: Semiotext.

Fowler, R., B. Hodge, G. Kress and T.Trew (eds) (1979) *Language and Control*. London: Routledge and Kegan Paul.

Friedson, E. (1986) *Professional Powers*. Chicago: University of Chicago Press.

Freidson, E. (1994) *Professionalism Reborn: Theory, Prophecy and Policy*. Chicago: University of Chicago Press.

Fuller, S. (1993) 'Disciplinary Boundaries and the Rhetoric of the Social Sciences'. In E. Messer-Davidow, D.R. Shumway, and D.J. Sylvan (eds) *Knowledges*. Charlottesville: University Press of Virginia.

Fuller, S. (2000) *The Governance of Science*. Buckingham: Open University Press.

Fuller, S. (2002) *Knowledge Management Foundations*. London and Woburn, MA: Butterworth-Heinemann.

Furedi, F. (2001) 'An Intellectual Vacuum'. *Times Higher Education Supplement* 5 (5 October).

Garlick, S. (1998) *Creative Associations in Special Places: Embracing the Partnership Role of Universities in Building Competitive Regional Economies*. Canberra: Department of Education, Training and Youth Affairs.

Garlick, S. (2000) *Engaging Universities and Regions: Knowledge Contribution to Regional Economic Development in Australia*. Canberra: Department of Education, Training and Youth Affairs.

Garlick, S. (2002) 'Creative Regional Development: Knowledge Based Associations between Universities and their Places'. Paper presented at the *Universities and Regional Engagement Forum*, University of Western Sydney, September.

Garlick, S. and G. Pryor (2002) *Compendium of Good Practice University-Regional Development Initiatives*. Canberra: Department of Transport and Regional Services.

Gibbons, M. (2003) 'Engagement as a Core Value in a Mode 2 Society'. In S. Bjarnason and P. Coldstream (eds) (2003) *The Idea of Engagement. Universities in Society*. London: Association of Commonwealth Universities.

Gibbons, M., C. Limoges, H. Nowotny, S. Schwartzman and P. Scott (1994) *The New Production of Knowledge – the Dynamics of Science and Research in Contemporary Societies*. London: Sage.

Goddard, J. (1997) 'Managing the University Interface'. *Higher Education Management* 9. 3: 7–27.

Goddard, J. (1997) 'Universities and Regional Development: An Overview'. Background paper to OECD *Project on the Response of Higher Education to Regional Needs*. Centre for Urban and Regional Development Studies, University of Newcastle upon Tyne. Available at http: //www.ncl.ac.uk/curds/univ/imhe-97.htm (accessed June 2005).

Goddard, J.B. (1998) 'Managing the University/Regional Interface'. *Higher Education Management* 9. 3: 7–28.

Goddard, J.B. (1999) 'How Universities Can Thrive Locally in a Global Economy'. In H. Gray (ed.) *Universities and the Creation of Wealth*. Buckingham: Open University Press.

Goddard, J.B. and P. Chatterton (1999a) 'Regional Development Agencies and the Knowledge Economy: Harnessing the Potential of Universities'. *Environment and Planning C*, 17: 685–99.

Goddard, J.B. and P. Chatterton (1999b) *The Response of Higher Education Institutions to Regional Needs*. Paris: OECD.

Goddard, J.B. and P. Chatterton (2001) 'The Response of HEIs to Regional Needs'. Paper presented at the conference *Universities and Regional Development in the Knowledge Society*, Barcelona, 12–14 November.

Goddard, J.B., D.R. Charles, A. Pike, G. Potts and D. Bradley (1994) *Universities and Communities*. London: Committee of Vice-Chancellors and Principals.

Goddard, J.B., M. Atkins, R. Vaughan, R. Firth, R.Tomlin, J. Dersey, J. Taylor, A. Parker (1997) *Universities and Economic Development*. Sheffield: Department for Education and Employment.

Gordon, I. and P. McCann (2000) 'Industrial Clusters: Complexes, Agglomeration and/or Social Network'. *Urban Studies* 37. 3: 513–32.

Gould, E. (2003) *The University in a Corporate Culture*. New Haven: Yale University Press.

Gouldner, A. (1973) 'The Sociologist as Partisan'. In A. Gouldner *For Sociology: Renewal and Critique in Sociology Today*. London: Allen Lane.

Graesser, A.C., M.A. Gernsbacher and S.R. Goldman (eds) (2003) *Handbook of Discourse Processes*. Mahwah, NJ: Lawrence Erlbaum Associates.

Graham, G. (2002) *Universities: The Recovery of an Idea*. Thorverton: Imprint Academic.

Gramsci, A. (1971) *Selections from the Prison Notebooks,* (edited by Q. Hoare and G. N. Smith). New York: International Publishers.

Green, M., P. Eckel and A. Barblan (2002) *The Brave New (and Smaller) World of Higher Education: A Transatlantic View*. Washington DC: European University Association EUA and, American Council on Education, Washington DC.

Greenwood, D. (1995) 'The Rhetorical Prison of Positivism and the Issue of Action Research's Professional Silence: From Spain to Scandinavia'. In C. Lisón Tolosana (compiler) *Antropología y literatura*. Zaragoza, Diputación General de Aragón, Departamento de Educación y Cultura.

Greenwood, D. (1996) 'Regímenes, universidades, y la "construcción" de la antropología en España y en los Estados Unidos'. In J.A. Fernández de Rota y Monter (ed.) *Las diferentes caras de España: Perspectivas de antropólogos extranjeros y españoles*. Colección Cursos: Congresos e Simposios, Servicio de Publicacións, Universidade da Coruña, La Coruña: pp. 23–44.

Greenwood, D. (1999) 'The Inhumanities and Inaction Research in Anthropology'. Society for Humanistic Anthropology, *Anthropology Newsletter*, 40. 4: 56.

Greenwood, D. (forthcoming) 'La antropología "inaplicable": El divorcio entre la teoría y la práctica y el declive de la antropología universitaria'. In J.A. González

Alcantud and M.L. Rivas (eds) *El sentido práctico de la antropología plural.* Granada.

Greenwood, D. and M. Levin (1998) 'Action Research and the Co-optation of Social Research'. *Studies in Culture, Organizations and Society*, 4: 237–61.

Greenwood, D. and M. Levin (1998) *An Introduction to Action Research Social Science for Social Change.* Thousand Oaks, CA: Sage.

Greenwood, D. and M. Levin (1999) 'Recreating University-Society Relationships: Action Research versus Academic Taylorism'. In O.N. Babüroglou and M. Emery (eds) *Educational Futures: Shifting Paradigms of Universities and Education.* Istanbul: Sabanchi University Press.

Greenwood, D. and M. Levin (2000) 'Reconstructing Relationships between Universities and Society through Action Research'. In N.K. Denzin and Y.S. Lincoln (eds) *Handbook of Qualitative Research*, Thousand Oaks, CA: Sage.

Greenwood, D. and M. Levin, M. (2001) 'Re-organizing Universities and "Knowing How"; University Restructuring and Knowledge Creation for the Twenty-First Century'. *Organization* 8. 2: 437–44.

Greenwood, D. and M. Levin (1998) 'The Reconstruction of Universities: Seeking a Different Integration into Knowledge Development Processes'. *Concepts and Transformation* 2 (2): 145–63.

Greenwood, D. and M. Levin (1999) 'Action Research, Science, and the Co-optation of Social Research'. *Studies in Cultures, Organizations and Societies.* 5 (1), vol. 4, no. 2, summer, 1998: 237–61.

Greenwood, D. and M. Levin (2000a) 'Recreating University–Society Relationships: Action Research versus Academic Taylorism'. In O. N. Babüroglu, Merrelyn Emery and Associates (eds) *Educational Futures: Shifting Paradigm of Universities and Education*, Fred Emery Memorial Book. Istanbul: Sabanci University: pp. 19–30.

Greenwood, D. and M. Levin (2000b) 'Reconstructing the Relationships between Universities and Society through Action Research'. In N. Denzin and Y. Lincoln (eds) *Handbook of Qualitative Research* (2nd edition). Thousand Oak, CA: Sage.

Greenwood, D. and M. Levin (2001) 'Pragmatic Action Research and the Struggle to Transform Universities into Learning Communities'. In P. Reason and H. Bradbury (eds) *Handbook of Action Research.* London: Sage.

Greenwood, D. and M. Levin (2002) 'Reorganizing Universities and "Knowing How": University Restructuring and Knowledge Creation for the Twenty-First Century'. *Organization* 8 (2): 433–40.

Grey, C. (2001) 'Re-imagining Relevance: A Response to Starkey and Madan'. *British Journal of Management* 12 (special issue): 27–32.

Griffith University (2002a) *Equity Plan and Indigenous Education Strategy.* Accessible at http://www.griffith.edu.au/equity/pdf/equity_strat_feb01.pdf.

Griffith University (2002b) *The Griffith Project.* Accessible at http://www.gu.edu.au/vc/key_issues/content_griffith project.html.

Gulbenkian Commission on the Restructuring of the Social Sciences (1996) *Open the Social Sciences.* Stanford, CA: Stanford University Press.

Gustavsen, B., H. Finne and B. Oscarson (2001) *Creating Connectedness: The Role of Social Research in Innovation Policy*. Amsterdam: John Benjamins.

Gustavsen, B., T. Colbjørnsen and Ø. Pålshaugen (1997) *Development Coalitions in Working Life: The 'Enterprise Development 2000' Program in Norway*. Amsterdam: John Benjamins.

Habermas, J. (1971) 'Technology as Science and Ideology'. In *Toward a Rational Society*. London: Heinemann Educational.

Habermas, J. (1992) *The Philosophical Discourse of Modernity: Twelve Lectures*. Cambridge: Polity Press.

Hall, J. (1999) *Cultures of Inquiry*. Cambridge: Cambridge University Press.

Hall, S. (1983) 'The Great Moving Right Show'. In S. Hall and M. Jacques (eds) *The Politics of Thatcherism*. London: Lawrence and Wishart.

Halliday, M.A.K. and J.R. Martin (1993) *Writing Science*. Pittsburgh: University of Pittsburgh Press.

Hammersley, M. (1995) *The Politics of Social Research*. London: Sage.

Harloe, M. and B. Perry (2004) 'Universities, Localities and Regional Development: The Emergence of the Mode 2 University?' *International Journal of Urban and Regional Research*, 28.1: 212–23.

Harris, M. (1998) 'The New Right'. In A. Lent (ed.) *New Political Thought: An Introduction*. London: Lawrence & Wishart.

Harsanyi, J. (1955) 'Cardinal welfare, individualistic ethics, and interpersonal comparisons of utility'. *Journal of Political Economy* 63: 309–21.

Harvey, D. (1989) *The Condition of Postmodernity: An Inquiry into the Origins of Cultural Change*. Oxford: Blackwell.

Held, J.R. (1996) 'Clusters as an Economic Development Tool: Beyond the Pitfalls'. *Economic Development Quarterly* 10. 3: 249–61.

Hellstrom T. and S. Ramen (2001) 'The Commodification of Knowledge about Knowledge: Knowledge Management and the Reification of Epistemology'. *Social Epistemology* 15. 3: 139–54.

Henkel, M. (2000) *Academic Identities and Policy Change In Higher Education*. London: Jessica Kingsley.

Henry, N. and Pinch, S. (2000) 'Spatialising Knowledge: Placing the Knowledge Community of Motor Sport Valley'. *Geoforum* 31: 191–208.

Herzfeld, M. (1992) *The Social Production of Indifference: Exploring the Symbolic Roots of Western Bureaucracy*. Chicago: University of Chicago Press.

Hesse, M.B. (1974) *The Structure of Scientific Inference*. London: Macmillan.

Hill, S. and T. Turpin (1995) 'Cultures in Collision: The Emergence of a New Localism in Academic Research'. In M. Strathern (ed.) *Shifting Contexts: Transformations in Anthropological Knowledge*. London: Routledge.

Hirschman, A. (1991) *The Rhetoric of Reaction*. Cambridge, MA: Belknap Press of Harvard University Press.

Holland, B.A. (2001) 'Measuring the Role of Civic Engagement in Campus Missions: Key Concepts and Challenges'. Paper presented at the *Universities and Regional Engagement Forum*, University of Western Sydney, September.

Hollis, M. (1970) *Tantalizers: A Book of Original Puzzles*. London: Allen and Unwin.

Holtta, S. (2000) 'From Ivory Towers to Regional Networks in Finnish Higher Education'. *European Journal of Education*, 35. 4: 465–74.

Holtta, S. and K. Pulliainen (1996) 'The Changing Regional Role of Universities'. *Tertiary Education and Management*, 2. 2: 119–26.

Hood, C. (1998) *The Art of the State: Culture, Rhetoric, and Public Management*. Oxford: Oxford University Press.

Howarth, D. (2000) *Discourse*. Buckingham: Open University Press.

Hudson, B.M. (1974) 'Regional Economic Effects of Higher Education Institutions'. *Socio-Economic Planning Sciences* 8: 181–94.

Huizinga, J. (1951) *Universiteit, Wetenschap en Kunst* [University, science and art]. (Collected Works, vol. 8). Haarlem: Tjeenk Willink.

Hunter, G.K. (2000) *The Discovery of the Molecular Basis of Life*. London: Academic Press.

Hymes, D. (1974) *Foundations in Sociolinguistics: An Ethnographic Approach*. Philadelphia: University of Pennsylvania Press.

Jacobs, K. (2001) *The Eye's Mind*. Ithaca and London: Cornell University Press.

Jay, N. (1992) *Throughout Your Generations Forever*. Chicago: University of Chicago Press.

Jensen-Butler, C., A. Shachar and J. van Weesep (eds) *European Cities in Competition*. Aldershot: Avebury.

Jessop, B. (2000) 'The State and the Contradictions of the Knowledge-driven Economy. In J. Bryson, P. Daniels, N. Henry and J. Pollard (eds) *Knowledge, Space, Economy*. London: Routledge.

Jimenez, J. and J. Zubieta (2001) 'Mexico and Japan: Linking Mechanisms between Higher Education Institutions and Knowledge Utilization'. Paper presented at the conference *Universities and Regional Development in the Knowledge Society*, Barcelona, 12–14 November.

Joint Declaration of the European Ministers of Education (1999) *The Bologna Declaration*. 19 June 1999.

Jones, B. and M. Keating (eds) (1995) *The European Union and the Regions*. Oxford: Clarendon Press.

Jongbloed, B. and L. Goedegebuure (2001) 'From the entrepreneurial university to the stakeholder university'. Paper presented at the conference *Universities and Regional Development in the Knowledge Society*, Barcelona, 12–14 November.

Kanter, R.M. (1995) *World Class: Thriving Locally in the Global Economy*. New York: Simon and Schuster.

Kappler, E. (2004): 'Universität als Universität der Studierenden: Anregungen aus einem Experiment mit einer tausendjährigen Vorlage' [The University as a university of students: insights from an experiment based on a 1000-year-old blueprint]. In S. Laske, T. Scheytt and C. Meister-Scheytt (eds) *Personalentwicklung und universitärer Wandel* [Human resource development in changing higher-education institutions]. München and Mering: Rainer Hampp-Verlag.

Keane, J. and J. Allison (1999) 'The Intersection of the Learning Region and Local and Regional Development: Analysing the Role of Higher Education'. *Regional Studies* 33. 9: 896–902.

Keeble D. and F. Wilkinson (1999) 'Collective Learning and Knowledge Development in the Evolution of Regional Clusters of High Technology SMEs in Europe'. *Regional Studies* 33: 295–303.

Kellogg Commission (1999) *Returning to our Roots: The Engaged Institution.* Washington DC: National Association of State Universities and Land Grant Colleges.

Kemp, D. (1999) *Knowledge and Innovation: A Policy Statement on Research and Research Training.* Canberra: Ausinfo.

Kerr, C. (2001) *The Uses of the University.* Cambridge, MA: Harvard University Press, Cambridge.

Kirp, D. (2003) *Shakespeare, Einstein and the Bottom Line.* Cambridge, MA: Harvard University Press.

KNAW (2004) *Historie KNAW* (The history of the Royal Dutch Academy of Arts Sciences). Available at http://www.knaw.nl/organisatie/trippenhuis/historie_ knaw.html (accessed May, 2004).

Knight, J. (2002) 'Trade in Higher Education Services. The Implication of GATS'. London: The Observatory of Borderless Higher Education. Available at http://www.obhe.ac.uk/products/reports/publicaccesspdf/March2002.pdf, (accessed May 2004).

Knight, J. (2003) 'GATS, Trade and Higher Education. Perspective 2003 – Where are we?' London: The Observatory of Borderless Higher Education. Available at http://www.obhe.ac.uk/products/reports/publicaccesspdf/May2003.pdf (accessed May 2004).

Knutstad, G. (1998) *Medvirkning og innrullering av sosiale – og teknologisake aktører I endringsprosesser* [Participation and enrolment of social and technological actors in change processes]. Unpublished PhD thesis (1998–7), University of Trondheim, Department of Industrial Economics and Technology Management.

Krause, Elliott, A. (1996) *Death of the Guilds.* New Haven: Yale University Press.

Kuhn, T.S. (1970 [1962]) *The Structure of Scientific Revolutions.* Chicago: University of Chicago Press.

Laclau, E. (1990) *New Reflections on the Revolution of Our Time.* London:Verso.

Laclau, E. and C. Mouffe (1985) *Hegemony and Socialist Strategy: Towards a Radical Democratic Politics.* London: Verso.

Lara, M.P. (1998) *Moral Textures.* Cambridge: Polity Press.

Laske, S. (1988) 'Auf der Suche nach der regionalen Identität der Universität' [In search of the university's regional identity]. In W. Marzen (ed.) *Die Betriebswirtschaftslehre in der Welt von heute* [Business administration in the world of today]. Spardorf: Wilfer-Verlag.

Laske, S. (1997) 'Führung als Management von Widersprüchen – Gedanken zur Steuerung von Bildungsorganisationen' [Leadership as the management of contradictions – thoughts on the control of educational organizations]. In R.

Benedikter (ed) *Wirtschaft und Kultur im Gespräch* [Economy and culture in dialogue]. Bolzano: Alpha & Beta.

Latour, B. (1987) *Science in Action*. Cambridge, MA: Harvard University Press.

Latour, B. (1996) *Aramis or the Love of Technology*. Cambridge, MA: Harvard University Press.

Lawton Smith, H. (2003) 'Knowledge Organizations and Local Economic Development: The Cases of Oxford and Grenoble'. *Regional Studies*, 37: 899–909

Le Galès, P. (2002) *European Cities: Social Conflicts and Governance*. Oxford: Oxford University Press

Leitner, E. (1999) 'Academic Oligarchy and Higher Education Research: Implications for the Reform of Institutions of Higher Education in Austria'. *Higher Education Policy* 12. 1: 27–40.

Levin, M. (1997) 'Technology transfer is organizational development: an investigation into the relationship between technology transfer and organizational change'. *International Journal of Technology Management*, 14(2/3/4): 297–308.

Levin, M. and D. Greenwood (1997) 'The Reconstruction of Universities Seeking a Different Integration into the Knowledge Development Process'. *Concepts and Transformation*, 2. 2: 145–63.

Levin, M and D. Greenwood (2001) 'Pragmatic Action Research and the Struggle to Transform Universities into Learning Communities'. In P. Reason and H. Bradbury (eds) *Handbook of Action Research Participative Inquiry and Practice*. London: Sage.

Levin, M. and G. Knutstad (2003) 'Construction of Learning Networks – Vanity Fair or Realistic Opportunities?' *Systemic Practice*, 16: 3–19.

Levin, M., E. Borgen, R. Gjersvik, R. Klev, I. Munkeby, M. Rolfsen, and H.J. Sæbø (1997) 'Creating Transdisciplinary Knowledge Learning from Working in the Field: How Engineers and Social Scientists Can Collaborate in Participative Enterprise Development'. *Concepts and Transformation*, 2. 2: 165–88.

Levin, M., E. Borgen, R. Gjersvik, R. Klev, I. Munkeby, M. Rolfsen, and H.J. Sæbø (1998) 'Integrating Engineering and Social Science Participative Enterprise Development'. In B. Gustavsen T. Colbjørnsen and Ø. Pålshaugen (eds) *Development Coalitions in Working Life*. Amsterdam: John Benjamins.

Lindholm Dahlstrand, Å. (1999) 'Technology-based SMEs in the Göteborg Region: Their Origin and Interaction with Universities and Large Firms'. *Regional Studies* 33: 379–89.

Loacker, B., R. Weiskopf, M. Auer and S. Laske (2005) 'In Würde wachsen – personalpolitische Spannungsfelder und Bruchlinien der österreichischen Universitätspolitik' [Growing gracefully – fields of tensions and yield lines in Austrian higher education policy]. Working Paper, Innsbruck: Department of Organization and Learning, Innsbruck University School of Management.

Lohmann, S. (2004) 'Darwinian medicine for the university'. In R. G. Ehrenberg (ed.) *Governing Academia*. Ithaca: Cornell University Press.

Lundvall, B.A. (1988) 'Innovation as an Interactive Process: From User-Producer Interaction to the National System of Innovation'. In G. Dosi (ed.) *Technical Change and Economic Theory*. London: Pinter.

Lundvall, B.A. (ed.) (1992) *National Systems of Innovation. Towards a Theory of Innovation and Interactive Learning*. London: Pinter.

Lundvall, B.A. and B. Johnson (1994) 'The Learning Economy'. *Journal of Industry Studies*, 1. 2: 23–42.

Lyotard, J.F. (1984 [1979]) *The Postmodern Condition: A Report on Knowledge*. (translated by G. Bennington and B. Massumi). Manchester: Manchester University Press.

Machiavelli, N. (1997 [1532]) *The Prince* (translated by A.M. Codevilla). New Haven: Yale University Press.

MacKenzie, D. and J. Wajcman (1985) *The Social Shaping of Technology*. Milton Keynes: Open University Press.

Mansell, R. and U. Wehn (1998) *Knowledge Societies. Information Technology for Sustainable Development*. Oxford: Oxford University Press.

Marceau, J. (1999) 'The Disappearing Trick: Clusters in the Australian Economy'. In J. Guinet (ed.) *Boosting Innovation: The Cluster Approach*. Paris: Organization for Economic Cooperation and Development.

Marginson, S. and Considine, M. (2000) *The Enterprise University: Power, Governance and Reinvention in Australia*. Cambridge: Cambridge University Press.

Marquand, D. (2004) *Decline of the Public*. Cambridge: Polity Press.

Martin, E. (1999) *Changing Academic Work: Developing the Learning University*. Buckingham: Open University Press.

Martin, R. and P. Sunley (2001) 'Deconstructing Clusters: Chaotic Concept or Policy Panacea?' Paper presented to the Regional Studies Association conference on Regionalising the Knowledge Economy, London, 21 November.

Marx, K. (1978) *Capital* (vol. 1). Harmondsworth: Penguin Books.

Maskell, D. and I. Robinson (2001) *The New Idea of the University*. London: Imprint.

May, T. (1994) 'Transformative Power: A Study in a Human Service Organisation'. *Sociological Review* 42. 4: 618–38.

May, T. (1999) 'From Banana Time to Just-in-Time: Power and Resistance at Work'. *Sociology* 33. 4: 767–83.

May, T. (2000) 'The Future of Critique: Positioning, Belonging and Reflexivity'. *European Journal of Social Theory* 3. 2: 157–73.

May, T. (2001) Power, Knowledge and Organizational Transformation: Administration as Depoliticization. *Social Epistemology*, 15: 3: 171–85.

May, T. (2005) 'Transformations in Academic Production: Context, Content and Consequences'. *European Journal of Social Theory* 8. 2: 193–209.

May, T. and B. Perry (2003) *Knowledge Capital: From Concept to Action*. Manchester: Contact Partnership.

Mayr, A. (1979) *Universität und Stadt. Ein Stadt-, Wirtschafts- und Sozialgeographischer Vergleich Alter und Neuer Hochschulstandsorte in der*

Bundesrepublik Deutschland [University and town. An urban, economic and social geographic comparison of old and new locations for university-level institutions in the federal Republic of Germany] Münstersche Geographische Arbeiten., vol. 1. Paderborn: Schöningh.

Meister-Scheytt, C. and T. Scheytt (2005) 'The Complexity of Change in Universities'. *Higher Education Quarterly* 59. 1: 76–99.

Merton, R. (1976) *Sociological Ambivalence and Other Essays*. New York: Free Press.

Messer-Davidow, E., D.R. Shumway, and D.J. Sylvan, (eds) (1993) *Knowledges: Historical and Critical Studies in Disciplinarity*. Charlottesville: University Press of Virginia.

Meusburger, P. (1998) *Bildungsgeographie. Wissen und Ausbildung in der räumlichen Dimension* [Educational geography. Knowledge and instruction in the spatial dimension]. Heidelberg: Spektrum.

Meyer, J.W. and B. Rowan (1991) 'Institutionalized Organization: Formal structure and myth and ceremony'. In W.W. Powell and P.J. DiMaggio (eds) *The New Institutionalism in Organizational Analysis*. Chicago: Chicago University Press.

Mintzberg, H. (1979) *The Structuring of Organizations*. Englewood Cliffs, NJ: Prentice-Hall.

Mitcham, C. (1994) *Thinking through Technology: The Path between Engineering and Philosophy*. Chicago: The University of Chicago Press.

Moldaschl, M. and D. Fischer (2004) 'Beyond the Management View: A Resource-Centered Socio-Economic-Perspective'. *Management Revue* 15. 1: 122–51.

Monbiot, G. (2001) *Captive State*. London: Pan Macmillan.

Morgan, K. (1997) 'The Learning Region: Institutions, Innovation and Regional Renewal'. *Regional Studies*, 31. 5: 491–503.

Morgan, K. (2001) 'The Exaggerated Death of Geography: Localized Learning, Innovation and Uneven Development'. Paper presented to the conference *The Future of Innovation Studies*, Eindhoven.

Morgan, K. and C. Nauwelaers (1999) *Regional Innovation Strategies: The Challenge for Less-Favoured Regions*. London: The Stationery Office/Regional Studies Association.

Müller, K. (1962) 'Die Standortbestimmung bei der Neugründung von Universitäten' [Locational decision-making in the foundation of new universities]. In *Universität neuen Typs?* [A new type of university] (papers presented at the evangelical academy, Loccum). *Schriften des Hochschulverbandes*, vol. 11. Göttingen; Schwartz.

Myers, G. (1990) *Writing Biology: Texts in the Social Construction of Scientific Knowledge*. Madison: University of Wisconsin Press.

National Committee of Inquiry into Higher Education (1997) *Chapter 12: The Local and Regional Role of Higher Education*. London: The Stationery Office.

Neef, D. (ed.) (1998) *The Knowledge Economy*. New York: Butterworth-Heinemann.

Nelson, B. (2002a) *Higher Education at the Crossroads*. Canberra: Department of Education, Science and Training.

Nelson, B. (2002b) *Varieties of Excellence: Diversity, Specialisation and Regional Engagement*. Canberra: Department of Education, Science and Training.

Newfield, C. (2003) *Ivy and Industry: Business and the Making of the American University: 1880–1980*. Durham and London: Duke University Press.

Noble, D. (1999) 'Academic Integrity'. In A. Montefiore and D. Vines (eds) *Integrity in the Public and Private Domains*. London: Routledge.

Nowotny, H., P. Scott and M. Gibbons (2001) *Re-Thinking Science, Knowledge and the Public in an Age of Uncertainty*. Cambridge: Polity Press.

Nuffic (ed.) (2003) *Nuffic Strategy 2003–2006. Outlook and insights*. The Hague: Netherlands Organization for International Cooperation in Higher Education (Nuffic), The Hague.

Observatory on Borderless Higher Education (ed.) (2002) *International Branch Campuses: Scale and Significance*. Briefing Note no.5, June 2002.

Ochs, E. (1997) 'Narrative'. In T.A. Van Dijk (ed.) *Discourse as Structure and Process*. London: Sage.

ODPM (Office of the Deputy Prime Minister) (2006) *State of the English Cities*. London: The Stationery Office.

OECD (1999a) *The Response of Higher Education Institutions to Regional Needs*. Paris Organization for Economic Cooperation and Development.

OECD (1999b) *Boosting Innovation: The Cluster Approach*. Paris: OECD

OECD (ed.) (2003) 'Key Developments and Policy Rationales in Cross-Border Post-Secondary Education'. Preliminary draft prepared for the forthcoming OECD report on cross-border post-secondary education, presented at the OECD/Norway Forum on *Trade in Educational Services: Managing the Internationalization of Post-secondary Education*' in Trondheim, Norway, 3–4 November.

Office of Economic and Statistical Research (2002a) *Regional Community Report. The Beaudesert (S), Logan (C), Redland Region(S)*. Brisbane: Queensland Treasury.

Office of Economic and Statistical Research (2002b) *Regional Community Report. The Gold Coast (C)*. Brisbane: Queensland Treasury.

Ohmae, K. (1995) *The End of the Nation State*. New York: Free Press.

O'Neill, O. (2002) *A Question of Trust*. Cambridge: Cambridge University Press.

One NorthEast (1999) *Regional Economic Strategy for the North East*. Newcastle upon Tyne: One NorthEast.

Orton, J.D. and K.E. Weick (1990) 'Loosely Coupled Systems: A Reconzeptualization'. *Academy of Management Review* 15. 2: 203–23.

Owens, L. (1985) 'Pure and Sound Government'. *Isis* 76: 182–94.

Palumbo, A. and A. Scott (2005) 'Bureaucracy, Open Access and Social Pluralism: Returning the Common to the Goose.' In P. du Gay (ed.) *The Values of Bureaucracy*. Oxford: Oxford University Press.

Parellada, F.S. (1999) 'The Responses of Higher Education Institutions to Global

Challenge: Innovative Universities and Human Resource Development'. *Higher Education in Europe* 24. 1: 67–79.

Parkin, F. (1974) 'Strategies of Social Closure in Class Formation'. In F. Parkin (ed.) *The Social Analysis of Class Structure*. London: Tavistock.

Parsons, T. (1971) 'Value-freedom and objectivity'. In O. Stammer (ed.) *Max Weber and Sociology Today*. Oxford: Basil Blackwell.

Paytas, J., R. Gradeck and L. Andrews (2004) *Universities and the Development of Industry Clusters*. Report for the Economic Development Administration, US Department of Commerce by Carnegie Mellon University, Center for Economic Development, Pittsburgh.

Pechar, H. (2003) 'In Search of a New Profession: Transformation of Academic Management in Austrian Universities'. In A. Amaral, L. Meek. and I.M. Larsen (eds) *The Higher Education Managerial Revolution*. Dordrecht: Kluwer.

Pechar, H. and A. Pellert (1998) 'Managing Change: Organizational Reform in Austrian Universities'. *Higher Education Policy* 11. 2: 141–51.

Pellert, A. (1999) *Universität als Organisation: Die Kunst Experten zu managen* [The university as organization: the art of managing experts]. Wien: Böhlau.

Pels, D. (2003) *Unhastening Science: Autonomy and Reflexivity in the Social Theory of Knowledge*. Liverpool: Liverpool University Press.

Pendergast, D. (2000) *Access to Griffith University: Evaluation of the 'success' of the Tertiary Access Course, 1989–1999*. Report to Griffith University. Accessible at http: //www.gu.edu.au/ua/aa/ss/equity/Tertiary.htm.

Perry, B. and A. Harding (2002) 'The Future of Urban Sociology: Report of Joint Sessions of the British and American Sociological Associations. *International Journal of Urban and Regional Research* 26. 4: 844–53.

Perry, M. (1995) 'Industry Structures, Networks and Joint Action Groups'. *Regional Studies*, 29. 2: 208–17.

Peters, S. (2000) 'The Formative Politics of Outreach Scholarship'. *Journal of Higher Education Outreach and Engagement* 5. 2: 23–30.

Peters, S. (2001) 'The Civic Mission Question in Land-Grant Education'. *Higher Education Exchange* 6: 25–37.

Peters, S. (2002a) 'Rousing the People on the Land: The Roots of an Educational Organizing Tradition in Extension Work'. *Journal of Extension*, vol. 40, no. 3. Available at *http://www.joe.org/joe/2002june/index.html*.

Peters, S. (2002b) 'Citizens Developing a Voice at the Table: A Story of Educational Organizing in Contemporary Extension Work'. *Journal of Extension* 40. 4. Available at *http://www.joe.org/joe/2002august/index.shtml* (accessed June 2005).

Peters, S. (2003) 'The Public Scholarship of a Weed Scientist'. H. Boyte and N. Kari (eds), *Intellectual Workbench: Perspectives on Public Scholarship*. Available at http://www.publicwork.org/2_4_cmp.html (accessed June 2005).

Peters, S., N. Jordan, T. Alter and J. Bridger (2003) 'The Craft of Public Scholarship in Land-Grant Education'. *Journal of Higher Education Outreach and Engagement* vol. 8, no. 1: 75–86.

Peters, S., N. Jordan, M. Adamek, and T. Alter (eds) (2005) *Engaging Campus and Community: The Practice of Public Scholarship in the State and Land-Grant University System*. Dayton, OH: Kettering Foundation Press.

Pickering, A. (ed.) (1992) *Science as Practice and Culture*. Chicago: University of Chicago Press.

Piore, M.J. and C.F. Sabel (1984) *The Second Industrial Divide: Possibilities for Prosperity.* New York: Basic Books.

Polanyi, M. (1983 [1966]) *The Tacit Dimension*. Gloucester: Peter Smith.

Porter, M.E. (1990) *The Competitive Advantage of Nations*. New York: Free Press.

Porter, M.E. (1998a) *On Competition*. Boston: Harvard Business School Press.

Porter, M.E. (1998b) 'Clusters and the New Economics of Competition'. *Harvard Business Review* 76. 6: 77–90.

Potts, G. (1998) 'The HESIN Knowledge House: A Front Door to North East Universities'. *Local Economy* 13: 267–271.

Powell, W.W. and DiMaggio, P.J. (eds) (1991) *The New Institutionalism in Organizational Analysis*. Chicago: Chicago University Press.

Power, M. (1997) *The Audit Society: Rituals of Verification*. Oxford: Oxford University Press.

Preliminary Bulletin of LeMoyne College, 1946–1947 and *1947–1948*. Syracuse: LeMoyne College.

Prichard, C. (2000) *Making Managers in Universities and Colleges*. Buckingham: Society for Research into Higher Education and Open University Press.

Putnam, R. (1993) *Making Democracy Work: Civic Traditions in Modern Italy.* Princeton, NJ: Princeton University Press.

Puukka, J. (2001) 'The external impact of the University of Turkuu – Evaluation and The Way Forward'. Paper presented at the conference *Universities and Regional Development in the Knowledge Society*, Barcelona, 12–14 November.

Queensland Government (1999) *Queensland. The Smart State*. Brisbane: Government Printer.

Raabe, H. (1999) 'A Strategic Framework for Creating Effective Demand Chain Management'. Unpublished PhD thesis, University of Trondheim, Department of Industrial Economics and Technology Management.

Rabinow, P. (1996) *Essays on the Anthropology of Reason*. Princeton: Princeton University Press.

Readings, B. (1996) *The University in Ruins*. Cambridge MA: Harvard University Press.

Rhoads, R. (1997) *Community Service and Higher Learning: Explorations of the Caring Self*. Albany: State University of New York Press.

Ricouer, P. (1984) *Time and Narrative*. Chicago: University of Chicago Press.

Ringer, F. (1969) *The Decline of the German Mandarins*. Cambridge, MA: Harvard University Press.

Risbourg, B. and M. Daumin (2000) 'L'Introduction du Contrôle de Gestion comme Facteur de Changement dans une Université Française de Taille Moyenne: le Cas de l'Université de Picardie Jules Verne' [The introduction of management control as a change factor in a medium-sized French university: The case of the Jules Verne University of Picardy]. Paper presented at the *IMHE General Conference*, Paris, September.

Robins, K. and F. Webster (eds) (2002) *The Virtual University? Knowledge, Markets, and Management*. Oxford: Oxford University Press.

Robson, B., K. Drake and I. Deas (1997) *Higher Education and Regions* (Report 9 to the National Committee of Inquiry into Higher Education). London: The Stationery Office.

Rorty, R. (1998) 'The Contingency of Language'. In M. Bernard-Donals and R. Glezjer (eds) *Rhetoric in an Antifoundational World*. New Haven: Yale University Press.

Rosenberg, J. (2000) 'Transformation of Universities in the Czech Republic: Experiences of the University of West Bohemia in Pilsen'. Paper presented at the *IMHE General Conference*, Paris, September.

Ross, D. (1992) *The Origins of American Social Science*. Cambridge: Cambridge University Press.

Ross, D. (ed.) (1994) *Modernist Impulses in the Human Sciences, 1870–1930*. Baltimore: Johns Hopkins University Press.

Ruch, R. (2001) *Higher Ed, Inc.: The Rise of the For-profit University*. Baltimore: Johns Hopkins University Press.

Rutten, R., F. Boekema and E. Kuypers (eds) (2003) *Economic Geography of Higher Education: Knowledge Infrastructure and Learning Regions*. London: Routledge.

Ryle, G. (1949) *The Concept of Mind*. Chicago: University of Chicago Press.

Salet W., A. Thornley and A. Kreukals (2003) 'Institutional and Spatial Coordination in European Metropolitan Regions'. In W. Salet, A. Thornley and A. Kreukals (eds) *Metropolitan Governance and Spatial Planning*. London: Spon Press.

Sapp, J. (2003) *Genesis: The Evolution of Biology*. Oxford: Oxford University Press.

Sassen, S. (1991) *The Global City: New York, London, Tokyo*. Princeton, NJ: Princeton University Press.

Saussure, F. de (1966) *Course in General Linguistics*. New York: McGraw Hill.

Savitch, H. (2002) 'What Is New about Globalization and What Does It Portend for Cities?' *International Social Science Journal*. 54.172: 179–89.

Scarborough, H. (2001) 'Knowledge à la Mode: The Rise of Knowledge Management and its Implications for Views of Knowledge Production. *Social Epistemology* 15. 3: 201–13.

Schimank, U. (2000): 'Welche Chancen und Risiken können unterschiedliche Modelle erweiterter Universitätsautonomie für die Forschung und Lehre der Universitäten bringen? [What are the opportunities and risks for research and teaching that various models of extended auronomy for universities may bring?]. In S. Titscher, G. Winckler, H. Biedermann, H. Gatterbauer, S. Laske, B. Kappller, R. Moser, F. Strehl, F. Wojda and H. Wulz (eds) *Universitäten im Wettbewerb: zur Neustrukturierung österreichischer Universitäten* [Universities in competition: on the restructuring of Austrian univiersities]. Munich: Rainer Hampp Verlag.

Schleicher, A. (2006) 'The Economics of Knowledge: Why Education is Key for Europe's Success'. Policy Brief. Brussels: The Lisbon Council asbl.

Schluchter, W. (1979) 'Value-neutrality and the ethic of responsibility'. In W. Schluchter and G. Roth (eds) *Max Weber's Vision of History: Ethics and Method.* Berkeley: University of California Press.

Schön, D. (1983) *The Reflective Practitioner: How Professionals Think in Action.* New York: Basic Books.

Schrag, C.O. (1997) *The Self After Postmodernity.* New Haven and London: Yale University Press.

Schutz, A. (1976 [1967]) *The Phenomenology of the Social World.* London: Heinemann.

Scott, A. (1995) 'Value Freedom and Intellectual Autonomy'. *History of the Human Sciences* 8. 3: 69–88.

Scott, A. (1997) 'Between Autonomy and Responsibility: Max Weber on Scholars, Academics and Intellectuals'. In J. Jennings and A. Kemp-Welch (eds) *Intellectuals in Politics: From the Dreyfus Affair to Salmon Rushdie.* London, Routledge.

Scott, A. J. (ed.) (2001) *Global City-Regions.* Oxford: Oxford University Press.

Scott, J.C. (1998) *Seeing Like a State: How certain schemes to improve the human conditions have failed.* New Haven: Yale University Press.

Scott, P. (ed.) (1998) *The Globalisation of Higher Education.* Buckingham: Society for Research into Higher Education and Oxford University Press.

Senker J., with K. Balázs, T. Higgins, P. Laredo, E. Munoz, M. Santesmases, J. Espinosa de las Monteros, B. Poti, E. Reale, M. di Marchi, A. Scarda, U. Sandstrom, U.Schimank, M. Winnes, H. Skoie and H. Thorsteinsdottir (1999) *European Comparison of Public Research Systems.* TSER Project No. SOE1 – CT96 – 1036.

Shepherd, W.R. (1923) *Historical Atlas.* New York: Henry Holt and Company, New York.

Shoemaker, A., J. Allison, K. Gum, R. Harmoni and M. Lindfield (2000) *Multi-Partner Campuses: The Future of Australian Universities.* Canberra: Department of Education, Training and Youth Affairs.

Shore, C. and S. Wright (2000) 'Coercive accountability: the rise of audit culture in higher education'. In M. Strathern (ed.) *Audit Cultures.* London: Routledge.

Shumway, D. (2000) 'Objectivity, Relativism and the Public Authority of the Scholar'. In R. H. Brown and J. Schubert (eds) *Knowledge and Power in Higher Education: A Reader.* New York: Teachers College Press.

Sil, R. and E.M. Doherty (eds) (2000) *Beyond Boundaries? Disciplines, Paradigms, and Theoretical Integration in International Studies.* Albany: SUNY Press.

Simmie, J., J. Sennett, P. Wood and D. Hart (2002) 'Innovation in Europe: A Tale of Networks, Knowledge and Trade in Five Cities'. *Regional Studies* 36.1: 47–64.

Simon, H. (1976) *Administrative Behaviour* (3rd ed.). New York: Free Press.

Simonyi, A. (1999) 'The Evaluation of University–Region Relationships'. *European Journal of Education*, 34. 3: 335–41.

Slaughter, S. (1988) 'Academic Freedom and the State: Reflections on the Uses of Knowledge'. *Journal of Higher Education* 59. 3: 241–62.

Slaughter, S. and L. Leslie (1997) *Academic Capitalism: Politics, Policies and the Entrepreneurial University*. Baltimore: Johns Hopkins University Press.

Smart, D. (1997) 'Reforming Australian Higher Education: Adjusting the Levers of Funding and Control'. *Educational Research and Perspectives* 24. 2: 29–34.

Smith, A. and F. Webster (eds) (1997) *The Postmodern University? Contested Visions of Higher Education in Society*. Buckingham: Society for Research into Higher Education and Oxford University Press.

Snow, C. and J. Hanssen-Bauer (1996) 'Responding to Hypercompetition: The Structure of and Processes of a Regional Learning Network Organization'. *Organization Science* 7. 4: 413–27.

Soja, E. (2000) *Postmetropolis. Critical Studies of Cities and Regions*. Oxford: Blackwell.

Soley, L.C. (1996) *Leasing the Ivory Tower: The Corporate Takeover of Academia*. Boston: South End Press.

Sporn, B. (1999) *Adaptive University Structures: An Analysis of Adaptation to Socioeconomic Environments of US and European Universities*. London: Jessica Kingsley.

Staber, U.H., N.F. Schaefer and B. Sharma (1996) *Business Networks: Prospects for Regional Development*. Berlin: DeGruyter.

Starkey, K. and P. Madan (2001) 'Bridging the Relevance Gap: Aligning Stakeholders in the Future of Management Research'. *British Journal of Management* 12 (special Issue): S3–S26.

State University of New York: Annual Catalog, Triple Cities College 1950–51. June 15, 1950. 1:1. Binghamton: SUNY.

Stehr, N. (1992) *Practical Knowledge: Applying the Social Sciences*. London: Sage.

Stehr, N. (1994) *Knowledge Societies*. London: Sage.

Stevenson, S., C. Evans, M. Maclachlan, T. Karmel and R. Blakers (2000) *Access: Effect of Campus Proximity and Socio-economic Status on University Participation Rates in Regions*. Canberra: Department of Education, Training and Youth Affairs.

Stevenson, S., M. Maclachlan and T. Karmel (1999) *Regional Participation in Higher Education and the Distribution of Higher Education Resources across Regions*. Canberra: Department of Education, Training and Youth Affairs.

Stoker, G. and K. Mossberger (1994) 'The Post-Fordist Local State: The Dynamics of its Development'. In J. Stewart and G. Stoker (eds) *Local Government in the 1990s*. London: Macmillan.

Storper, M. (1995) 'The Resurgence of Regional Economies, Ten Years Later: The Region as a Nexus of Untraded Interdependencies'. *European Urban and Regional Studies* 2. 2: 191–221.

Storper, M. (1997) *The Regional World: Territorial Development in a Global Economy*. New York and London: The Guilford Press.

Strathern, M. (ed.) (2000) *Audit Cultures*. London: Routledge.

Swyndegouw, E. (1992) 'The Mammon Quest: "Glocalisation", Interspatial Competition and the Monetary Order – The Construction of New Scales'. In M. Dunford and G. Kafkalis (eds) *Cities and Regions in the New Europe: The Global-Local Interplay and Spatial Development Strategies* (pp. 39–67). London: Belhaven Press and New York: J. Wiley & Sons.

Taylor, P. and J. Blaik (2002) *Project Report: What Have We Learned? The Logan Campus 1998–2001*. Nathan: Griffith Institute of Higher Education.

Taylor, P. J. (1996) 'Embedded Statism and the Social Sciences: Opening up to New Spaces. *Environment and Planning A* 28: 1917–28.

Taylor, T., J. Gough, V. Bundrock and R. Winter (1998) 'A Bleak Outlook: Academic Staff Perceptions of Changes in Core Activities in Australian Higher Education, 1991–96'. *Studies in Higher Education* 23. 3: 255–68.

Thanki, R. (1999) 'How do We Know the Value of Higher Education to Regional Development'. *Regional Studies*, 33. 1: 84–9.

Thompson, E.P. (ed.) (1970) *Warwick University Ltd.: Industry, Management and the Universities*. Harmondsworth: Penguin.

Thompson, J. (1990) *Ideology and Modern Culture*. Stanford: Stanford University Press.

Toulmin, S. (1995) 'Concluding Methodological Reflections. Elitism and Democracy among Sciences'. In S. Toulmin and B. Gustavsen (eds) *Beyond method*. Amsterdam: John Benjamins.

Toulmin, S. and B. Gustavsen (eds) (1996) *Beyond Theory*. Amsterdam and Philadelphia: John Benjamins.

Traweek, S. (1988) *Beamtimes and Lifetimes*. Cambridge, MA: Harvard University Press.

Triple Cities College Bulletin, 1947–1948. 1:1. Binghamton: SUNY.

Tsoukas, H. and S. Cummings 'Marginalization and Recovery: The Emergence of Aristotelian Themes in Organization Studies'. *Organization Studies* 18. 4: 653–83.

Turner, S. (2003) *Liberal Democracy 3.0: Civil Society in an Age of Experts*. London: Sage.

Van der Sijde, P. and F. Schutte (2000) *The University and its Region: Examples of Regional Development from the European Consortium of Innovative Universities*. Twente: Twente University Press.

van der Wende, M.C. (2001) 'Internationalization Policies: About new trends and contrasting paradigms'. *Higher Education Policy* 14: 249–59.

Veysey, L.R. (1970) *The Emergence of the American University*. Chicago: University of Chicago Press.

VSNU (eds) (2002) *Universiteiten in cijfers. Branchejaarverslag universiteiten 2001* [Universities in numbers. Branch report, universities 2001]. Utrecht: VSNU.

Wenger, E. (1999) *Communities of Practice*. Cambridge: Cambridge University Press.

W.K. Kellogg Foundation (2002) *Engagement in Youth and Education Programming*, Michigan. Accessible at http: //www.wkkf.org.

Wachelder, J.C.M. (1992) *Universiteit tussen Vorming en Opleiding: de Modernisering van de Nederlandse Universiteiten in de Negentiende Eeuw* [Universities between formation and education: Modernizing Dutch universities in the nineteenth century]. Hilversum: Verloren.

Washington Research Council (1999) *The Economic Value of Higher Education*. Special Report of the Washington Research Council, Washington, DC: *http:// www.researchcouncil.org/Reports/1999/EconomicValueofHigherEducation/ EconomicValueofHigherEducation.htm*.

Weber, L. (2000) 'La Gouvernance des Universités Suisses en Chantier: l'Effort est-il Suffisant?' [The governance of Swiss universities in process: is sufficient effort being made?] Paper presented at the *IMHE General Conference*, Paris, September.

Weber, M. (1918) 'Parliament and Government in Germany under a New Political Order'. In P. Lassman and R. Speirs (eds) *Weber: Political Writings*. Cambridge: Cambridge University Press, 1994.

Weber, M. (1919) 'Science as a Vocation.' In H. Gerth and C. Wright Mills (eds) *For Max Weber*. London: Routledge, 1948.

Weber, M. (1919a) 'Science as a Vocation'. In P. Lassman and I. Velody (eds) *Max Weber's 'Science as a Vocation'* (pp. 3–31). London: Unwin Hyman.

Weber, M. (1919b) *From Max Weber: Essays in Sociology.* (Translated, edited and with an introduction by H. H. Gerth and C. Wright Mills). London: Routledge.

Weick, K.E. (1976) 'Educational Organizations as Loosely Coupled Systems'. *Administrative Science Quarterly* 21. 1: 1–20.

Weingart, P. (1997) 'From "Finalization" to "Mode 2": Old Wine in New Bottles?' *Social Science Information* 36: 591–613.

Weller, G.R. (1998) 'The Impact of a New University in a Developing Region: The Case of the University of Northern British Columbia'. *Higher Education Policy*, 11: 281–90.

Wenger, E., R. McDermott and W.N. Snyder (2002) *Cultivating Communities of Practice.* Cambridge, MA: Harvard Business School Press.

Williams, M. and T. May (1996) *Introduction to the Philosophy of Social Research.* London: University College of London Press.

Willmott, H. (1993) 'Strength is Ignorance; Slavery is Freedom: Managing Culture in Modern Organizations'. *Journal of Management Studies* 30. 4: 515–52.

Willmott, H. (1995) 'Managing the Academics: Commodification and Control in the Development of University Education in the UK'. *Human Relations* 48. 9: 993–1028.

Willmott, H. (2003) 'Commercialising Higher Education in the UK: The State, Industry and Peer Review'. *Studies in Higher Education*, 28. 2: 129–41.

Wilson, G. (1997) 'Multi-Campus Universities'. In J. Sharpham and G. Harman, (eds) *Australia's Future Universities*. Armidale: University of New England Press.

Winter, R. (1995) 'The University of Life plc: The 'Industrialisation' of Higher Education. In J. Smyth (ed.) *Academic Work: The Changing Labour Process in Higher Education*. Buckingham: Society for Research into Higher Education and Open University Press.

Wittenburg, E. (1989) 'The Crisis of Science in Germany in 1919'. In P. Lassman and I. Velody (eds) *Max Weber's Science as a Vocation*. London: Unwin Hyman.

Woolgar, S. (ed.) (1988) *Knowledge and Reflexivity*. London: Sage.

Zabusky, S. (1985) *Launching Europe*. Princeton: Princeton University Press.

Index

public sector institutions, role of 45
publication of academic work 174–5

quality assurance 100
quality of life 117
quasi-markets 20
Queensland 64–7, 177, 179

Rabinow, Paul 129
ranking systems for university performance 99–100, 105
Rau, Johannes 198
regional development 7, 11, 36, 41–50, 53, 96, 102–7, 110–11, 165–6, 177–8, 182
regional development agencies 57, 60, 63, 68
regional problems 109–10
relevance of universities 2–3, 7–11, 21–2, 122–3, 126, 130, 133–4, 138–42, 145, 154, 160
Research Assessment Exercise 14, 64, 116
research bids 9
Ringer, Fritz 11–13, 16–17
Roosevelt Academy 82–3, 85–6
Ryle, Gilbert 40–1

Sabel, C.F. 43
Salford University 33
Schön, D.A. 44
Schorr, Ira 117
Schrag, Calvin 136
Schutz, A. 41
science, nature of 143–7, 153–6
scientists, role of 153
Scott, Alan xiii; *co-author of Chapter 1, co-interviewer for Chapter 12 and co-editor*
Scott, James 16–17, 21, 108
Scott, P. 33, 37
secularization 72–3
self-promotion by universities 1–2
Sen, Amartya 108
service-learning involvement 110
Sheffield universities 58
Shore, Chris 15
Shumway, D. 154, 158
Silicon Valley 55
Simon, H. 153

Slaughter, S. 97, 99
small and medium-sized enterprises (SMEs) 56, 60, 167, 170
Smith, Christine xiii–xiv, 21; *co-author of Chapter 11*
social capital 165
social constructivism 55
social functions of universities 102–10
social sciences 107–9, 134–6, 148, 156
Sontag, Susan 159
Sorbonne Declaration (1998) 29
Southern Cross University 66, 116
specialization, academic 15, 74, 85
  see also flexible specialization
spin-off firms 56, 165–6
'stakeholders' in universities 20–1, 32–3
Starkey, K. 151
Stehr, N. 28, 132
Storper, M. 179
student numbers 9–10, 73, 75–6
students seen as 'customers' 100–1, 157
Sunderland University 61
Sunley, P. 54
supranational policy-making 31
Sznaider, N. 5

tacit knowing 40–1
tax subsidies 104
Taylor, Frederick Winslow (and Taylorism) 107–10
teamwork 107
techne 41, 111–15, 147
technology, concepts of 40
technology transfer
  see knowledge transfer
Thatcher, Margaret 115
Thompson, E.P. 120, 126
Total Quality Assessment (TQA) 14
Toulmin, Stephen 41, 111
tradition, embodiment of 13, 18, 102
Tsoukas, H. 153
Twente University 82
twinning programmes 84

United States 5, 87, 99–100, 103, 115, 159
Utrecht University 73, 82

value-based and *value-free* academics 150–60